W9-BUU-298

Also by Judith Jones

WITH EVAN JONES

The Book of New *New England Cookery*

The Book of Bread

Knead It, Punch It, Bake It!

WITH ANGUS CAMERON

The L. L. Bean Game and Fish Cookbook

The Tenth Muse

The Tenth Muse

MY LIFE IN FOOD

Judith Jones

ALFRED A. KNOPF   NEW YORK

2007

THIS IS A BORZOI BOOK
PUBLISHED BY ALFRED A. KNOPF

Portions of *The Tenth Muse* have appeared, some in slightly
different form, in *The New York Times*, and in *Anteus, Bon
Appetit, Gastronomica, Saveur,* and *Vogue* magazines.

Library of Congress Cataloging-in-Publication Data
Jones, Judith.
The tenth muse / Judith Jones.
p. cm.
"A BORZOI BOOK."
Includes bibliographical references and index.
ISBN 978-0-307-26495-4
1. Jones, Judith.   2. Women cooks—Biography.
3. Cookery, International.   I. Title.
II. Title: 10th muse.
TX649.J66A3 2007
641.59—dc22   2007006789

Manufactured in the United States of America
Published November 2, 2007
Second Printing Before Publication

FOR EVAN

who was singularly inspired by the Muse

The Muses

1 POETRY *Calliope*

2 HISTORY *Clio*

3 MUSIC *Euterpe*

4 DANCE *Terpsichore*

5 LOVE POETRY *Erato*

6 TRAGEDY *Melpomene*

7 COMEDY *Thalia*

8 GEOMETRY *Polyhymnia*

9 ASTRONOMY *Urania*

And, in the words of Brillat-Savarin,

Gasterea

is the tenth muse.
She presides over all the pleasures of taste.

Contents

1   *Growing Up*   3

2   *Paris—the First Time*   17

3   *Paris for Keeps*   27

4   *Julia to the Rescue*   48

5   *Voices in the Kitchen*   73

6   *Food as Memory*   90

7   *American Cooking*   106

8   *What Is Taste?*   132

9   *Treasures of the Good Earth*   160

10   *The Pleasure That Lasts the Longest*   181

Recipes   199

Index   283

The Tenth Muse

1

Growing Up

When my mother was well into her nineties, she announced that she had an important question for me and wanted an honest answer. I steeled myself for something weighty, perhaps about whether I believed in heaven and hell.

Then she looked at me and asked: "Tell me, Judith, do you really like garlic?" I couldn't lie. Yes, I admitted, I adored garlic. She looked so crestfallen at that moment that I was sure she felt a sense of finality about the wayward path her younger daughter had taken.

To her, garlic represented everything alien and vulgar. It smelled bad, and people who handled it or ate it smelled bad. Moreover, it covered up the natural flavor of honest food—and that was suspect. Those French chefs, for instance, why did they have to put a sauce on everything, anyway? No doubt to disguise the taste because what was underneath wasn't very fresh to begin with.

In my mother's house we were always being told to get rid of the smells, to make sure that the kitchen door was shut, that the windows were open. Not only was garlic banned, onions were permitted only when a lamb stew was being prepared, for which two or three well-boiled small white onions per person were deemed appropriate. That's all that were purchased; Mother didn't want our cook, Edie Price, sneaking a little chopped onion into her meatloaf. And heaven forbid that indigestible, raw pieces might find their way into a tuna-fish sandwich.

Still, I have to admit that the unadulterated English-style food I grew up on had its merits. I always loved our Sunday dinner prime rib roast with Yorkshire pudding, which my British grandfather, whenever he was present, would carve at the table, deftly cutting thin—too thin, I always thought—rosy slices. My father, Charles Bailey, who was called Monty because he grew up in Montpelier, Vermont, somehow never lost the mischievous charm of a small-town boy after he had to settle in New York City. When he married into the Hedley family, he made a point of carving clumsy, thick slices, and so was banished as the family carver. My mother took over. I can still see her standing at the head of the table honing her knife on a sharpening steel, and I would always try to sneak a nibble from the platter when she wasn't looking. The knuckle-bone meat on a lamb roast was irresistible.

I am grateful, too, that those organ meats that people spurn today often graced our table: liver and bacon, beefsteak and kidney pie, breaded sweetbreads—I lapped them up and still find all forms of innards an earthy delight. Frugality was considered a virtue. One never let things go to waste, so Edie learned to turn leftovers into wonderful dishes: crispy croquettes with creamy lamb, ham, or chicken inside; shepherd's pie of ground-up leftover lamb with a mashed-potato topping; minced meats in cream on toast; stuffed vegetables. We also had a meatless night once a week, either for the sake of economy or because it was good for us to forgo the pleasure of flesh, I'm not sure. For quite a few years after I graduated from the nursery table to the grown-up dinner table, I thought when we were served breaded and fried eggplant or broiled mushrooms that

The Hedley sisters: my mother in front;
with her middle sister, Helen, and her older sister, Hilda

they were a form of meat. Of course, I didn't dare ask, because one wasn't supposed to talk about food at the table (it was considered crude, like talking about sex). And if we indulged in appreciative sounds like "yum-yum," we just might be sent from the table.

Nor could we make disparaging remarks if something displeased us. I remember how endlessly long the winter seemed when all that Mr. Volpe, our Italian fruit-and-vegetable vendor on the corner, could produce was overgrown root vegetables, sprouts and cabbage, and tired potatoes. Then what greens we could get were cooked so long that an unappetizing cabbagy smell permeated the air, and it was hard to get down our due portion. But we weren't allowed to say a word. It did take me some time, though, to appreciate parsnips and broccoli. When, finally, spring broke through and we tasted our first asparagus, even though slightly overcooked, it was a treat worth waiting for. And we were allowed to pick up the spears with our fingers.

But I don't remember ever going shopping with my mother in the city to pick out the first vegetables and fruits of the season. Food shopping was invariably done by phone, as though to keep a distance from the things of the earth. In the summer, though, a truck with fresh farm produce would do a tour of the lake in Vermont where we had our summer cottage, and it was fun to go out and greet the local farmer and get a look at what he had just pulled from the soil. Every week the butcher's truck would stop by, and I once persuaded him to let me ride with him as he made his rounds. I was impressed with the way he wielded his knife and would lop off a slab of meat which, when he put it on the scales, would always come within an ounce of what the customer had ordered. The back of the truck was chilled only by a block of ice, and as the warmth of the summer day penetrated, the smell of raw meat became tantalizingly strong.

Meat was such an important part of everyone's diet that when we were plunged into World War II and were suddenly confronted with rationing, there was a sense of deprivation. I was away at college in Bennington, Vermont, in those years, and we had a huge Victory Garden in which all had to participate. I remember how the erudite critic Kenneth Burke insisted that he conduct his class out in the burgeoning fields, because he felt that having our feet planted firmly in the soil and nurturing the fruits of the earth would encourage our minds to soar. We were also asked to volunteer for poultry duty, and I felt very virtuous beheading and plucking and eviscerating chickens by the dozens—all in expectation of a good dinner, of course. Bennington was known for its superior food, and I'm not ashamed

*Little Judy Bailey—was I going to be
the plump one of the family?*

to admit that, after sampling the fare at a number of sister colleges, I just may have chosen Bennington because I liked to eat well.

Meanwhile, back home in New York, meat was scarce. My parents had acquired a Kerry blue terrier, no doubt to fill the gap left by their last daughter's going off to college, and they were finding it so hard to get enough meat to feed this hungry animal that they finally gave him to Albert, the butcher. Or so the story goes. The other version is that my mischievous father, now that there were no children around, had to take the dog out every night for what seemed increasingly long walks. Now, in those days, Third Avenue in the East Sixties was still a thoroughly Irish neighborhood; the el rattled through, and there was a pub on every corner. During the daytime, when my mother walked the dog, she began to notice how he would stop at several of the nearby pubs and pull her in, tail wagging in happy anticipation of a doggy treat. Then it dawned on her why those evening walks were taking Monty so long. She quickly made an arrangement with the butcher.

But back to those earlier childhood memories at the table. Above all, we always ate what was put in front of us, especially if we wanted dessert. To me those homemade desserts of British ancestry were the crowning glory of the meal, and I wouldn't have missed them for anything. I still feel nostalgic for the warm chocolate steamed pudding with foamy sauce, the bread pudding with its crusty top and raisins bursting inside, the apple brown Betty made with good tart country apples, the floating island with its peaks of egg white swimming in a sea of yellow custard. Then, when summer came, there were the summer puddings, a bread-lined mold steeped in gently cooked blueberries, raspberries, or blackberries as each came in season, pressed, chilled, and unmolded, with thick unpasteurized cream poured over each serving. Edie had some specialties of her own, such as individual warm nut-and-date cakes, and meringues (which we called kisses) topped with bananas and slathered in hand-beaten whipped cream.

I loved watching Edie with a big mustard-colored ceramic bowl cradled on her hip as she would beat a batter with her strong brown arm, her wooden spoon hitting the bowl with a plopping sound. In fact, the kitchen was where I headed as soon as I got off the school bus and threw down my books. Not only did I want to know what was for dinner and to watch it all magically come together, but I was fascinated by Edie's other life. She came from Barbados and at my urging would tell me about the foods she grew up on—strange fruits I'd never heard of, hot peppers that made one sweat, and, of course, garlic. I'd sometimes get cheeky enough to ask what she was going to make for her boyfriend on her Thursday night off, and as she described the food, I would long to have her spirit me off to Harlem with her. Instead, to spare my mother having to cook, we were taken to a prissy little restaurant on Lexington Avenue called Susan Prince that served the kind of food we had at home.

When I was asked during my middle-school years what I would like for lunch on Fridays—the day when we had to stay in school until only one o'clock—I knew exactly what I wanted: a whole artichoke, spaghetti and cheese, and fresh fruit or applesauce for dessert. The spaghetti and cheese that Edie made was more sauce than pasta (a term we didn't even know then—it was either spaghetti or macaroni), enriched with massive gratings of good Vermont Cheddar cheese, then baked in a casserole with buttered crumbs and more cheese on top. I made a ritual of slurping down those hot creamy strands of spaghetti and alternately picking off artichoke leaves, one by one, dipping them in lemony butter or hollandaise, and scraping off the flesh with my teeth. I did it slowly, often turning the pages of a book. Then, when I got to the heart, I would carefully pull off all the thistles and revel in that concentrated, slightly grassy-tasting artichoke flesh. If I had a sip of milk, it was curious how the artichoke flavor distorted the taste of the milk. I found the same true when I graduated to wine. So this was one taste treat better just enjoyed on its own.

My father soon recognized that I inherited the food genes from his side of the family and decided to treat me to more adventurous fare. So on Saturdays he would take me to lunch at La Petite Maison, a typical French restaurant near us in Manhattan's East Sixties, and there I was able to wallow in onions as I broke through the cheesy toasted crust of a *soupe à l'oignon* or to savor seafoods wrapped in delicate warm crêpes, to say nothing of mopping up those winey sauces that hid who knows what. The only trouble was that quite often by mid-afternoon I would start throwing up. I could just hear my mother saying: See what happens to a child when she eats those foreign foods. But I was not to be deterred: We gradually isolated the culprit and found that I was allergic to scallops.

Incidentally, for many years I had to forgo those wonderful sea-briny mollusks, but when I was in my forties, my husband, Evan, who didn't really believe in allergies, started experimenting to see if he could wean me. Unbeknownst to me, he would slip just a shaving of a scallop into my serving of a fish soup he had made, and when there was no adverse reaction he would sneak a larger portion into whatever seafood dish he made next time. After several years of increasing doses, I was able to consume happily a whole plateful of fresh scallops, and I have been making up for my years of deprivation ever since. The moral of this story is not only that you shouldn't cling to childhood prejudices—try to get over them—but also remember that the body changes, and what poisoned you at ten years old may well nourish you pleasurably in middle life.

I think my most important awakening to the pleasures of cooking came when I was about eleven and bargained with my parents to let me spend one winter with my grandmother in Montpelier. After I'd convinced them, my mother blurted out anxiously: "But what if you get sick?" My answer was that I had no intention of getting sick. And, of course, I didn't. Instead, I grew up.

I particularly loved spending time with my Aunt Marian, who lived a little way down the street from my grandmother's house. After school and on weekends, I would stop by and settle into her warm, sweet-smelling kitchen and watch as she prepared dishes she knew her husband liked. Uncle Doc was a popular GP in town, and often his visits to patients would last into the evening. But no matter the hour, Aunt Marian always had a hot dish and all the accompaniments ready and waiting for his return. I marveled not only at how she could be so flexible and have everything turn out just right, but also at the love she seemed to express in cooking. She kept notebooks of her favorite recipes, some clipped from the *Ladies' Home Journal* and *Good Housekeeping,* and she would tuck in alongside them a poem she liked, or some pressed flower or herbs that might have decorated that particular dish. The household had a hired girl who did some of the chores, but to Aunt Marian the idea of anyone aside from his own devoted wife cooking for Uncle Doc, or even ironing his shirts, was unthinkable. One thing she made that I always loved was timbales created out of scraps of ham she had in the icebox mixed with eggs, milk, and breadcrumbs. It seemed so magical that you could put these simple ingredients together, bake them in buttered custard cups, and, when they were done, turn them upside down and see the perfectly formed timbale plop neatly onto the plate. As we took these trembling timbales out onto the porch to eat for lunch in summer, Aunt Marian would pluck off an edible flower or two to decorate the plates.

My grandmother wasn't anything of a cook. In fact, after she produced four children, she more or less took to her bed and was content to let others serve her. Her housekeeper, Mrs. Cooney, was the kind whose menus followed the same pattern every week: roast pork on Monday, hash on Tuesday, macaroni and Velveeta on Wednesday, tough steak on Thursday, and then the dreaded boiled salt cod with boiled potatoes on Friday. Saturday might be a slab of ham, and Sunday a roast chicken. But she did make those delicious, spicy cookies known as hermits, which I'd always find in the big cookie jar in the pantry, and her heart was in the right place. That was brought home to me one night after I'd gone to bed and I heard noises in the kitchen below. Fortunately, the house had heat registers in the ceiling, and when I opened the slots of the register on the floor above the kitchen, I could look down on the scene below. There at the kitchen table were two strange men bent over big bowls into which Mrs. Cooney had ladled ample portions of the stew we'd had for supper, and they were slurping it up happily. Mrs. Cooney seemed to beam with pleasure as they laughed and slapped her back and thanked her. The next day, I asked about what I had seen and she told me the men were "hoboes"—sad, hungry, out-of-work men who wandered from town to town looking for a job; and they were always hungry. She said my grandmother wanted her to feed anyone who asked for food. Then she took me outside and showed me the mark that had been made on the trunk of the elm by the back door. It was a code indicating to other wanderers that this was a place that welcomed strangers. Suddenly I felt a surge of pride that I was part of that generous house on the street that bore my father's family name: Bailey Avenue.

Perhaps it was that awareness that cooking is a way of sharing, even expressing love, that prompted me, one summer when

I was in my early teens, to announce that I intended to cut short my summer vacation and return to New York so I could cook for my abandoned father. Every summer, my family took off for at least three months to northern Vermont, where the air was clean and the dreaded polio virus was unlikely to strike. But Monty had a measly two weeks off from his law firm. We would get funny, sad letters from him telling of the heat in our apartment (no air conditioners in those days), of the mosquitoes who found their way up to the eighth floor, and of the pathetic meals he tried to cook for himself. I suspect my magnanimous gesture was prompted as much by the fact that it had rained for days in the Northeast Kingdom and I was also fed up with the social life, but anyway I took off on the overnight *Montrealer* and arrived in the scorching city without a clue as to how to even turn on the oven.

By the end of a week or so, I had managed, I thought, to master steaks and hamburgers and other simple fare with accompanying vegetables. Then my mother was due to return from Vermont, and I wanted to celebrate with a cake. It seemed so easy, mixing everything and beating the batter as I had watched Edie do, and I popped the cake confidently into the oven. But after ten minutes we smelled burning, and when I opened the oven door the cake was hopelessly blackened on top. What happened, as Mother pointed out gently (maybe secretly hoping that this might dampen my cooking enthusiasm), was that I had lit the broiler, not the oven. In fact, I hadn't known the difference; all week I had been happily cooking everything under the broiler.

Fortunately, that experience didn't deter me from future efforts at cooking, but I was somewhat inhibited by the dread of becoming a fat young lady. One summer when I was about twelve, my mother and Auntie Hilda had instilled that fear in me. It was on one of those cold end-of-summer Vermont days, and we had all climbed into the same bed together to keep warm. Suddenly I felt them pinching my thighs and laughing, and Hilda exclaimed, "Oh, she's going to be the plump one of the family." And my mother chimed in, "Yes, indeed, she's a true Bailey." Now, though I relished being a Bailey, the plumpness was worrisome. Was this the price I would have to pay for loving food?

A year or so later, when I went to the Brearley School, I became close friends with a fellow newcomer, little Eleanor Freedley, whose father was a Broadway producer. Her parents seemed wonderfully glamorous, living as they did in the Ritz Towers and coming home with stories about Ethel Merman being spanked in the new Vinton Freedley musical *Red, Hot and Blue!* Once, when we all rode down in the elevator, we stopped to pick up a beautiful, secretive-looking woman, and I realized it was Greta Garbo. Mrs. Freedley immediately fixed us with a stern look and said softly but firmly, "Eyes down, girls. Keep your eyes down."

So I was thrilled one summer when the Freedleys invited me up to their country place in Pomfret, Connecticut. It was a sprawling old farm that had been turned into a beautiful estate, and life there was full of parties and good food and galloping over the meadows on thoroughbred horses. There was a special large shed with a grand piano and polished hardwood floors where Fred Astaire danced when he was visiting and many a new tune was tried out. But what particularly delighted me was the pleasure the Freedleys took in good food. In the afternoons, there would be small tables around the lawn with pitchers of iced tea and little sandwiches and pastries. And that was just for nibbling between meals. Dinner was always a feast, with an abundance of things fresh from the garden, good warm rolls, and rich desserts. At one point, the handsome Mr. Freedley turned to me after I had filled my plate with second helpings, and said, "You really like to eat, don't you?" Then he asked me what I weighed. When I told him I was about 112 pounds, he laughed and, right in the middle of dinner, took my hand and led me to his bathroom scale. The dial kept going up, and when the arrow reached 122 pounds, I was mortified. For only five foot three, that's a lot of pounds.

As a result of that humiliating experience, I spent my suc-

As a teenager with a friend (right),
Anne Woodward, in Vermont

ceeding school years strictly monitoring my intake. Invariably
I had no more than a raw carrot and a glass of milk for lunch
at school. I would sometimes go with a few classmates to
Schrafft's, one of the chain of genteel restaurants where the
waitresses were all of Irish descent and dressed parlor-maid-
style in black with a starched white apron and headpiece. But I
would sip a ginger ale while everyone else guzzled thick chocolate milkshakes or ice-cream sodas. I could easily have become
anorexic—a term not even in the current vocabulary then, but
for which the seeds were certainly being laid. Fortunately, my
food genes cried out for satisfaction, and instead of starving
myself I learned discipline as well as a sense of balance in what
I ate. It was really the years in France that taught me how. But
that came later.

Meanwhile, I continued to make discoveries on my own. When
I first ventured forth to a real Italian restaurant with a girlfriend,
I couldn't believe the relaxed pleasure we enjoyed, savoring
course after course—an assortment of antipasti with garlicky
sausage, pasta with strands so long you had to roll them around
a fork or just slurp them up (at home, our spaghetti was always
cut into ladylike pieces), then tender veal scaloppini, plus
dessert, all washed down, of course, with a hearty Chianti. I
couldn't wait to go home and try to recapture these wonderful
flavors, but the only cookbook we owned was *Fannie Farmer,*
and that hardly provided guidance on lusty Italian fare. Moreover, how could I possibly cover up the odor of garlic?

So I bided my time.

2

Paris—the First Time

Even though I had a promising job after college as a junior editor at Doubleday, the call of *la belle France* was irresistible. I admired the easy chic of French women and the way they treated their men—not something I had experienced at home. As for the men, who could resist the suggestive voice of Maurice Chevalier or the seductive charm of Charles Boyer? But most compelling was the memory of those meals at La Petite Maison that had stirred my gastronomic juices and made me yearn to know more about the pleasures of French food.

As single girls in New York, my Bennington College roommate Sarah Moore and I loved to give little dinner parties in the summer, when we took over her family's vacated apartment on Riverside Drive. Our hope was to meet some new, exciting people and, for me, to break out of the mold that my conservative parents had projected for me. And good food seemed to me a naturally seductive enticement. Besides, I loved to cook. Sarah was good at making a potent martini—several of them, in fact, to loosen things up—and I would prepare a casserole of chicken and vegetables or a dish we called bitki (meatballs smothered in onions and sour cream), inexpensive dishes that just needed reheating when we were all ready to stagger to the table. I always got compliments for the food, but I knew how limited my repertoire was. Clearly a trip to Paris was in order.

In the spring of 1948, I met Arthur Koestler at some literary event, and he took an interest in this *jeune fille*'s ambition. It also happened that my cousin Jane had just married the writer John Gunther, and they were celebrating with a trip to Europe on the *Vulcania*. With them as chaperones, armed with letters of introduction from Koestler to a number of his friends (Jean-Paul Sartre, Albert Camus, and André Malraux, no less), and with Sarah as a companion, my family couldn't help but approve this adventure.

The voyage on the *Vulcania* that summer was not an auspicious beginning. The Gunthers were ensconced in a first-class cabin, but Sarah and I were traveling what was billed as third class. Later, I wrote home to my parents:

> *The trip over was something you'll never believe. What luck that you didn't have a glimpse of the hole where we were quartered. It was no tourist class—not even third—just plain steerage. The deck space was not even large enough for standing room and on rough or rainy days even that was closed off, so thousands of misery-eyed souls were confined to their 2 × 4 cabin spaces, rocking and moaning and vomiting on the floors where a bit of sawdust was thrown on top to cover the mess.*

But we survived by enchanting a young steward, who brought us oranges each morning and helped us find a back way up to first class, where Gunther arranged deck chairs for us. He would also take us at dinnertime into the elegant first-class dining room, where he would tell the waiter in a conspiratorial way that he'd need a table for four, since he was dining with his wife and two mistresses. The waiter, deadpan, would seat us at a fine table, and we'd hungrily consume enough to last us through the next day.

When we landed in Naples, the crowd pushing its way off the ship was so desperate that the sleeve was torn right out of a nice dress my mother had made for me. Our luggage was thoroughly searched. Hoping to find nuggets of cocaine or something, the customs man dug his way into our cosmetics bags. When he came upon a box of tampons, he started tearing each one apart, and we were helpless to stop him and explain their purpose. Just then a distinguished man from the American consulate, who had been delegated to meet the Gunthers, came to the rescue, explaining that tampons were a form of medication and should be left alone.

Then an Italian chauffeur took us on a hair-raising ride down the Amalfi Drive. We were all to stay with friends of the Gunthers in Positano, in a lovely villa that spilled down the rocks to the blue, blue Mediterranean. That evening we ate a seven-course meal that lasted until well after midnight, and then we fell into soft, quiet beds.

But, for all the seductions of Italy and the Côte d'Azur that Sarah and I traveled along by train, stopping at little seaside towns like Cassis, it was Paris that captured my heart. The moment we taxied across that magical city, bathed in early-evening light, I knew somehow that I belonged. Soon after we'd settled in at the Hôtel Montalembert, on the Left Bank, I wrote my parents enthusiastically:

> *Paris is such a wonderful city. It is the first place, and don't let this frighten you, where I'd really like to settle down and work. . . . In the evenings one sits around in cafés, eats in small and always good little restaurants,*

then dances perhaps—but in inexpensive and unelabo-
rate places. Nobody has much money; nobody drinks
much, except wine, but that is more for the taste to go
with good eating. . . . And my appetite is fantastic. I am
no longer content with a fish or meat course; it has to be
both. Another thing I find happy is that almost all
Frenchmen are bachelors until well into their thirties,
and have a good time until they are well established
before getting married. So there is a fortunate number of
gents about, gay [a favorite word of mine that had
quite a different meaning then] *and attractive, and*
one doesn't have to look to the forty-years-olds for
charm.

One of those older attractive bachelors was Pierre Ceria,
who had worked for *la résistance.* Malraux had given Koestler's
letter of introduction to his secretary, suggesting she invite me
to the weekly reunion of resistance heroes who met at a local
bar (it was the only letter, incidentally, that Koestler had written
that bore fruit; Sartre never answered, and Camus handwrote a
one-line note saying he was out of town—probably a good
thing for this susceptible young creature).

Pierre and I took a shine to each other, no doubt because I got
him talking about food. He took great pleasure in cooking and,
in spite of his hectic life as a journalist, zipping around town in
his little *deux-chevaux* Renault to do stories for the Gaumont
Actualités newsreels, he always had time for the long, lingering
lunch so dear to a Frenchman. Most evenings, on his way home,
he would pick up ingredients and then prepare a delicious meal.
He delighted in the challenge of introducing this curious young
American girl to the *vraie cuisine française.* His kitchen was

*Pierre Ceria, the French journalist,
who became chef of Le Cercle
du Cirque*

minuscule, as were most French apartment kitchens, but he would put together several courses, deftly switching frying pans over the limited number of burners, and tossing ingredients in the air with the jerk of his wrist.

One Sunday lunch, we had a fine *sole meunière* at a little *auberge* in the country, and a few days later he made it for me, first showing me at the market how to pick the right fresh sole, and then how to carefully scale and sauté it. I was in heaven. Moreover, he didn't speak a word of English—and had no desire to—so my culinary vocabulary grew rapidly.

Once, we drove to Brittany to visit friends of Pierre's in the small fishing village of Port Manech. The stone house was very primitive, and we had to pump water from the neighbor's well.

Each morning, after warming ourselves with big bowls of café au lait, we would all go fishing. Whatever we caught or gathered on the rocks—shrimps, mussels, mackerel, sardines, langoustines, sea urchins—would be prepared for lunch, everyone pitching in, opening the shells and cleaning the fish. There was always a jug of cider on the table to wash down those strong, briny flavors. I innocently thought I was just swilling down apple juice until I learned what a kick it had.

One evening we went out to a restaurant in nearby Riec-sur-Belon, which I described in one of my carefully composed letters to my parents as "the home of one of the most marvelous cooks in the world, Melanie. She is a lovely, gross woman who has dedicated her whole life to the art of eating in its finest forms." I went on to tell how "she showed us her amazing collection of modern paintings which artists from all over had given her in return for tasting of her marvelous cuisine," and added that the town was near Pont-Aven, where Gauguin lived and started the Pont-Aven school of painting—ever hopeful that my parents would see the connection between art and cuisine. "As to the food"—I did persist in telling them what I ate—

> First, oysters—a dozen of them, the best I have ever tasted—and there were no ill effects [that last remark was aimed at my mother, who in typical English fashion always worried about our digestive systems]; then, a kind of tiny clam the size of my little fingernail; next, lobster, enormous pieces, all hot in a fabulous sauce, a secret of Melanie's—and I couldn't possibly detect what was in it; then cold chicken with chicken liver pâté; and finally, a chocolate mousse, sort

of like one that Edie made but Melanie's was terribly
thick and chocolaty and rich with gobs of cream on top.

I didn't have to write my parents the details of the unexpected trip that Sarah and I made to Mont-Saint-Michel,
because they would soon be reading all about it in an upcoming
issue of *Life*, and I wanted them to be surprised. The magazine
was doing a feature on the many young Americans who were
flocking to Europe that summer of 1948. But evidently, despite
the premise, there weren't too many Americans to be found on
the streets of Paris, so when Barbara O'Conner, the writer for
Life, and Yale Joel, the photographer, spotted us poking around
Saint-Germain, they approached us and asked if we would be
willing to be featured in the story. They both liked the idea of
posing us in front of Mont-Saint-Michel, building a sand castle,
and we were more than willing to be their models in return for
such a glorious trip. Off we went toward the Atlantic in their
rented car, and after hamming it up on the beach for the camera,
we enjoyed the famous puffy omelette made by Mère Poularde
over the open hearth at her restaurant, and roamed the steep,
narrow streets of that storybook place. But what seemed so
rewarding, as we drove through the Loire countryside, was
stopping for lunch or dinner and finding in every village a small
bistro where the food was prepared to order with care and with
simple, good ingredients: a homemade pâté or maybe *rillettes;* a
thick, meaty soup; a sautéed freshly caught trout; a flavorful,
slightly chewy *entrecôte;* beautifully made French fries; and
always good local cheese.

This idyllic awakening to the delights of French life seemed
to pass all too quickly, so I bargained with Doubleday for an
extended leave. Sarah had to return, but we made a brief trip to

The picture that appeared in Life *of Sarah and me building a sand castle on the beach in front of Mont-Saint-Michel*

Stopping for lunch at a little café

London together, where I found the food (at the Connaught, no less) as "depressing as it is famed to be. Endless trays of quivering and jellied desserts and stewed fruits!" I confessed only to my father, fearing my mother would take offense.

Back in Paris, I reveled in the pleasure of being on my own. I found cheap lodging at the Hôtel Lenox, four flights up, with one shared bathtub on the second floor, and I learned to enjoy a meal by myself with half a bottle of wine in little local bistros. I could really only afford one meal a day, so I had to choose carefully.

One time, I settled down at an outdoor table on the Quai Voltaire and, after studying the menu, decided that the something of veal would be a good choice. After polishing off the first *plat*, I was presented with what were unmistakably brains—that something I didn't recognize was *cervelle de*. They were unadorned, so I could see the contour of each lobe, and they confronted me on a white plate in a pool of brownish butter speckled with what turned out to be a few capers. But this was my only meal of the day, so I dug in. And I'll never forget the first surprisingly delicious bite, much like the soft creaminess of sweetbreads. I licked the platter clean and blessed my heritage for having exposed me to the offal that most Americans shun.

Sometimes I would buy just a little charcuterie or cheese and a baguette and sit in one of the nearby squares or parks to eat. I marveled at the lines in the food shops, people waiting in old carpet slippers with maybe a toe sticking through—no matter how hard the times, they had to have a good noonday meal. I would feel abashed as I ordered only a stingy *tranche de pâté maison* while all around customers were filling their string shopping bags with *rillettes* and *terrine de canard* or foie gras.

I remember one day standing in line at a local *boulangerie* when suddenly a cry went up and everyone joined in. One of the regular customers, upon breaking open his baguette and seeing that it was made of pure white flour, shouted out his approval and passed the loaf around to others who shared his delight. For longer than anyone cared to remember, the bread had been a dirty gray, made from inferior flour and the leavings of the granary floor, and the pleasure the French people took in the recovery of their proud past after the humiliations of the Occupation was so contagious that I felt near tears.

A few days before my Paris sojourn was due to end, I was sitting in the Tuileries on a bench, reading. As I looked up at the sky, reveling again in that end-of-day light and wishing that I could stay forever, I felt a stranger eyeing me, so I got up hastily, tucking the book under my arm. What I didn't tuck under my arm was my purse, and I didn't realize until I'd walked away from the area where I'd been sitting that I had left it hanging on the bench. Of course, when I went back it was gone, and with it the ticket for my passage home, my American Express checks, my passport—in short, my identity. Little Miss Bailey no longer existed.

Even as I headed for a nearby *préfecture de police* to report my loss, I felt a certain calm, as though this disaster was an act of fate and I had better heed it. The police, after scolding me mildly and telling me to report next day to the United States Embassy, gave me a *jeton* so I could take the metro back to my hotel. Once there, I took stock of my situation and cagily left my door open, hoping someone would take pity on me. Sure enough, a bunch of fellow Americans, one of whom just happened to be from Greensboro, Vermont, where we had our summer home, took pity on me and they invited me out to dinner. By the time I went to bed that night, on a full stomach, my mind was made up.

3

Paris for Keeps

It was not easy to persuade my parents that staying on alone in Paris was a good idea. Where would I live? How could I get a job with no green card and only schoolgirl French? Could I manage all by myself? I tried to sound confident and reassuring:

> *Sweeties—*
>
> *Being in Paris is something I believe in and I hope you are convinced that it is a really good thing. I think I will get some exciting and interesting work, and I shall be a well-educated girl really knowing for once something that goes on in the world. Meanwhile I am not starving—only shivering, and the trunk is a must.*

As I was awaiting word about that trunk full of warm clothes, I stopped one chilly fall morning at the American Express on rue Scribe, then a hangout for Americans abroad, and by another stroke of fate I ran into Paul Chapin, a young Bard College student whom I had known during the weeks he interned at Doubleday the summer before. When he heard that I was down to my last *sou*, he immediately invited me to move into his aunt's spacious apartment, where he was staying. His aunt was the Princess Caetani, a patroness of the arts who sponsored a literary magazine, *Botteghe Oscure*, in Rome, where she was now living. The only other occupant was an older painter who had a room there, thanks to the Princess's largesse, but was off working in his studio all day. Without hesitation, I loaded up my few worldly goods and moved in. The painter turned out to be Balthus (of course, I'd never heard of him), and he seemed amenable when I was shown around. I was particularly taken with the wonderful big kitchen with tile floors, a huge stove, and copper pots hanging from the rafters. Balthus was suffering from a mysterious virus he had picked up somewhere in his travels—malaria, I was led to believe—and on days when he was having chills and fever he welcomed my bringing him a bowl of soup; I loved preparing it on the ancient range, which had obviously fed a large family for decades.

After I was comfortably settled in—we even acquired a handsome poodle named Nikki to complete the ménage—it seemed the logical next step for Paul and me to figure out a way we could manage our daily sustenance. Maybe we could pay for feeding ourselves by feeding others? It was a shame not to share the lovely ambience of the rue du Cirque, so why not have a little circle of homesick Americans come there several evenings a week to enjoy good food. We immediately started converting the large living room into a *salle à manger,* gathering up all the small tables we could find around the apartment, embellishing them with red-checked tablecloths and candlesticks improvised from empty champagne bottles dripping with wax (Paul had another aunt who had married into the Moët-Chandon family). Angèle, the building's concierge, joined in, polishing the hardwood floors by skating across them with a rag under her sturdy shoes to spruce things up for what she thought would be a dinner party. Even the reclusive Balthus, when he returned from his studio that evening, seemed to approve.

As to the chef, who could be better suited than my friend Pierre? He was captivated by the idea of donning an apron and educating the palates of Americans at the end of his hectic day pursuing news stories, particularly since he could lean on Paul and me as his two eager sous-chefs.

After targeting an opening night, Paul lined up as our clientele some Marshall Plan employees, an American *chanteuse* from a nearby nightclub, and a visiting Scotsman with several compatriots in tow. My contribution to the guest list was my cousin Jane, who just happened to have landed in Paris with her famous husband.

However, by the morning of the opening we still didn't know what the menu would be. When I pressed Pierre, he brushed me off with Gallic hauteur, responding that he couldn't possibly know until we'd gone to the market to see what was fresh and particularly enticing. That morning, he picked me up at about six in his little car, and we raced through the traffic to an open-air market to examine the day's produce before prodding fingers could bruise it. I understood about the prodding when Pierre demonstrated the proper way to judge the freshness of fish: Press your fingers into the flesh; if it springs back, he told me, *ça va bien,* but if an impression remains, *ça ne va pas,* the fish is tired. Also, he told me to bring the fish up to my nose and smell it. He carefully selected about eight pounds of shiny-skinned rascasse, grondin, daurade, turbot, and merlan, which he tossed whole into my waiting shopping bags. When I asked whether fish was to be the main course, he was dismissive. *Non, non, non*—only for the soup. Then we stopped to select several plump rabbits, hanging on hooks, still enrobed in their fur. Moving quickly among the fresh greens and herbs, I learned about the importance of savory and saffron, fennel and leeks and shallots—all new to me—and what they would impart to each dish.

As soon as we were back in the rue du Cirque kitchen, Pierre shot off rapid instructions about preparing our haul and took off to work, saying he would be back at lunchtime to check on our progress. It was then, after we had carefully simmered the catch of the day in aromatic broth, that he told us to strain all the fish through a *tamis,* a large, fine-meshed sieve that was conveniently hanging from a hook on the kitchen wall. So we pushed and scraped the flesh of the resistant fish through the *tamis* until it was reduced to a pulp, a labor-intensive process that took the two of us several hours. Fortunately, we had had the rabbits skinned in the market, and Pierre expertly disjointed them, not entrusting that task to us. Off he went again, leaving us with an afternoon of *éplucher*-ing and *couper*-ing the herbs and vegetables.

I have no memory of the impression that the *soupe de poisson* and *civet de lapin* made on our guests. The kitchen was too far from the salon, and I was busy dishing up (Paul got to serve drinks, so he was there for the applause). But when the last plate had been whisked away, I staggered up front. There was our chef, a Gauloise drooping from his mouth, talking intensely with John Gunther about the state of Europe. When Gunther looked up approvingly at me and remarked, "So—when are you going to open in New York?," I knew we were a success.

We were such a hit, in fact, that the following morning the phone was ringing and our instant regulars were trying to make reservations for the next night. We booked a full house again— and then we learned that Chef Pierre had to be out of town on an assignment. *Tant pis:* I would cook.

In one of those carefully worded letters to my parents, I confessed: "Meanwhile—and this will really alarm you—I have found a temporary means of support." I went on to describe "our truly bang-up opening night" and to regale them with details of the repeat performance when I had to manage the cuisine alone. I even reproduced the menu, describing my "hors d'oeuvre of lobster, crab, and a white fish in a rich, warm sauce with soft boiled eggs and shrimps in their shell all around." I didn't admit that I had to extend the martini hour (on the house, of course) so that the "poulet en crème" could become tender; evidently I hadn't made myself understood at the market, so I ended up with boiling hens, not broiling chickens. I boasted instead of "the dessert I invented, made with apples, crushed black grapes, sugar, and rum, all baked with a foamy sauce on top," and of how, after dinner, in front of the fire, we served "mulled wine, made sizzling with a hot poker."

But I realized that my attempts to persuade my family that feeding others was a noble calling fell on deaf ears. In my next letter, I cajoled, "I know you didn't send me to an expensive college to have me become a cook. But you must understand that in France cooking is not regarded as demeaning. It is an art."

Before they could book passage to come over and put a stop to my foolishness, the Princess Caetani had done the job. Unbeknownst to us, as Pierre continued to play chef to what we called Le Cercle du Cirque over the next few weeks, turning out *daube de boeuf, blanquette de veau,* and *cassoulet,* Angèle became increasingly suspicious of the goings-on on the *deuxième étage* and wrote to the Princess that she suspected the apartment was being used as a restaurant. The Princess was on the next train.

When we met, she took Paul and me out to a neighboring bistro, and she was very diplomatic, explaining only that she needed the apartment for relatives who were coming for a family wedding. There was not a word about "the restaurant," only a slightly condescending mention of the fact that Angèle had said that I was a good cook.

After I moved out, we decided as consolation to pool our

meager resources and take a quick trip to Monte Carlo. Paul
knew a young American couple with a car, and we piled in along
with our poodle, Nikki, and headed toward the Côte d'Azur.
After we had passed Lyon, we were getting hungry and noticed
a big sign on the highway announcing a restaurant called La
Pyramide in nearby Vienne. We'd never heard of the place, but
we decided to pull off and take a look. In the town's square
there was a large pyramid but no La Pyramide restaurant visi-
ble. Then we noticed, across the street, a wall with a gate on
which was posted a discreet sign: "Fernand Point, Restaura-
teur." That might be our destination, so we decided to take a
peek. Inside was an elegant courtyard filled with trees and flowers and herbs, and a building that might have been the house of
a modest country estate. When we were about to retreat, feeling
far too scruffy for such an elegant place, a very large man—
well over six feet and more than three hundred pounds, I'd
guess—approached us. His eyes were on Nikki, and he asked if
our *caniche* was hungry. I piped up and said yes, and so were we,
but I was afraid that we were not properly dressed for this
lovely place, and, of course, we didn't have a reservation.
Maybe it was because of our tawny-colored poodle (I learned
later that he had one) that he reached out his hand, said that he
was Fernand Point and wanted to feed us, so please come in.
Deep down, I believe that he not only wanted to show these
untutored Americans what a good French lunch could be but
also to express the profound sense of gratitude that he felt
toward the Americans who had brought an end to the Occupation, during which La Pyramide had closed its doors.

So he led us in and settled us at a comfortable table. Nikki
was fed first—an ample bowl of who knows what delicious tid-
bits. Then a succession of glorious dishes was placed in front of
us—pâtés, foie gras, *saucisson en croûte,* all made on the

premises, with piquant sauces; then a trout, and a *poulet de Bresse.* The wines flowed, a different taste sensation for each course. Toward the end of the meal, when the restaurant had emptied out, Monsieur Point sat down with us for a *digestif.* I wish I could remember more clearly all the details, but this was before I quite dared to take the subject of food entirely seriously. So I didn't even make notes. I just knew unconsciously that it was an experience that would help to shape my life. As to the bill, which we were naturally nervous about, it was no more than a medium-priced lunch we might have had in Paris.

When I learned later all about Point, particularly from Joseph Wechsberg's delicious Profile in *The New Yorker* that came out only a year later, I was so glad I hadn't known beforehand who this giant was.

Back at the good old Hôtel Lenox, another extraordinary act of fate decided my future. Trying to find a job, I had made a list of at least a half-dozen valuable people to see—Jeff Parsons at the *Herald Tribune;* Fleur Cowles, who was starting a new magazine; some high-up (not Howard Hunt) at the ECA (Economic Cooperation Administration)—and one by one I had crossed them off after interviews that produced no hope of a job. There was just one name left: a Mr. Jones, editor of *Weekend* magazine. He was my last hope, but where to find him? There was no office listed in the phone book, and I couldn't locate a magazine by that name on the stands. Then, late one afternoon, I walked into the lobby of the Lenox, where the single phone for the hotel was located, and I heard a female American voice loudly asking: "*Weekend?* Is this *Weekend* magazine?" As soon as she finished her business, inquiring about possible work in the art department there, I grabbed the phone from her. Within minutes I had wangled an interview. The next day I managed to find the offices of *Weekend,* located in an old residence behind a courtyard on the less fashionable end of the rue Saint-Honoré. Mr. Jones greeted me in what seemed like a nicely messy private study with a fire going in the grate. Pinned on the walls were dozens of photographs taken in Germany of two adorable little girls. He introduced me to them and said that this was his way of celebrating younger daughter Pamela's birthday. Both girls had returned to the States with their mother, and it was clear that he missed them. By the end of a long interview in which he diligently read some jacket copy I had written and brought along while we sipped a glass of dark, chicory-laden coffee, I had a job as his assistant.

The magazine, which started out as a weekend picture magazine for *Stars & Stripes,* the military newspaper, had had to strike out on its own when the deutschmark was devalued and

Me with Evan (center) *and the German photographer Hanns Hubmann, who shot many a brilliant photograph for* Weekend

there were no longer sufficient funds to underwrite it. The editors all put their meager savings into it and moved the publication to Paris, eventually changing the name to *Now,* and they were struggling to keep afloat in the face of the oncoming invasion of *Life* and *Look* magazines. So my pay was minimal, but I loved playing girl Friday to the editor—Dick Jones, as he was called then, although I came to prefer his middle name, Evan, with its unmistakably Welsh ring.

We quickly discovered that we shared the same passion for food. Our first lunch together, in cold, gray December, was at a bistro near the *Now* offices on the rue Saint-Honoré. Seeing *boudin blanc* listed on the menu, we asked what it was, and the waiter gave us a detailed description of this special holiday sausage made with white poultry meat, veal, cream, and bits of black truffle. We both thought it tasted marvelous, delicate and succulent, and somehow it sealed a bond between us. Taste can do that. (Later, when we were back in New York and couldn't find *boudin blanc,* we would make them for Christmas Eve. Evan would push the ground meat through a big sausage-plunger we brought back with us, and I would catch it in the casings—quite a sight [see page 226].)

Soon I moved into the large, comfortable apartment on the rue Lauriston in the upper-bourgeois 16th arrondissement that Evan shared with Sterling Lord, his young managing editor. Evan's brother and another reporter from Germany were in and out, so it was a full, lively household. I tried explaining the situation to my skeptical parents (remember, this was 1948):

> *Dearest ones—*
> *About the question of co-habitation, one might call it. I know it is hard for you to accept the idea of gents*

*and ladies all under one roof, but practically in terms of
expense it is not possible for me to live alone. The only
way you can beat the rent racket is to get a large place
and share it. And I couldn't stand living with four or
five girls, dormitory fashion—stockings drying all over
the place, etc. . . . They have a little Alsatian maid,
who babbles a strange combination of French and German and is a most economical cook.* [I remember how
she would bring us free shaved ice from the fish market, where her husband worked, for our martinis,
which always had a distinct fishy taste to them as a
result.] *That means I shan't be cooking for the boys,
which you were distressed about.*

Of course, secretly, I would have been delighted to cook for
the boys, but that was not in the cards. The magazine went
under, and the next few years in Paris were challenging, just trying to keep afloat.

After we left the rue Lauriston, we lived in a number of different *quartiers,* often with meager kitchen facilities—maybe
two burners, no oven, no refrigerator, just a metal storage box
under the kitchen window that kept food only as cool as it was
outside. So I learned to shop at least twice a day, like a Parisienne. In the mornings, I would go out to get milk for café au lait
and fresh bread or croissants (I can still see the *boulanger,* his
face and hands covered with flour, coming up the stairs from the
ovens below, where he had been baking all night so his customers would have fresh bread in the morning); then, in the
evenings, we would stand in line at the *charcuterie,* the *boucherie*
or *poissonière,* the *épicerie,* and sometimes, if we were feeling
flush, the *pâtisserie,* to say nothing of the *fromagerie* and the

marchand du vin. We could never buy too much at one time, because our little string shopping bags didn't accommodate much and we had so little storage room. But this kind of shopping was a way of life, and everyone seemed to enjoy it, particularly as cherished items that had been rationed for so long, like sugar, rice, and coffee, became more available. I thought the coffee was dreadful and described it in a letter home as "strange, greasy, dark beans to which I add chicory to make it go further," hoping, of course, for a care package of Maxwell House.

But in other ways my palate was constantly being awakened and honed. There was seldom a cookbook in the various places we rented. Only once did I discover on someone's shelf a copy of *Tante Marie,* the *Fannie Farmer* for the French housewife. But when I consulted it on *béchamel,* I was horrified to find that Tante Marie said it was all right to make it with water instead of milk. Even I knew better than that, so I decided to follow my better instincts. I learned primarily to ask questions. The first time I purchased a white, glistening, silver-toned daurade, I asked the fishmonger how to cook it and, with customers waiting, he described exactly how it should be done: left whole, of course, head and tail intact, and sautéed in lots of butter with a little white wine splashed in the pan and fresh herbs, preferably *estragon,* strewn on top. And when is it done? "When you tickle a fin and it pulls out easily. *Voilà*—it will be perfect." And it was. One day, as I bought an *entrecôte,* the chewy cut I had grown very fond of, I envisioned crisp French fries alongside, so I asked the butcher's wife at the cash register what her secret was for good *frites.* It's all in the fat, she assured me, whereupon she scooped up a combination of beef and pork fat in just the right proportion for me to take home.

The open-air markets were a revelation, bursting with fresh

produce. I always tried to follow the advice of Marie Clare McDonell, a thrifty Breton married to *Now*'s charming business manager, who told me that the only way to shop was to walk the length of the market to observe and compare before buying a thing. Sometimes it was hard to resist when the first spring morels, or baby artichokes, or tiny *fraises des bois* were decoratively displayed—delicacies that seemed so out of this world to me that I was always afraid they would all be snatched up before I could make the return trip.

But our income was limited, to say the least, so we learned to be frugal and inventive—the key to good French family cooking, I found. Evan was writing a novel, and I had finally managed to get a job advertised in the Paris *Trib* with an outfit called Rogers American Motors. When I showed up at the fancy address on the avenue Franklin Roosevelt and was interviewed by this short, heavy, gangster-looking man with a deep scar across his face, I quickly realized that he was looking for a genteel American girl to give respectability to his operation. And I fitted the bill. He had also hired a highly intelligent-looking, attractive young woman, Bettina Roth, who had a desk across the aisle from me; we got to know each other when our boss, Charlie Rogers, was off at the races and we could talk. She had been recently married to Jacques Roth, a German Jew who as a teenager had managed to escape across the border into Switzerland and had spent the war years hiding out in Occupied France and in Switzerland. Bettina's own family had gotten out of Germany in time and moved to London, where she finished her education. Her Oxford accent appealed to Charlie's notion of respectability, and he had hired her on the spot. It was a lucky thing, because she and her husband had almost no money then. Later, when I got to know Bettina better, she told me that during this period they had a nice rented room in an apartment on the Ile Saint-Louis but there wasn't much money left for food after they paid the rent. More often than not, supper would be a kind of faux hamburger made with thick slices of *gros pain*— a coarse bread made from inferior flour—on top of which Bettina would place a "hamburger" consisting 90 percent of yesterday's *gros pain* crumbled and mixed with 10 percent butcher's scraps of meat ground up. At least it was filling, and while they chewed, they would read "fantastic recipes," Bettina said, from books borrowed from the American Library, pretending that what they were eating was one of those dishes.

We wanted to meet each other's male counterparts, so I invited the Roths to come to dinner with us at the little atelier that we'd just moved into. In a letter to my mother and Aunt Hilda, I described the place as "utterly bewitching, actually the garage or carriage house of a very nice old Parisian mansion, set back off the street in a nice little court full of greenery and a gravel walk. It is located in the more elegant part of the Left Bank, an extension of the rue de Bellechasse where Doris Duke has a place and where Paul Chapin now stayed at his countess-cousin's." Clearly I thought that would impress them. I didn't, of course, mention my roommate.

The night the Roths came, they took a bus, and by chance Evan was on the same bus, so they sized each other up across the aisle. When they both got off at the same stop, Evan said, "You must be our guests." It was the beginning of a lifelong friendship. I remember that I had splurged and bought little langoustines for a first course, and a good steak. But before I could cook it on our tiny electric stove, the power suddenly went off, as it did so often in those postwar years in Paris. Fortunately, I had prepared the langoustines ahead of time, so we had them cold, followed by lots of cheeses, and the Roths didn't go home hungry.

The trouble with Charlie Rogers's enterprise that was providing Bettina and me with a measly wage was that he didn't have a permit from the French authorities to rent cars, and yet that was the business he was in. To lure customers, he hired a little plane to circle the ships when they arrived at Le Havre, floating a banner that said "Charlie Rogers American Motors— Welcome" followed by the avenue Franklin Roosevelt address. So the rich Americans were drawn there only to find that they had to buy one of his Cadillacs or Buicks outright. But that didn't bother the Hollywood types like John Garfield and Franchot Tone, or the director Anatole Litvak, all of whom dropped by. They would sign the papers and take off for the Riviera, expecting that when they returned they would get their money back minus a fair fee. But too often Charlie would have squandered everything at the racetrack and couldn't pay up. Nor could he always pay his employees, and more than once we went home empty-handed on Saturday night. Furthermore, the future was uncertain: We worried not only about irate customers wanting their vengeance but also about the very real possibility that the French gendarmes might show up one day and haul us all off to the clink. And eventually they did come, but only Charlie was arrested. Fortunately, his manager had called the help that morning and warned us not to come to work. Otherwise who knows how long I, who signed many an illegal document for him, might have lingered in the Santé prison, where Charlie was held for months before he was brought to trial.

Still, those impecunious days were full of inventiveness and fresh discoveries. I learned a lot about lesser cuts of meats for braises and stews; we would taste different kinds of innards at inexpensive neighborhood bistros, then try them at home—kidneys in a mustardy sauce, slow-braised tripe, tender little lambs' tongues, succulent neck meat and cheeks. They were all delicious, and we were fearless.

One Christmas, when we were living in a tiny apartment at the Porte de Saint-Cloud—one of the numerous small flats we heard about that could be rented for a very short time very inexpensively—on the outskirts of Paris, we had invited the Roths to have a *réveillon* feast with us. But just the day before, as Evan was coming home on the train, somehow a small stash of francs had slipped through a hole in his pocket, and we had hardly a *sou* left to buy the comparatively expensive turkey we planned to roast. So we scrounged around and put together enough to purchase at the open market a bargain goose, direct from the farm, that had not been plucked or even eviscerated. When we got it home and started to pluck, we discovered just how recalcitrant those feathers could be, and we had to resort to scalding the creature in a bathtub full of warm water to loosen them up. Moreover, we'd never cooked a goose and were astonished at the fat that gushed out of it. Yet somehow instinct prompted us to draw it off (and save it!), and the goose was a *succès fou,* surrounded by chestnuts, which could be had for a song, and served with sauce made from its giblets. Even its plump liver, which we sautéed in butter and shallots and a little Marsala, made a fine hors d'oeuvre spread on toast. It was a meal none of us will forget.

Another meal I will always cherish, not for its gastronomic importance but as a very French gesture of understanding and support, was a dinner given to welcome my mother when she finally decided to come to Paris to check up on her wayward

A view of Paris from the roof of our apartment in Saint-Cloud

daughter. My early food mentor—Aunt Marian, my father's sister, who shared his kind of mischief and loved to see the wheels go round—accompanied her (Monty pleaded busy, not wanting the confrontation). We were living then in a rented room in an apartment on the rather bourgeois Boulevard Péreire, and the proprietor had taken a liking to us. It was clear that she had a fondness for Americans when one opened her kitchen cupboard. It was crammed with all sorts of goodies, including Spam and tuna and canned asparagus and soups which some American GIs in Paris at the time of *la libération* had given her in appreciation of her generosity, taking them in and feeding them on her meager rations.

One of those cans of asparagus turned out to be a lifesaver. Madame Damianos had a handsome standard-size black poodle, whom she adored. But one day his greed got the better of him. He found Evan's razor, and in his eagerness to lick the shaving cream off it, he managed to chew up and swallow a whole razor blade. The vet was immediately called, and when he tentatively asked Madame if she had any asparagus—it wasn't the season for it—she remembered those cans. That will do it, the vet said. Stuff every last spear of asparagus down the dog's throat, he said. The fibers would form a ball, he hoped, catching the slivers of the razor blade and sending them safely right through— and out. I couldn't help but think what a French remedy this was, as Evan coaxed the whole large can of asparagus into the dog's mouth, spear by spear, and I stroked its throat, while Madame D. wrung her hands in anguish. But it worked. Next day, she assured us, the stools were evidence that it had all been flushed out, and she was eternally grateful.

So it wasn't surprising, when I confessed to her my desperation about Mother's finally discovering that Evan and I were living in sin, that she rose to the challenge and reassured me everything would be all right. I was to move all Evan's clothes into her already overstuffed closets, hide his writing materials in her desk, and clean up the bathroom so no trace of him could be found. Then she would put on a dinner for Mother and Auntie, and they would be completely taken in. I can't remember exactly what we ate, but when I told Madame D. that my mother was of English descent, that was all she needed to know. After Mama had inspected my living quarters, we all sat to a good soup and a well-done roast in Madame's candlelit dining room. It was a most civilized evening.

During those Boulevard Péreire days, we would usually head for the Left Bank when we wanted dinner out. There were so many little restaurants on those backstreets where you could linger over a leisurely meal all evening. One night, when Evan's brother, Russ, was in town, we went to an Algerian place on the rue de la Huchette to try couscous, and we stayed there drinking wine until everyone else had left. When we got the bill, we asked if we could pay in travelers' checks, but the rate of exchange the proprietor was trying to get away with was absurdly low. So Russ said he'd go around the corner and use a cash machine, but when he got to the restaurant door, he found it locked. At that point, the waitress, obviously sensing trouble, came with the key, opened the door, and let us out. However, the tough-looking proprietor, who had a bludgeon known as a *matraque* in his hand, followed us, and as Evan crossed the street and then turned, the guy cracked it down full-force on his forehead. When we finally got home—toward dawn, after an excruciatingly bumpy ride in a police wagon and a hearing at headquarters as the blood dripped from Evan's forehead— Madame Damianos took charge. She not only got us to her doctor, who sewed up the mess with a dozen or so deft stitches (sans anesthetic), but as we tucked our wounded man into bed, she laid her hand gently on the bandage and told me how it was a mark of our union and that I would cherish the scar it left for the rest of my life.

Of one thing I was certain: I was not to be lured home until after Evan had succeeded in getting a divorce and we could return as a legitimate couple. We were in no hurry. We dabbled in a literary agency and, ironically, had one big success selling a French publisher *Live Longer, Live Better* by Gaylord Hauser. He was what we used to think of as a health nut—not something the French fall for, at least in those days—and he'd been a paramour of Garbo. Whether that helped, I don't know, but soon, to my astonishment, *Vivez Jeune, Vivez Longtemps* was in bookshop windows all over Paris.

Other ways we earned our keep included publishing a little book called *How to Live in Paris on Practically Nothing*, which Evan wrote and to which I contributed a few food tips. Then, in 1950, I heard that Doubleday was opening a Paris office, and I persuaded Frank Price, who was to manage the office, that he needed me as an assistant. The first few months, he operated out of his rooms at the Hôtel de l'Université, and a fascinating world unfolded as Truman Capote, Jimmy Baldwin, and others would drop by in the late morning and gossip about the goings-on the night before in the gay bars. I particularly remember how Capote would appear at noon, still in his maroon bathrobe, to regale us with what had transpired the night before in the Latin Quarter, gesturing with his hands and giggling with delight.

But Frank soon realized that he needed a more respectable front, and he found an elegant apartment on the rue de la Faisanderie, near the Bois de Boulogne, to serve as both office and living space. He hired a hearty Yugoslavian maid, Baritza, who always made a nice substantial lunch for us and for visiting Doubleday authors, such as Somerset Maugham and Daphne du Maurier. Although I was paid a pittance, the perks made up for it. I enjoyed the leisurely pace, reading French submissions, typing French letters, getting to know some of the French publishers, and partaking of Baritza's cooking.

One day, when Frank had gone off into the heart of Paris for a literary lunch, I set to work on a pile of submissions that he wanted rejected. As I made my way through, I was drawn to the face on the cover of a book Calmann Lévy was about to publish. It was the French edition of *Anne Frank: The Diary of a Young Girl*. I started reading it—and I couldn't stop. All afternoon I remained curled up on the sofa, sharing Anne's life in that attic, until the last light was gone and I heard Frank's key at the front door. Surprised to find me still there, he was even more astonished to hear that it was Anne Frank who had kept me. But he was finally persuaded by my enthusiasm and let me get the book off to Doubleday in New York, urging them to publish it.

It didn't take much urging, and we were given the go-ahead to offer a contract. Otto Frank, Anne's father, who had discovered her manuscript when he returned from a concentration camp after the war, wanted to meet with us to make sure of our intentions, so we invited him to come down from Amsterdam for lunch.

After Baritza had served us one of her long, leisurely midday meals, so conducive to talk, he made just one stipulation. He wanted to have a say in the dramatic rights, because he admitted, with tears in his eyes, "I couldn't bear the thought of some actress playing my Annie."

Our wedding picture, with Russ on the right, Vienna, 1951

. . .

In the fall of 1951, Evan's divorce came through, and when the final papers were issued, the judge said solemnly: "*Ne mariez pas avant neuf mois.*" We looked baffled about the nine-month delay he was imposing, so he added, wagging his finger, "*Période de vacuité, vous comprenez*"—and then it dawned on us that the womb had to be empty. Well, given that it had been more than three years since Evan's wife had returned to the States with their two little girls, the *vacuité* was not an issue. But the French law is the French law. So we took the train for Vienna, where we managed to get a marriage license and to have a taste of Viennese food before we were married in a civil service with Evan's brother and sister, both working as journalists in Vienna at the time, as witnesses.

4

Julia to the Rescue

Back in New York, I was eager to maintain the French way of life. Evan and I would put together a delicious, carefully prepared meal every night for the two of us—something to begin with, a main course (in modest portions), salad and cheese (where they belong in a meal), and fruit. He had started cooking tentatively in Paris, and I'd encouraged him—mostly by leaving him alone. I find that men tend to have a different style at the stove: They usually read a recipe, or several, then take off on their own. And they like fast heat. Fortunately, because I'd had domineering women in my family and Evan had had his fair share of them, I didn't say a word when it looked as though a precious steak was going to catch fire. But his bolder approach invariably produced good results, and it was always more creative to have two cooks at work. We loved making an ambitious, elegant dinner for friends that would last well into the night, with the wine flowing, and we thought nothing of cooking for the better part of a Saturday or Sunday to prepare it.

I was often frustrated, though. So many ingredients I'd come to take for granted couldn't be found in American supermarkets: no shallots, no leeks, no fresh herbs; no delicate, slim *haricots verts*, seldom fresh mushrooms; big heads of iceberg lettuce were the prevailing salad green; cheeses were mostly processed, and even imported varieties seemed bland; butter was overly salted, and there was no lovely crème fraîche; garlic, if you could find it outside of Italian neighborhoods, came in nasty little boxes so you couldn't tell how dried up the cloves were (garlic salt or powder was the poisonous substitute called for in most recipes). Butchers were generally surly, and if you asked for anything out of the ordinary, like cheeks or brains, you were met with a shrug. Wines were expensive, and one thought twice about emptying a whole bottle into a beef stew. As for a crusty baguette to mop up the sauce on the plate, I searched in vain and had to settle for Pepperidge Farm rolls or soft, so-called Italian bread from the deli.

But it wasn't just the quality or lack of ingredients that seemed to make it difficult to re-create a dish with that unmistakable French touch. One needed certain essential equipment. Fortunately, I had bought a well-seasoned cast-iron cocotte at the flea market in Paris and lugged it home with me, and that served us well for browning and braising stew meats with vegetables in the same heavy pot. But we were sorely in need of an authentic omelette pan, really sturdy sauté skillets, straight-sided soufflé dishes and ramekins, a copper bowl and balloon whip, an adequate mortar and pestle, and those fine sieves so necessary for puréeing (this was, of course, well before the food processor came to the aid of the home cook), to say nothing of really sharp, well-balanced knives.

I also realized how much I didn't know. What made that *blanquette de veau* we served at our Cercle du Cirque so suave? I cursed myself for not having taken more notes, but Pierre had not been the kind to linger over details. What gave the *boeuf bourguignon* that winey depth of flavor? What made a great cassoulet so rich that even the beans tasted *onctueux*? I had been bumbling along through trial and error, asking questions but getting inadequate answers. For the French, it seemed, cooking was instinctive, absorbed at *mère* or *grandmère*'s knee. But I'd not been so lucky, and I realized I would have to find a way of learning these secret techniques. So I searched through all the old standby cookbooks, like *Joy of Cooking* and *Fannie Farmer,* and a few current ones that dabbled in French-sounding recipes, but I found nothing genuinely instructive. It was still the era of fast and simple. The prevailing message was that the poor little woman didn't have time to cook, and, moreover, it was beneath her dignity to waste time cooking if she could reach for a frozen product or a ready-made substitute. This was a message that the food industry had been skillfully promoting since the nineteenth century. Cookbooks boasted of the number of recipes they had crammed between the covers. A short recipe was encouraged, because, presumably, the briefer it was, the quicker it was to make. Who cared about the quality of the instruction? In fact, we were almost made to feel guilty for indulging in such a mundane occupation when we could be pursuing higher goals.

There were two voices of sanity out there in this wilderness: James Beard, the pioneering spokesman for good American cooking, and Helen Evans Brown, the advocate for fresh and sophisticated California food, and their correspondence during the 1950s gives a chilling picture of the taste of America at this low point in our gastronomic history. In 1955, Jim wrote to Helen about *The Dione Lucas Meat and Poultry Cook Book:* "It is so full of wrong attacks on the standard things that it made me feel something should be done to make this a better world for honest cookery." But he became so discouraged by the prevailing mood that he was almost ready to capitulate. Writing to her about a book they might do on entertaining, he added: "And much as I hate to say it, I am coming to the point of saying that we have to follow some of the trends and give quick-and-easies, and perhaps time each recipe and give short cuts for most of them. Even here [he was writing from Mexico] they are supermarket mad and frozen food mad. I'll hate us for taking the easy way out, but I know damn well we'll make money if we can make things easy better than the others can, and I think that is probably our mission in life." Later, Helen complained of the insidious power of the home economist: "Home economists! . . . Nothing I do is right anymore. . . . 'Lovely is not a word to apply to food.' 'Don't say stale bread, say day old bread,' etc. See what I mean? I am so self-conscious about everything I say that I can't write. . . ."

I wondered if the contempt for cooking was more pervasive in sophisticated metropolitan areas, and I secretly hoped that if we got out into the heartlands it would be a different story. But one summer in the mid-fifties, when Evan's father was ill, we left New York and spent several months in Northfield, Minnesota, helping out on the weekly newspaper that his family ran, and I was appalled to find that there in the breadbasket of America, with its rich fields of corn and wheat stretching across the horizon, you couldn't get any fresh seasonal produce in the supermarkets. There weren't even farm stands along the back roads. One could only assume that farmers had a little patch somewhere out back for raising family vegetables. Or did they? Judging from the food pages of the Twin City papers then, a casserole of canned string beans mixed with a can of mushroom soup and topped with canned fried noodles was more to everyone's liking. My mother had told us that Midwesterners ate out of cans, but I thought she was just reflecting the usual Easterner's snobbery.

Still searching for a good way of life, we decided to try country living, and through friends who were city dropouts, we rented a little house in Alstead, New Hampshire. Evan had a book to do that would keep bread and butter on the table, and I found occasional odd jobs, such as writing "fashion" stories and photographing the subjects for *Yankee* magazine as well as substituting as a teacher at the local grammar school. We had been in Alstead almost a year when we had a rude awakening. One day we got an unexpected call from the local plumber, a member of the school board, who said he had been delegated to ask us a few questions. The McCarthy Communist witch-hunting era had had an insidious effect that had not worn off by the late fifties, and in a small New England village outsiders were regarded with even more suspicion than usual. It seems that, while teaching one day, I had tried to explain to the class what the word "allies" meant, and I gave as an example England and Russia being our allies in World War II. Obviously some eager fifth-grader had run home with the news that his teacher had said the Soviets were our friends. How did I explain that? our friend the plumber asked. Then there were questions about why Evan had a beard, and why I wore my hair long and loose. Also, it seemed strange to some of the villagers that the shed adjoining our little house always had the shades drawn. What was going on there? (It was my improvised darkroom for developing my photographs.) And just as our interrogator was leaving, he shot one last remark at Evan: "I hear you like to cook, too." Did he mean to say that that was a suspicious, unmanly thing to do? I'll never know. But we managed to field the questions quite successfully, and the plumber left seemingly satisfied.

However, the incident left an uncomfortable taste. Also, the only job I was finally able to get in that rural community, since I clearly couldn't teach now, was at Gay's Express Trucking,

On our penthouse terrace. Evan is pouring wine into some newfangled wine dispenser.

across the river, in Bellows Falls, Vermont. What clinched things was when I was called in by my boss one day and offered a promotion and a slight raise. Somehow I couldn't see myself dispatching trucks around New England for the rest of my life. It was time to return to the big city.

The timing was good, too. Not long after we settled into a small penthouse apartment that we put together out of several tiny maid's rooms on the roof of the building where I'd grown up, I heard via the publishing grapevine that Blanche Knopf was looking for an editor. She had just fired a very capable young man and would have preferred, I'm sure, a male replacement. But fortunately I seemed the right person to fill the spot, particularly when she learned that I was responsible for Doubleday's publishing of *Anne Frank: The Diary of a Young Girl*. It still rankled that her editors, including, I presumed, the one just fired, had turned it down. When she interviewed me, she pulled out from a drawer a thick file of reports including that calamitous one as well as many others she had been hoarding. I think she also liked the fact that I had succeeded in introducing French women to Gaylord Hauser and his formula for *Vivez Jeune, Vivez Longtemps*. So she offered me a job.

Things were looking up, too, in the world of food. Craig Claiborne had taken over as editor of the food page of the *New York Times* and was producing some wonderful stories about real people who cooked—and enjoyed it. He managed to ferret out interesting home cooks in ethnic neighborhoods who were proud of their heritage and wanted to share it with fellow Americans. It looked as though the days of the "home ekkers" might be numbered. He also went out of his way as the restaurant critic to discover little hole-in-the-wall eating places, and would go back in the kitchen to observe and chat with the chef. After I got to know Craig, he would quite often suggest lunch at some place he was exploring, making the reservation in my conveniently anonymous name. Fortunately, he had a rather anonymous face, so he could poke around freely behind the scene without being recognized. James Beard was now touring the country, enthusiastically sizzling steaks on a little portable Skotch Grill he was promoting, participating in local cook-offs, and getting the message across that it was okay for men to cook. In Sonoma, California, Chuck Williams opened the first kitchen shop filled with good French pots and pans and other equipment that he personally selected. The response from home cooks was so positive that he soon expanded into San Francisco and launched a mail-order catalogue flavored with his personal recommendations that spoke to people all over the country. Clearly there was a need, and Chuck Williams sensed it. He operated out of his own deep love of cooking and his respect for really good pots and pans and other useful equipment that was hard to come by in those days.

The idea of working on cookbooks never even occurred to me when I settled in as an editor at Knopf. Blanche had hired me primarily to work with translators of French authors she had signed up after the war, such as Jean-Paul Sartre and Albert Camus. I particularly enjoyed immersing myself in the French translations and encountering the problems that each different voice presented as we tried to make that writer's style come alive in English. The lovely sound of French was dancing in my head again. But the thrill—and the presumption—of editing as distinguished an author as Elizabeth Bowen was something I had not anticipated. Blanche and Elizabeth were good friends, and I understood without being told that when Blanche asked me to act as her editor any editorial suggestions I might have would be strictly anonymous—that is, they would be passed along to Elizabeth Bowen as Blanche's ideas. But that didn't matter to me. However, after I had worked on three books by Bowen, I was included in a lunch the Knopfs gave to celebrate the publication of *The Little Girls* at one of Alfred's clubs. There were about ten people at the event, mostly from Knopf, and Bowen was very much at ease, regaling us with stories of the London literary scene as she gobbled down one appetizer after another, served on small plates. Then, suddenly, the accordion-pleated wall of the reception room we were in was pulled back, and there before us was an elegant table laid out for a multicourse lunch. Elizabeth let out a whoop of distress, saying she thought we'd eaten lunch, but nevertheless she sat down and devoured everything put before her. Later, when we were in the coatroom pulling on our boots, I felt her looking at me intently. Finally, when we were alone, she pointed a finger at me and said with her characteristic stammer, which she never let deter her, "You . . . you . . . you are the one." I was mortified. What had I done? And then she explained that she knew it wasn't Blanche who had been editing her these past several years. "Let's have lunch," she whispered conspiratorially. So, later that week, we did have a long, leisurely lunch that lasted well into the afternoon, during which, I was embarrassed to realize, she had managed to pry out of me my whole life story. She was that kind of insatiably curious novelist, and she did love a good lunch.

Alfred's approach was entirely different. When he selected one of his editors to take over a Knopf author of long standing, his first concern was for the author. He wanted to make sure that the writer would be well served by the editor. Some years later, when he asked me if I would like to handle John Hersey, before he made a commitment he invited not just me and Hersey to lunch but our respective spouses as well. We all met at the Old Drovers Inn, midway between New York and New Haven, where Hersey was teaching. The food and wine were good (although Hersey was strictly a beer man and stuck to his guns), and we all got along swimmingly. So I was anointed to take over, and I worked with Hersey on his last six books. It was a close working relationship, something I felt he had missed, and we had particular fun putting our heads together over the recipes tucked in that remarkable book he did called *Blues*, which celebrated the full cycle of life, from the chase and the catching of one of those magnificent bluefish to the gutting, filleting, and cooking of it. I was even honored to have a favorite Jones household recipe included, in which the deliciously oily,

Lunch at the Old Drovers Inn. Right to left: *Barbara Hersey, John Hersey, Alfred, me, and Evan*

strong-fleshed fish is broiled over a bed of fennel. In the dialogue between the Stranger and the Fisherman (i.e., Hersey) in the book, the Stranger exclaims when he tastes it, "This is superb." And the Fisherman answers, "Be careful. You'll inflate me with hubris.

> "I am in truth a God, I bring the dead
> By mere scent of my food, to life again."

On a more practical level, I learned the Canadian rule for determining how long to cook a fish: "Measure the fish at the thickest part, and then cook ten minutes to the inch." Even so, the Fisherman admits that, since the great crime is to overcook fish, he always cooks it a little less and tests with a fork. "If the fork goes straight through without resistance it's done; if it hits rubber, cook a bit longer." Now, there's a fisherman-writer who knows how to cook.

One day early on during my tenure at Knopf, Blanche called me in and asked me to handle a cookbook for which she had bought the American rights. It was Elizabeth David's *Italian Food*, and it had been enthusiastically recommended to us by Avis De Voto, who lived among the academics and literati of Cambridge, Massachusetts, and acted as a scout for Knopf. I was immediately captivated by the book, loving the way David managed to weave history, story, and personal experience into a collection of recipes, peppering it all with opinionated comment. My role was simply to see the book through production, since it had already been published in England and Avis was doing the necessary Americanizing of measure and terminology. But I couldn't resist getting into it and even making a few suggestions. Ingredients were not listed, for instance, and there were no serving amounts, which I thought might be daunting for an American audience. Moreover, in one of the recipes I tried, I ended up with three times the amount of stuffing I needed to fill the suggested number of courgettes, as the English called zucchini. I had the audacity to mention this in a letter to David, and I got a curt, condescending response putting down Americans and their need for precision. The implication was that you'd never be a real cook if you were so fussy about details like that—and the leftover stuffing could always be put to another use. Later, on the subject of translating the recipe titles she answered me with this gem:

> *Inconsistencies are inevitable in a cookery book and preferable, I think myself, to absurdities brought about by overzealousness in the matter of literal renderings. As*

you yourself so rightly observed, the English names often do not sound very appetizing, or convincing. Some of the Italian dishes in question are so well known that to translate them would be rather as if a Frenchman were to call Churchill "Eglisecolline." It has always been one of my criticisms of American cook books, if I may be forgiven for saying so, that the authors in the name of consistency, often go too far in this matter, thus divesting sometimes beautifully named old dishes of all their associations and evocative charm, so the reader no longer feels the urge to cook them.

I don't think one does any harm in crediting one's readers with a little imagination and knowledge of their own.

I mentioned my dilemma to Blanche, and her retort was "Then let's walk away from it." (This was one of her favorite tactics when things went amiss.) But the idea of walking away from Elizabeth David when she had just opened up a whole new world to me in the art of food writing was an appalling thought. So we went ahead and published it—quietly.

The only other cookbook I remember our publishing during my first couple of years at Knopf was *The Classic French Cuisine* by Joseph Donon. The book had been acquired by Alfred Knopf, who was a member of the Food and Wine Society and a friend of Samuel Chamberlain and other amateur connoisseurs of food and wine. Looking at the perfunctory recipes in the book, I could only conclude that Joseph Donon was writing for such gentlemen, who admired the art of cookery at a safe distance from the kitchen. As chef for the wealthy Mrs. Hamilton Twombly, of Vanderbilt descent, he presided over the kitchens of her many mansions. He was said to be the richest private chef in the world. So he wasn't really interested in luring his employers into his domain. Herbert Weinstock, to whom the book had been assigned for some mysterious reason (he was our erudite music editor, who didn't know or care beans about cooking), was puzzled, as was I, at the amounts the recipes yielded even though the number of people served was the normal six or eight. When he questioned the chef about this, the answer was that, of course, there had to be enough to feed the help in the kitchen, too.

Clearly Donon was not the answer to my quest.

Then, one day in the summer of 1959, a huge manuscript on French cooking by Mesdames Julia Child, Simone Beck, and Louisette Bertholle landed on my desk, courtesy of Bill Koshland, who was then the secretary of the Knopf establishment and a good friend in court. He was a genuine hands-on amateur cook, and we'd often compare notes on meals we'd made. He knew how much I loved French cooking, so he thought I might respond to this impressive tome. And, indeed, I did. From the moment I started turning the pages, I was *bouleversée,* as the French say—knocked out. This was the book I'd been searching for.

I started taking home recipes and trying them, and my faith was vindicated. I made the *boeuf bourguignon,* and before I even put on my apron, I learned all about the right cuts of beef to use (first choice as well as second choices, in case you were out in the sticks with no obliging butcher). I was introduced to *lardons,* the little pieces of pork fat that give that *onctueux* texture to the braising sauce, and learned that you could use bacon as a substitute but you had to blanch it first to subdue the smoky flavor. I discovered that it was important to use a combination of bacon fat and oil—not butter, which burns too easily—and that one should pat dry each chunk of beef first and brown only a few at a time (otherwise, the meat would merely steam and not get brown). I was admonished not to try to get away with some old jug of California red, that the Burgundy you cook with must be as good as what you would serve for dinner. I realized that I had to sauté to a golden hue the little white onions and the mushrooms, separately, so that they would caramelize and add flavor to the sauce, even if this did mean using two more pans, and I followed faithfully the final instructions for removing the fat and boiling down the cooking liquid to reduce it to a rich sauce. *Et voilà!* Evan and I agreed that it was the best *boeuf bourguignon* we had tasted since leaving France.

Soon I was absorbing the secrets to clarifying stock, whipping egg whites to seven or eight times their volume, making a perfect hollandaise (and knowing how to rescue it when it curdled), blanching vegetables to intensify their color, and prebaking a tart shell with little stones to weight it down so the bottom crust wouldn't buckle.

I realized, too, that the genius in these pages lay not only in explaining all the techniques so meticulously but in the structure, which was based on master recipes and their variations. Once you had done the basic *boeuf bourguignon* and absorbed all the essential information, you could apply that know-how to other stews and braises in almost any cookbook. It dawned on me that that might be a very good selling point in persuading the skeptics who would undoubtedly take issue with such a demanding cookbook written by three totally unknown ladies with no particular credentials.

After a month of steeping myself in the manuscript, I knew we had to publish it. But first, of course, I had to persuade Alfred Knopf that this was a work of genius and that the house of Knopf was the right publisher to launch it successfully. The fact that it was sponsored by Avis De Voto, who was the wife of the distinguished historian Bernard De Voto, helped considerably. Avis had first learned of the project after her husband, obviously at her urging, had written a piece for *The Atlantic Monthly* bemoaning the disappearance of good carbon-steel kitchen knives. This was a subject right up the alley of French-cooking enthusiast Julia Child, who was living in Paris; she spotted the story and wrote a fan letter that led to a heady correspondence. Avis soon learned that Julia, after graduating from the famous Cordon Bleu cooking school, had joined a little circle of *gourmettes* where she met up with two French women who were trying to write a book on French cooking for Americans, and they had asked Madame Child to join them.

Julia was the perfect person to take on such a challenge. When this tall gal from Pasadena, California, had arrived in France, she didn't speak a word of French and knew nothing about cooking. But after tasting her first impeccably cooked *fillet de sole meunière* en route to Paris, she was so smitten that she was determined to learn the secrets of French cooking. Encouraged by her husband, Paul, who worked for the State Department and had a sophisticated palate, she befriended all the neighborhood purveyors around their rue de l'Université apartment and soon became fluent enough in French to enroll in Cordon Bleu. It proved to be a rather unsympathetic institution, but Julia was undaunted. She had a highly analytical mind, and she was determined to understand all the techniques involved to make a recipe work. The chefs she worked with respected her, and soon she was giving little classes for fellow Americans in Paris, teaching the fundamentals she had learned. She realized, therefore, that a good book on French cooking for Americans had to be more than a collection of recipes. Her role should be to *translate* classic cuisine for the American home cook, explaining to them all the things she had needed to know—what to expect, what the rules were, viable substitutes for ingredients not then available in the States, and, to make life just a little easier, what steps could be done ahead. Simca, as Simone Beck was known, was an instinctively gifted and more impulsive cook, and Louisette Bertholle's role was limited (she was the one who had the useful contacts in America).

After Avis De Voto read the manuscript she received from the threesome in January 1953, she wrote that she was in "a state of stupefaction." She recommended that they forget about Sumner Putnam, a contact of Bertholle's, who had offered a modest advance for the original project but hadn't even responded when they sent him the manuscript, and she persuaded them to let her submit it to Houghton Mifflin. Dorothy de Santillana, an editor there, was impressed with the work. However, on the advice of the men in her company she told the authors they had to trim its encyclopedic length to a more manageable size. They tried to comply, but after six years of hard work, when they turned in the heavily revised version, the editor-in-chief, in a firm rejection letter, wrote that they had not come up with the "short simple book directed at the American housewife chauffeur" that Julia had promised. "The present book," he went on, "could never be called this. It is a big, expensive cookbook full of elaborate information and might well prove formidable to the housewife."

"I sighed," Julia noted in her memoir. "It just might be that The Book was unpublishable. . . . Maybe the editors were right. After all, there probably weren't many people like me who liked to fuss around in the kitchen."

But there was one. Me. And I was convinced that, if the book was so right for me, there were bound to be maybe thousands like me who really wanted to learn the whys and wherefores of good French cooking. Ordinary Americans, not just the privileged, were traveling to Europe now, in droves, and their taste buds had been awakened. I hoped we'd had our fill of quick-and-easy, and there was an appetite for the real thing. I felt the time was right.

I enlisted the help of my Knopf colleague Angus Cameron. He not only loved to cook but had been at Bobbs-Merrill when *Joy of Cooking* was published and knew a good deal about marketing a cookbook. To help persuade the Knopfs, he used my argument that this book was so thorough that its teachings could make recipes in other books work—even Chef Donon's. I was too junior an editor to attend the editorial meeting, so Angus made the pitch. Finally, Alfred said, "Well, let's give Mrs. Jones a chance." Whereupon Blanche walked out of the meeting, no doubt miffed that her French editor was going to be wasting her time on culinary pursuits.

At last I could write Mrs. Child that Knopf would be very proud to publish this unique work, confessing that the manuscript had "already revolutionized my own efforts in the cuisine." After Julia's delighted acceptance of our offer, letters flew back and forth between New York and Oslo, where Paul Child was now posted. We chewed over everything, including the need for more beef recipes (in deference to the American male appetite), the size of the portions (was two pounds of meat enough to serve six? Angus didn't think so), and how we could make the design of the book accommodate Julia's novel approach of running the ingredients in a column alongside the instructions, so they appeared only as they were used in the recipe. I loved the way Paul and Julia wanted to do the illustrations, photographing over the cook's shoulder so that what the reader sees—and what the illustrator would work from—is as the cook does it instead of a mirror image that the reader has to translate.

During that time, I got several elegantly handwritten letters from Paul addressed to me at home about the kind of line drawings we wanted. One day, when I picked up the mail, which was left on a table in the hall outside our apartment and another small penthouse much like ours that a young newly married couple had rented, I automatically reached for an envelope that had Paul's immediately recognizable writing on it and was postmarked Oslo before I realized that it was addressed not to me but to our penthouse neighbors, the Prud'hommes. When I delivered it to them, I couldn't help asking what their connection was with the Childs, and I learned that young Mr. Prud'homme was Paul's nephew. It seemed uncanny—as though my relationship with the Childs had been somehow foreordained. Forty years later, it was the son of the Prud'hommes, Alex, who would help Julia in the months before she died to finish the memoir I had been urging her to do, *My Life in France*.

From the late spring of 1960 through the next year, Julia became an increasing presence in our kitchen. I served as her sleuth, tracking down what ingredients and equipment were available in America, and would let her know that it was okay to include mussels (surprisingly, *Gourmet* magazine had just devoted a whole issue to them). I practiced fluting mushrooms, reporting to my mentor that I was "fluting two mushrooms a night and improving rapidly though I can't yet cry Eureka," and I tried all three of the ways of making omelettes by practicing, as Julia suggested, the jerking and tossing techniques using dried beans instead of eggs. I did it on our terrace to spare the kitchen floor, and, lo and behold, in the spring the beans sprouted, and young shoots popped up through the slats of the deck as a reminder of Julia's exactitude and my clumsiness.

We didn't always see eye to eye. When I ventured the suggestion that maybe the book might include a few more earthy peasant dishes, I got a dressing-down:

> *Neither Simca nor I are enthusiastic about including more of these. What with cassoulet, beef daubes, braised lamb with beans, braised sauerkraut and cabbage, boiled dinner, etc. the ground has about been covered. Perhaps Americans think French peasants are more peasanty than they are?? Absolute peasants boil everything. Farm people, concierges, and policemen cook like everybody else with fricassées à l'ancienne, blanquettes, bourguignons, and Orloffs.*

Actually, I had suggested the cassoulet recipe, having loved it in France, and to that they responded readily. But I didn't realize I was opening a Pandora's box. This was an area in which Simca clearly thought that she was the expert, and she wouldn't give an inch. Julia confided:

> *I never realized myself until I went into it how much controversy and deep feelings there were about the dish. My colleague, Simca, is one of those who feels passionately that it is not a Cassoulet unless it contains goose, and so far no amount of authoritative background to the contrary will budge her. (Ah, so French she is.) How-*

*ever I am hoping she will relent because goose is not
practical for the U.S.A.*

More and more I realized that Julia was the strong guiding
force behind the book and that she would not compromise the
vision she had of the book. It had to work for Americans, for
cooks as lacking in knowledge as Julia had been. She welcomed
the idea of my giving one of the office secretaries (as assistants
were then called) a recipe to try, to see if it made sense for a
complete neophyte. When a barrage of questions came back—
how hot was hot? why did the onions turn so dark? why did the
surface of the meat become dry?—Julia was quick to apologize
that she'd neglected at one point to say to turn down the heat
and to cover the pot in the oven. Horrors!

But at the same time, she did not suffer fools gladly. She
chided me when I suggested that home cooks might object to
the number of bowls and pots and pans she called for (all of
which someone had to clean up). "You'll never be a good cook
if you worry about that," she admonished. And she always
resisted giving in to the flimsies, as she called the not-serious
cook. Once, I told her about a man who late in life took a cooking class for beginners. He complained to his teacher, Marion
Cunningham (our latter-day Fannie Farmer), that recipe directions seemed so baffling. For example, he wasn't certain what it
meant "to toss the onions into the pan." So he decided to position the pan on the other side of his kitchen and toss the onions
into it, figuring that they were supposed to be aerated as they
sailed through the air. When Julia heard that, she howled in
derision and said: "Don't ever let that man into a kitchen
again."

As publication of the book was drawing near, we were still

wrestling with the right title. Julia sent me lists of suggestions, everything from *French Food at Last* and *A Map for the Territory of French Food* to *How, Why, What to Cook in the French Way* and *Method in Cuisine Madness.* Back to the drawing board. We liked the idea that French cookery was something to be mastered, but *The Mastery of . . .* sounded like an accomplishment— too daunting. Finally, I arrived at *Mastering the Art of French Cooking* and airmailed the title to Julia. She and her French colleagues were sold. "It implies scope, fundamentality, cooking, and France," she wrote. "The present participle saves the day."

However, when I triumphantly showed our title to Mr. Knopf, he scowled and said, "Well, I'll eat my hat if that title sells." I like to think of all the hats he had to eat.

By the summer of 1961, Paul had decided to retire from the State Department, and he and Julia had bought a handsome old house in Cambridge, Massachusetts, where they thought they would lead a quiet life, with Julia continuing her culinary pursuits, perhaps teaching a small group of students, and Paul painting and taking photographs. Little did they realize how *Mastering the Art of French Cooking* would change their lives.

The first time Julia walked into my office after our months of correspondence, through which we got to know and trust each other (although we still wrote "Mrs. Child" and "Mrs. Jones," as was the proper form of address then), I was struck immediately by the sheer force of her personality. She was a good head taller than Paul, who accompanied her, and she was very Smith College–American–looking in tweed skirt, sweater, and sensible shoes, with trim hair, tightly permed. But it was her voice, rising and falling with disarming forthrightness, that gave her authority as well as a certain unpredictability—you never quite knew what was going to emerge. And her earthiness, her unabashed love of food when she talked about it, was so refreshing. Paul was more measured and very sure. I immediately wished I had tidied up my office for him (and in future visits I always did). He seemed to observe everything and took careful notes, and I felt that he was a true partner, who both supported and challenged Julia.

In spite of my enthusiasm for our project, I knew next to nothing about launching a cookbook, and the house of Knopf didn't have much experience with this kind of publication. So when the first finished books appeared (Julia proclaimed them "perfectly beautiful . . . Who could dream of anything more satisfying to clasp to one's bosom?"), I boldly telephoned James Beard, and to my surprise he answered the phone himself. I described our book and he seemed intrigued, saying he would love to see a copy, and hoped he could help. He did, by persuading Dione Lucas to put on a dinner at her restaurant, The Egg Basket, and Jim personally invited what was then a very small nucleus of food and wine people and magazine editors.

I also called Craig Claiborne, whom I didn't know, and asked him to lunch. Being the good reporter that he was, over lunch he managed to get me to tell him about how Evan and I would fire up the grill on our terrace and cook a meal while neighbors stared with envy from their apartment windows. He felt there was a good story there for the *Times* food page and offered a bargain: If the Joneses would agree to put on a cookout so he could write about it, then, in return, he promised to give his attention to *Mastering* . . . And, if he thought it worthy, to review it.

It was a steamy hot day in late August when Craig arrived

with a photographer to watch Evan turning a roast lamb on the spit, while I filled seashells with cockles and mussels in a creamy sauce and ran them under the broiler for a starter. We were celebrating Welsh dishes that we'd discovered during a recent trip there, but we hadn't anticipated how hot it would be, the noon sun pounding down on our rooftop coupled with the glowing coals. It was worth it, though. Craig created an appealing story, and about six weeks later we opened the *New York Times* to find that he had written an extraordinary review. After calling *Mastering the Art of French Cooking* "comprehensive, laudable and monumental," he went on to praise the "glorious" recipes "painstakingly edited and written as if each were a masterpiece," and he ended declaring that this book would become a classic.

It couldn't have been a better send-off. After an initiation on the *Martha Deane* radio show, Julia and Simca, who came over for the launch, were invited to appear on the NBC *Today* show, and some four million Americans watched as they deftly flipped an omelette over a not-so-hot hot plate. It was a triumph, and Julia felt herself seduced by television.

The early sixties were well before the days when publishers launched a big book with an extensive author tour, and putting a cookbook author on the road was unheard of. But Julia had a natural instinct for publicity, and she and Simca set forth, armed with their own knives and pots and pans and an emergency hot plate. They stopped first at Grosse Pointe, Michigan, where Simca's very Frenchness had wowed the local ladies on a previous visit, and their performances together were such a hit that there were never enough books for all those they converted. Then they went on to the West Coast, where their days were filled with local radio and newspaper stories and demonstrations in department stores. Paul was always there, acting as stage manager, and more than once cleaning up the dishes behind the scenes, occasionally having to resort to washing them in the ladies' room.

But the miracle that occurred late the following spring was something that no one was prepared for. Julia was asked to go on what she called an egghead public-television show in Boston called *I've Been Reading*, and, fearing she wouldn't have enough to talk about to fill the half-hour, she brought along her trusty hot plate and made omelettes as well as demonstrating some fancy knife work. She was an immediate hit. The station got more letters than they'd ever received for a show, the gist of which was, Get that woman back on television. And WGBH heeded the call. By late fall, they started filming a series of twenty-six shows called *The French Chef,* and soon a star was born.

Clearly Julia had something that was unique in the fledgling television industry. She was completely natural, and the earthy observations, the slapping of the meat, the smacking of her lips, the satisfaction she got out of handling ingredients, and the way she let us into the intimacies of her kitchen gave license to all who watched her to enjoy the sheer *pleasure* of cooking.

I remember, some years later, when we were filming a series on Julia's techniques from *The Way to Cook,* I had the chance to watch her in action. The contents of each tape would be roughed out, but her script was totally unrehearsed. When she fished out a little cheesecloth bag full of herbs and aromatics— the *bouquet garni*—that had stewed a long time with the meat, and she held up the tired gray mass for all to see, she muttered, "Looks like a dead mouse," before throwing it in the trash can. Another memorable Julia moment of truth came when I was on the set as she as was preparing suckling pig. She was explaining how the ears and the tail could easily burn while the piglet was roasting in the oven, so the thing to do was to wrap a piece of foil around each. Then she paused, looking at the creature in front of her, and said that there was an even easier method for the tail. Fortunately, she pointed out, there's a natural little hole below the tail, so just tuck the tail into that and it won't burn.

As *The French Chef* went nationwide in 1963, Julia's name became a household word. Soon people who couldn't even boil an egg were feeling empowered by her. We had friends who had never before cooked a meal suddenly feeling confident enough to give a small dinner party à la Julia. When one was invited out to dinner, we would speculate, before setting forth, which of her dishes we might be served that evening. People began talking about food—where to get a good imported French cheese or a croissant, what wines went with what—and, sure enough, as the demand grew, even supermarkets started stocking ingredients such as fresh parsley and shallots. As Julia would admonish, if you can't find something, just talk to the manager. You're the customer.

What was most heartening to me was that food—and the pleasure of cooking it—was a subject at last out in the open. After more than a century of being told by the food industry that it was too much trouble and too demeaning for women to cook, we were all getting in the act now and loving it.

5

Voices in the Kitchen

While Julia was fast winning her way into the American hearth and home, in our kitchen a few new presences were materializing. I think that as an editor I was particularly interested at the time in trying to lure men into the kitchen. After all, if the challenge of preparing meals was shared, it would be less "work" for the "beleaguered" housewife. Also, I sensed what pleasure Evan got from cooking. He was in his element in the kitchen, and the more he was challenged, the more he liked it. He was particularly creative at making something delicious for a lonely writer's lunch out of bits of leftovers I stashed in the fridge. So I was drawn to a manuscript that came my way entitled *The Master in the Kitchen* by an American cook, Donn Pierce, an enthusiastic amateur who had traveled a lot and absorbed different styles. He also wasn't afraid to boast of male superiority in the kitchen.

> We men who cook seriously and not just when the spirit moves us are, in my opinion (and that of many women), better cooks. Maybe this is because few of us are married to the kitchen through sheer necessity. None of us is hampered by past cooking conventions. When we cook we are seldom out to save time but to spend it, if not recklessly, at least proudly. When more effort is involved than that

spent in just whipping up a meal, there is one great difference in the results: a far better meal. We have learned to be at ease in the kitchen—one of the secrets of good living.

What I didn't pay sufficient attention to was the admission in his introduction that he had been "a recipe-robber, undercover-sniffer, and pot-snooper in many kitchens" since childhood. The sniffing and snooping were, of course, okay, but recipe robbing should have sent up a red flag. Not long after the book was published, it came to light that Pierce had lifted verbatim several recipes from Peggy Harvey, a particular embarrassment since Knopf had published her cookbook shortly before I started working there.

Frankly, at that point I hadn't thought much about the copy-righting of recipes. I had just assumed that every recipe was derivative, and that the way a cookbook writer made it his own was in the interpretation, the language in which it was written, and the personal touches that the author-cook would be bound to add. And, in a sense, my instinct was right. Only the text of a recipe can be protected by copyright, not the ingredients used. But Pierce's versions of Peggy Harvey's recipes were a little too close for comfort. And I learned the hard way that one really had to know a lot about the author, question his ways of working, and make the rules of the game clear. When the voice is as unmistakable as, say, Julia's, there isn't any question of originality; it may be a classic *coq au vin* she is writing about, but it is *her* interpretation and *her* instructions every step of the way. In any event, when I had proudly sent off an advance copy of *The Master in the Kitchen* to Julia, she had called it "nifty . . . full of good and original recipes."

Then along came the Baron de Groot. If ever there was a distinctive voice, his was—seductive and delightfully persuasive, albeit a bit self-congratulatory. He had done one cookbook on the Rockefeller diet (whatever that was) and no serious writing about food as far as I knew, but I was immediately won over by his definition of the true meaning of "gourmet" in his proposal. Derived from "grommet," he explained, the term originally referred to the skilled manager of one of the household departments in the court of Louis XIV. In the new kitchen-speak, "gourmet" had become debased to an advertising slogan. I particularly disliked it when one of my Vermont cousins would say to me, "Oh, but you're a gourmet cook," as if the ordinary home cook and the gourmet cook were a world apart. That was precisely the barrier that Julia had so determinedly tried to break down, and I felt in de Groot a new champion. In the introduction, his three-part definition of a gourmet was "one who could expertly judge food in the market, who has skill and flexibility in the kitchen, and who shows, at the table, an exquisite sensitivity to the needs and desires of his guests. To develop these three qualities is the objective of this book." And he ended quoting Dr. Samuel Johnson: "He who does not mind his belly will hardly mind anything else." How could I resist?

When I made an offer for the book, which was to be titled *Feasts for All Seasons*, the agent told me that de Groot wanted to take me to lunch to make sure we were compatible. I was also informed that he had gradually turned blind after being wounded in the London blitz. So that he wouldn't have to deal with the menu, he would call me ahead to plan what he should order. When he did, he asked me if there was anything I could not eat, and the only thing that came to mind was my old nemesis—scallops—which I mentioned.

We were to meet at the elegant French restaurant Le Chambord in the East Fifties, and when I arrived, there he was, a large, imposing figure ensconced in a corner table with a big, well-behaved Seeing Eye shepherd at his feet. The service was attentive, and the first course came quickly. And it turned out to be, of all things, *coquilles Saint-Jacques*—plump scallops bathed in a *sauce parisienne* and gratinéed in their shells! Their fragrance was seductive, but I knew better. Fortunately, because de Groot could not see, I was able to sign-language my distress to the waiter, shaking my head vehemently and making a little upchucking gesture. The dish was swept quietly away and supplanted with something else, and the Baron never knew what had gone on.

Despite that inauspicious start, it turned out we were compatible, and I spent many hours in the de Groots' cozy walk-up apartment on Bleecker Street in Greenwich Village, helping him to formulate—and to make a touch more accessible—his ambitious, all-encompassing *Feasts for All Seasons*. His goal was to encourage families to cook together, to make every meal a celebration, to use seasonal produce, and to draw on regional dishes from all over the world, not to get stuck in the rut of cooking a single cuisine. He had two daughters, who had been taught to try anything, and who often shopped and cooked when their mother, Katherine, a Scots-Irish actor, was working. Together they devised ways to use leftovers creatively, and to manage the food budget, although, considering the number of rather costly ingredients called for, I often wondered how. But the manuscript pages were bursting with information about new (to me) seasonings and products, along with a wide-ranging directory of wines and cheeses, and an elaborate countdown system for planning one's time and working ahead. De Groot was proud that his family celebrated feast days from all over the world—another way of opening up the palates of young people—and he offered menus for an Arab Feast Day, a Spanish Fiesta Supper, and a Chinese New Year Dinner, among others. The Indian meal alone called for deep-fried dumplings, sole in spiced batter, chicken biryani, Persian rice, and flaky sweetmeats. But everybody could pitch in. And it seemed at the time as though that was just what many of us were eager to do.

When I was finally able to send the finished book to Julia, she seemed to agree:

> *My heaven, this book is a whole way of life! What care, love and work has gone into it. I am finding it*

De Groot shopping with his dog, Nustra

fascinating. . . . It is intensely personal, original, throbbing with sincerity and the earnest wish to communicate fully to the reader. I would think people would just love it as it is not like anything else.

Sometimes my faith in de Groot was a bit shaken. I had always been so impressed by his description of how he organized his refrigerator and freezer so that he had everything he needed easily at hand; there was even an illustration in the book of his perfectly stocked fridge, which I longed to emulate. Then, one day when I was down at his Bleecker Street apartment overlooking a common garden, he asked me to get something from the kitchen, and I sneaked a look inside his refrigerator. What I found was mostly empty shelves—no dark, smoked bacon, few containers of "encore" foods, no neat rows of garnishes and pickles. It was not only as haphazard as my refrigerator, it was surprisingly empty.

A few months after *Feasts for All Seasons* had been published and enthusiastically received, Roy Andries de Groot was given a special award by the Society for the Blind, and there was a luncheon at the Plaza to which he begged me to go. After much speech-making, the awards were bestowed, and then de Groot was led to the podium by his skillful dog, Nustra. When he returned to our table, he didn't even sit down. "Let's get out of here," he said. As he strode down Fifth Avenue, with Nustra parting the waves of pedestrians, he announced that he couldn't stay and hear more of such saccharine talk. I knew what he meant—that tone of condescension praising the wonderful blind man for such an inspirational book, a cookbook of all things. In a loud, arrogant voice, de Groot declared: "I won't be treated that way. I am a bastard. I've always been a bastard. And I will always be a bastard."

I discovered that quite a few people had encountered his more difficult side. One afternoon, when I was coming down the stairs from the de Groot apartment, the landlady on the ground floor beckoned to me. "You work with him," she said. "Do you really think he is blind? And do you really think he is a baron?" Yes, I could assure her, he was really blind. As to his being a baron, I didn't know and didn't care. I just knew that he loved food and wrote about it in an enthusiastic and persuasive way, and that was what counted.

To round out what became my triumvirate of male culinary mentors B.B. (Before Beard) there was Michael Field. In the mid-sixties, his first book, *Michael Field's Cooking School,* was published, and he quickly became a presence on the American culinary scene. We didn't make contact until later, when Knopf published his book of essays on the compositions of various foods and how to cook them. I was impressed with the depth of knowledge and extensive research that went into these pieces that had been published by *McCall's,* then a typical woman's magazine. If Middle America was being fed such interesting fare, that was a good sign of the times, and we rounded out the book *All Manner of Food* with recipes to put into practice what Field was teaching.

Michael Field started his career as a concert pianist and was known internationally as part of the duo piano team of Appleton and Field. I am not sure what made him switch to the kitchen, but he always had the flair of a performer when he was waving his pots and pans. When I attended one of his classes, it was as though at least three pianos were all playing at once, and I remember a middle-aged, very puzzled-looking woman in the back of the room furiously trying to take notes. She asked me if I wouldn't intervene and persuade the maestro to go back and revisit that first recipe for veal scallops—she was lost. The few times we had dinner at the Fields', Michael never sat down, and it troubled me that he was missing an important part of what made cooking so rewarding. But that fervent energy he had did serve him well in the pursuit of the mysteries of the egg, the versatility of the lemon, the strident voice of garlic, and he would hop a plane at the drop of a fork to taste and test some exotic ingredient in its own *terroir*. He could be preachy and overly opinionated, but he wrote with such authority that his voice was often heard in our kitchen: "Michael says never salt the steak before cooking," I'd proclaim. "But Jim says to salt first," Evan would remind me. Which way to go? Well, that's how you become your own cook.

In the late sixties, I published a book by Michael on a subject I have always felt strongly about—leftovers. They get short shrift in most cookbooks and food magazines, because leftovers have such a bad connotation. The emphasis is always on the dish that will impress your guests, and yesterday's lamb, even topped with mashed potatoes and called shepherd's pie, is not likely to do that. Yet so many of the world's great dishes, like cassoulet and moussaka, were born out of leftovers. Moreover, using effectively those odds and ends that are left over is part of the rhythm of home cooking and challenges the creativity of the cook. So together we devised a fancy title that would give dignity to the subject, *Culinary Classics and Improvisations,* and I worked hard to try to get Michael to focus his musical talents on improvising. But his heart was not quite in it. Instead, he did a splendid book on some of the great classic dishes that were based on an already cooked ingredient. Often his second-round creation was three times as demanding to make as the original dish, but no matter—the recipes were first-rate, and there were lots of good "odds and ends" suggestions.

Michael Field with M.F.K. Fisher

Meanwhile, Julia was working full steam ahead with Simca on Volume II of *Mastering*. I was more intimately involved in the development of this book, and Julia would send sections in rough form as she and Simca went along. (Bertholle, who had married again, was not a co-author this time.) Our most intense work sessions were during the times when I would go up to the Childs' house in Cambridge and we would huddle together over the manuscript spread out on the kitchen table. The kitchen was unmistakably the center of activity in that old, rambling house, with pots and pans and equipment hanging from the walls all around us. Paul would be in and out, always at the ready with his camera if there were intricate procedures to be recorded for the illustrations.

I remember a frequently used phrase of Paul's—"Submit it to the test, Julie"—and one day I could see clearly how she heeded that admonition. I had asked if she and Simca could do a section on charcuterie in Volume II, because there were so many items in that category that were an essential part of French cooking—sausages of all kinds, including my favorite *boudin blanc,* and *saucisson de Toulouse,* which lent flavor to cassoulet, to say nothing of preserved goose, and pâtés and terrines, which, of course, the French housewife could purchase ready-made around the corner. So the first thing I saw next time I walked into the Cambridge kitchen was a wall on which Julia had posted a large chart marked "Sausage-making." There were columns in which she had cited ancient French charcuterie sources followed by her test results, the final column devoted to her own formulas along with a critical analysis of each effort. I was impressed, but she assured me that if you didn't use casings sausage-making was really no harder than making hamburger patties. Well, maybe, after she had done all the investigative work to arrive at the right formula.

Those work sessions in Julia's kitchen were labor-intensive, to say the least, and I always learned something new. Once, when I told her that I had not understood a fine point in her manuscript instructions for making puff pastry—something she was determined that the serious home cook should master— she put me to the test. "Just try it out, dearie," she said, and handed me her giant-size rolling pin and stood me in front of her pastry marble. As I struggled with the scary process of smearing the butter onto the dough—too cold and it wouldn't budge; too warm and it would leak through the pastry when it was rolled out—she watched my every move and then fine-tuned her instructions where I had faltered.

Often we worked so hard through the day that we hardly stopped for lunch—maybe just threw together a tuna-fish sandwich, or corned-beef hash straight from the can (and even then I learned an important *truc* from Julia: Add a little stock when cooking the hash, to give it a nice glaze). Finally, at ten or

Working with Julia in her kitchen in Cambridge

eleven in the evening, Julia would sweep everything aside and declare, "Time for dinner." Paul would set the table—in the kitchen, of course—and make the cocktails, I'd be asked to make a nice little potato dish and perhaps a salad, Julia would whip up a delicious simple main course, and in no time we would be sitting at the table enjoying a *soigné* (to use one of her favorite words) dinner with a good bottle of wine from Paul's cellar. Well after midnight, we would fall into our beds, and then, at six the next morning, I would be awakened by the thump-thump-thump of Julia and Paul doing their morning exercises on the floor.

I also asked, as they were winding up work on Volume II, if Julia and Simca could see their way to giving a workable recipe for French bread. I felt that a good baguette was such an integral part of a French meal, and it was not something you could buy readily in those days, even in New York. Julia agreed, but was still so immersed in *marmites* and *matelotes* and *pithiviers* that she didn't have time to throw herself into bread-baking, and Simca thought it was all nonsense (that was what *boulangers* were for). So the task was assigned to Paul, who used to make bread when he was in college. Poor Paul. I think he produced over sixty loaves, several of which he mailed to me in New York, and they arrived looking like the sad, twisted limbs of a gnarled olive tree. But Julia would not be defeated. She sought out the renowned Professor Calvel of the Ecole Française de Meunerie, packed up the American flour and yeast and salt she and Paul had been using, and set off for Paris. "And it was like the sun in all its glory suddenly breaking through the shades of gloom," she wrote in the book's introduction. To me she sent a postcard saying simply, "It's all in the shaping of the loaves." Right, but there was also, she discovered, the important business of the long, cool rising of the dough, simulating a baker's oven, slashing the loaves correctly after shaping them, and creating steam. No wonder the recipe was eleven pages long—an example of the kind of carefully spelled-out instruction that Julia developed to an art. I treasure it, and still often make my own baguettes, even though today I have only to walk down the street to find one equally good or better. But if I buy one that someone else has made, I don't have the fun of tearing off a hunk of dough after it has risen to make a small pizza or a focaccia for lunch.

It became clear to me, in working so closely with Julia, that her relationship with Simca was growing more and more strained. How much Simca realized what a celebrity Julia had become is hard to determine (surely she must have seen her as *Time* magazine's cover girl in the fall of 1966). As Julia was becoming more and more confident and was looked to as an expert on everything French, Simca was more condescending and difficult. I was in Julia's Cambridge kitchen once when Volume II was just about completed, and a fat letter from Simca arrived. Julia started reading it aloud, doing a hilarious imitation of the French hauteur (*non, non, non, ce n'est pas français*), and finally she threw the letter on the floor and stamped on it. "I will not be treated like dog Tray any more," she cried. Paul cheered. This was something he had been waiting for. And I knew it was a turning point in her life.

When the second book was published, Simca participated in some of the promotion but not as much as she had before. It was Julia whom everyone wanted now, and her tour schedule was packed with appearances.

She was so in demand that at Knopf we even took turns squiring her and Paul around, and in San Francisco I had a taste of being on the road with her. At one point, we were in a large, crowded elevator, and as Julia said something to me, someone in the back recognized that throaty voice and cried, "Why, it's Julia Child." All eyes turned. I was glad Simca was not along.

After an all-day round of cooking demonstrations and interviews, by evening Julia and Paul were eager to dodge the crowds and would head toward Chinatown. Chinese cooking was their second love—they had met in the Far East during the war—and they could always sniff out a good place and know instinctively how to order. For me a new world opened up as steaming platters of colorful, heady-scented dishes, all served at once, were plunked down in the middle of the table, often on a lazy Susan, so all could dig in. And dig in they did. The only trouble was that I had never really used chopsticks before, and while I was still trying to balance them between my thumb and fingers and get a good grip, most of the dish I was aiming at had been consumed. Julia was a voracious eater, and she and Paul were completely adept at the art of plunging chopsticks into a slippery stir-fry and coming up with a substantial, well-balanced mouthful. And they were so ravenous they hardly noticed I was going hungry. Oh well, another useful lesson learned. When I got home, I cooked and ate only with chopsticks for weeks, until I could hold my own with the most adept.

To celebrate the launching of *Mastering II*, Julia persuaded Evan and me to come to Provence for Christmas. She and Paul had recently finished building as a second home a lovely, typical Provençal country house on property that Simca and her husband, Jean, had offered them. Evan and I stayed at a country *auberge* not far from their village of Plascassier and had fun sampling the local fare: the *pâté de bécasse* in oval crocks with the woodcock's head and long beak emerging at one end and the two clawed feet at the other; whole *alouettes*, little larks embedded in jelly; terrines of hare, duck, pheasant; and whole stuffed piglets with *"joyeux Noël"* written in strips of fat along their glistening sides; and, of course, our sentimental favorites, *boudins blancs*. Ernest's, the favorite charcuterie in Plascassier, had lines around the block, and at one point when a delivery truck hurtled down the narrow passage, the arm of a kind man reached out and flattened me for protection against the building. Christmas, particularly in the provinces, created a special kind of camaraderie among the French, and it all seemed to spring from an unabashed pleasure in food.

We had to restrain ourselves to be able to enjoy the repasts at Julia's. On Christmas Day, I went over to La Pitchoune (The Little Thing), as the Childs called their house, to help stuff the goose for dinner. After showing me how to judge the approximate age of the bird by pressing the breast and breast bones, which should not be too rigid, Julia pointed out how important it was that the feet were still attached. Only that way could you get at those pesky tendons, which had to be pulled out in order to make the legs tender enough to enjoy. Whereupon she cracked one of the ankle bones with a single solid whack, slit open the skin enough to reach in and wind her fingers around the tendons, then plunked the bird on the floor, positioned a broomstick over the ankles, and, straddling it, pulled. Lo and behold, after only one hefty tug, the tendons came out whole. "Just like pulling the cork out of a bottle," she declared. It was another lesson to tuck away, although when I would have the chance to use it, I wasn't sure.

For Christmas dinner we were treated to a new apéritif that Paul created of French vermouth, Dubonnet, orange essence, and dark rum.

There was a first course of *jambon persillé* made by the local *traiteur*, and then the goose, cooked to perfection with its stuffing of gizzards (which I'd been instructed to peel carefully), sausage, whole chestnuts in their own syrup, and preserved prunes steeped in brandy. And for dessert a splendid *bûche de Noël*.

The *réveillon* for New Year's Eve was chez Simca and Jean. When we arrived at nine-thirty at their *vieux mas*, just a stone's throw away from La Pitchoune, the French guests were already there, the ladies well settled into comfortable chairs circled around the fireplace, awaiting the celebration—namely, the arrival of the food. It started with a procession of *amuse-gueules* to titillate the palate—caviar, shrimp in flaky pastry, smoked salmon, a pâté of *grives* (thrushes), and foie gras that Simca had prepared. It seemed like an endless cascade, and Jean passed these delights one by one to the ample French women, who never stirred from their chairs and, unlike the puritans I'd grown up with, clucked with delight, licking their fingers and reaching for another bite.

Knowing how much more there was to come, since we had been told by Jean how he had killed with his own hand their obviously well-fed year-old hen to make their annual *potée normande*, a specialty of Simca's native Normandy, I wondered how on earth we were going to tuck away more rich food. But the secret lay in one of the great appetite-revivers—the broth from the *potée*, so fragrant and restorative with its marrow and earthy root vegetables that it seemed to pick up the leaden appetite and stir new juices of—was it possible?—hunger. Whereupon we had a plateful of everything that had gone into the big copper cauldron: a good piece of that meaty hen, a slice of pork, another of well-larded beef, a chunk of garlicky Provençal sausage, surrounded by leeks and carrots, and over all a spoonful of lovely, creamy sauce. This last plate kept us eating until almost midnight, when champagne corks popped and we toasted in the New Year, embracing friend and stranger, and kissing each of them on both cheeks. And then we danced off some of our evening-long gorging to fox-trots played on an old Victrola. I felt in every fiber of my being that I was back where I belonged.

Simca and Julia were like sisters who had long nourished each other but were ready now to go their separate ways. Which they did. Simca wrote a beguiling book, *Simca's Cuisine*, aimed at people "who adore to cook and partake of *la véritable cuisine à la française*" (to which she alone had the key?), and I experienced firsthand what Julia had endured those many years of their collaboration. No wonder that Julia called her *la super française*. Deep down, it was hard for Simca ever to believe that Americans could really cook the French way, and it was no easy task translating what she did so brilliantly and instinctively to workable recipes.

At one point, after a dispute about terminology, I wrote in exasperation: "My dear Simca, we do know the difference between a tart and a cake." But I never ceased to be amazed at her output—the number of recipes she zipped through in a day, feeding them all to Jean for him to critique (I even cautioned her that maybe she was stuffing him beyond redemption), then waiting impatiently for me or her American collaborator to try them and, for the most part, disdaining whatever criticism we might have. Even Jim Beard pitched in after I had repeated trouble with the raspberry sorbet made with cooked meringue (he had tasted it and thought it so delicious he couldn't bear not to perfect it so that it would work, as he said, for any fool). And that was it—everything was so delicious and original that you wanted it to succeed. Simca had an extraordinary palate. She managed to wed the *normande* side of her nature (lots of cream, eggs, cheese) with the more assertive flavors she came to love in Provence (garlic, anchovies, peppers). She could taste a chef's new creation and know in a flash what went into it and how to simulate it at home. It was the analytic part and the details that she didn't have the patience for.

Meanwhile, Julia, no longer having to speak for her French colleagues, found her own separate voice, embracing new ideas, new products, and always hand-holding and inspiring the American home cook.

6

Food as Memory

By the late sixties, the American food scene was undergoing some radical changes. New waves of immigrants were encouraged to express their culinary heritage rather than suppressing it or modifying it to suit presumed American tastes. Chinese restaurants started offering more enticing fare than chop suey and egg rolls and bland, sweetish stir-fries. You might even be able, if you persisted, to order from the special menu reserved for the Chinese clientele. Regional Hunan and Szechuan places started sprouting up, too, giving us a taste for spicy-hot. A Greek proprietor, who in the past might have run a simple steakhouse, would now embellish his menu with stuffed grape leaves, hummus, spanakopita, and moussaka. Indian restaurants gradually came into their own, and we learned what curry was in all its variety—not just a bright, yellowy powder that came in a jar. Italian food took on new life when regional foods emerged, and soon our palates, jaded by spaghetti and meatballs, were welcoming the different flavors of Bologna, Tuscany, Friuli, and Trieste. Restaurant Associates played with the idea of theme restaurants, such as the Forum of the Twelve Caesars and La Fonda del Sol in Rockefeller Center, designed around a huge hearth with an open grill where suckling pigs turned on a spit and the blending of pre-Columbian and South American was the accent; alas, the concept was before its time, but it did open our palates to the excitements of Latin American cooking, which had been heretofore ignored.

Inevitably, cookbooks were picking up on the new trends, and I felt that it was more important than ever that these cuisines be presented so that we had a sense of how they had evolved and how they could be translated to our own home kitchens, using ingredients that were locally available or else substitutes that actually worked. With a new, exotic, unfamiliar style of cooking, more than ever we are flying blind—we may never even have tasted the dish we are trying to reproduce—and we need a lot of hand-holding. So I kept my eyes and ears, to say nothing of my taste buds, open to the kind of writer-cook who was particularly gifted, like Julia, at explaining the techniques of a different cooking culture. Among those I eventually worked with, I discovered one characteristic they had in common: They were amateur cooks who had had to learn for themselves and so could identify with the home cooks' needs. Moreover, being transplanted to another land, they were driven by a yearning to reproduce the foods that formed them in childhood. And they wanted to share that journey of discovery with all of us to help keep those memories and that food tradition alive.

In the early seventies, when Evan's brother, Russ, was a news correspondent in Tel Aviv, he came across *A Book of Middle Eastern Food* by Claudia Roden, which everyone in Israel seemed to be cooking from. He sent us a copy, and we found it enchanting—full of history and family stories and a wide range of delicious-sounding recipes from the Middle East and North Africa. It had been written by a young woman who had grown up in a Sephardic family in Cairo. As an art student in Paris, she found herself homesick for the activities of preparing and eating those special, flavorful foods of her childhood, so she

Claudia Roden

started contacting family and friends all over to collect recipes. When her family was forced out of Egypt during the Suez crisis and migrated to London, her quest became even more urgent, for she discovered that celebrating these dishes was a way to get together to "rejoice in our food and summon the ghosts of the past." In the introduction to the book, she wrote:

> Each dish has filled our house in turn with the smells of the *Muski*, the Cairo market, of the *cornice* in Alexandria, of Gropi's and the famous Hati Restaurant. Each dish has brought back memories of great and small occasions, of festivals, of the emotions of those times, and of the sayings invariably said. They have conjured up memories of street vendors, bakeries and pastry shops, and of the brilliant colors and sounds of the markets. Pickles and cheeses have re-created for us the atmosphere of the grocery shop around the corner, down to which a

constant flow of baskets would be lowered from the windows above, descending with coins, and going up again with food. It is these smells, emotions, habits, and traditions, attached to and inseparable from our dishes, a small part of our distinctive cultures that I have tried to convey with food.

Soon American kitchens, I was convinced, would be filled with these new smells and taste sensations as we launched the book here. When I sent James Beard an advance copy, he pronounced it "a landmark in the field of cooking" and insisted that we get Claudia Roden over from London so that the food world could get to know her. He would give a party to introduce her. It was held in the garden of his Greenwich Village house, where a luscious array of Middle Eastern *mezze,* such as stuffed vine leaves and taramasalata and little meat pies, all those sumptuous bites that are a way of life in that part of the world, were spread out on low tables to seduce the uninitiated.

I went to meet Claudia at the airport when she arrived, because I sensed that as a sheltered Middle Eastern wife and mother she would be somewhat awed by her first venture to America. As I saw her coming up the escalator, she looked so radiant that I was sure this was an important moment in her life. The next day, she called me and confessed how thrilled she was spending her first night alone in New York in a hotel room. It was as though she knew that her journey with food had finally given her a passport to freedom and to finding herself.

It was Craig Claiborne, with his instinct for ferreting out hidden culinary sources, who discovered Marcella Hazan, a native of Emilia-Romagna. She was a biologist who had turned to cooking after she came to this country, and she was giving small classes on Italian regional cooking in her East Seventies apartment in Manhattan, one of those modern buildings that gave such short shrift to the kitchen that you could barely get two people into it at the same time. But that didn't bother Marcella— in fact, it was an advantage, because it kept the students out, and she did not believe in participation classes. Craig was impressed at all he learned from her, and he wrote such a persuasive piece about Marcella for the *Times* that she was quickly offered a book contract. Unfortunately, it was with a publisher who had no experience in marketing cookbooks, and when her *The Classic Italian Cookbook* came out, Marcella was frustrated at the lack of publicity it got. So she turned to—who else but?— Julia, and Julia took charge. She advised the Hazans to talk to me about having Knopf take over the book, and I was invited to lunch. Marcella produced a rich and flavorful lunch, with both *primo* and *secondo* courses, and her husband, Victor, pedaled home on his bicycle from where he worked in the fur district to partake of both the good meal and the serious book talk.

I soon realized what an integral role Victor had in their success. As a noncook, but with a fine critical palate and a knowledge of Italian food and wine, he could ask the questions that the neophyte cook needed answers to and pin Marcella down about details, as well as judge the results critically. Moreover, he wrote eloquently, whereas Marcella was not at home in English—and didn't seem to want to be. They were singularly attuned, sharing the same rigidities and condescension toward the average American's knowledge of, and taste in, food. It was a perfect mating, and I felt myself to be an intruder—with good reason, as it turned out.

The Hazans had managed to extricate themselves from their contract so that Knopf was able to take over subsequent printings of the first book. With the attention Marcella was getting, the book was selling successfully and continued to do so. Then, when we started working on the second volume, *More Classic Italian Cooking,* I, as usual, flung myself into the whole process, trying out many of the wonderful recipes, and for a while the Joneses' kitchen was happily full of Marcella. But there was one dish that I felt was too saturated in fat and looked a bit unappetizing, with pools of fat circling the plate. It was a recipe from Bologna, where they are known to enjoy the combination of butter and olive oil in generous amounts along with any accumulated fat from the meat; for Americans, particularly when the fear-of-fat mania was beginning to spread, it seemed like too much of a good thing. So I spoke up the next time we were working together in their apartment. There was a silence, and then Marcella turned to Victor and cried indignantly: "Vut did she say?" I got up quietly, and as I was putting on my coat, I tried to explain that the cookbooks I had worked on had been the result of a healthy collaboration between author and editor, that my role was to play the devil's advocate and ask questions. Clearly that was not what Marcella wanted. As I reached the elevator, Victor came running after me, and I did return. But it was never an easy give-and-take relationship, which is so important in creating a cookbook.

One time, when Marcella was trying to develop a workable Italian bread, she showed me the recipe and I suggested that, instead of calling for fresh cake yeast, which was very perishable and which most supermarkets did not carry then, she recommend active dry yeast. In my own experience, I had found it perfectly satisfactory and couldn't tell the difference in the final loaf. She looked at me dubiously and then decided the only way to put the matter to the test was to have a panel of experts sample the different results. So one afternoon she summoned to her apartment Jim Beard and his friend Carl Jerome, a fellow cook, and the chef who did the breads at the elegant Four Seasons restaurant, and Evan (who declined tactfully), along with Victor and me, and we had a blind tasting. Not one of us could tell the difference between the *pane all'lio* that she made with fresh yeast and the one made with dry. Yet, in the final book, cake yeast is what she calls for, claiming that she finds it produces "a warmer-tasting, less sour bread," although admitting that she has never conducted "large scale tests to substantiate it." (We were only small-scale, evidently.) Years later, however, in her *The Essentials of Classic Italian Cooking*, the updated compendium of the two books that was published in 1992, only dry yeast is listed.

For all our minor disputes, I admired the way that Victor and Marcella managed to get across the idea that the best Italian cooking is in the home, and that, if you are going to enjoy this daily pleasure, "You must give liberally of time, of patience, of the best raw materials. What it returns is worth all you have to give." It was a philosophy I wholeheartedly shared. Soon Evan and I, like so many other enthusiasts across the country, were making our own pasta, rolling out the dough and cutting the strands, which the children in our household loved to catch as they poured out of our Italian-made hand-cranked machine. Marcella made it clear that she preferred hand-rolling, claiming the machine produced "slick and inferior quality." Oh, the guilt, but still we persevered—and loved the results.

· · ·

When Madhur Jaffrey's manuscript came to me at Knopf, I was immediately persuaded that food-conscious Americans were ready for authentic Indian food, particularly if they had someone as skillful as Madhur guiding them. She was canny enough to realize, it was apparent, that she had to seduce us slowly, step by step. She knew that not everyone was willing to spend hours in the kitchen, to chase down unfamiliar ingredients, and to hand-grind spices. So she started each chapter by offering the simpler dishes, figuring that once we were hooked we would move on to the more complex. She tried to persuade us, for instance, that using eight spices was really no harder than using two. It was a somewhat disingenuous argument, of course, because in Indian cooking it's not necessarily the number of spices but the way they are used; one spice might be added in three different ways—some of it in the initial paste that is blended and fried, some in the stewing of the meat, and some of it toasted and strewn on top before serving. It's all a matter of technique, and Madhur details every step of each technique, carefully explaining why it is important. I was struck by how one lamb *korma* can taste so different from another lamb *korma* when many of the same ingredients are used, but it became clear that the difference came from *how* each ingredient was treated.

As a child, growing up in Delhi, Madhur was an appreciative and curious eater, relishing not only the meals enjoyed together by her large extended family, where her grandfather presided at the table, but embracing all the different ethnic foods that her schoolmates brought in their lunch boxes, and the forbidden goodies that she savored from local street vendors. All of these delights formed her food memories, but that wasn't enough to sustain her when she went off to England, and later America, to pursue an acting career. She wanted to bring these dishes back to life, but she had hardly ever set foot in the kitchen. So she persuaded her mother to write down the recipes in full detail, and, little by little, she found she could reproduce them. All of these careful efforts eventually found their way into *An Invitation to Indian Cooking*.

Despite the enthusiasm for the book expressed by those who recognized its quality, it took some time to catch hold. I suggested that Madhur try giving some classes that might attract attention and get written about, and once again Jim Beard opened his doors and offered to have the Indian cooking classes in his house. At first not many signed up, so I recruited a number of people who worked at Knopf to enlist, and soon word of mouth spread.

What Madhur exemplified to me was that if you have the love, the motivation, and the drive you can always find time to cook and enjoy it. Working as an actress in the theater and in film, raising three daughters, and now doing cooking classes, she seemed to produce effortlessly a dazzling array of dishes in her tiny kitchen, where she filled so many serving plates and bowls they would have to be stored on ceiling-high shelves and retrieved at the last moment by the tallest guest available. Then everything would be served so elegantly Indian-style. She and her violinist husband, Sanford Allen, would always gather interesting friends from their different worlds, and the deliciousness of the food was a binding force. When we went there for dinner, we didn't even have to remember the number of their apartment; we would just follow our noses down the long hall and we would be pulled to the right doorway by the enticing smells that wafted out.

Some years later, when I was working with her, on her *World-of-the-East Vegetarian Cooking*, we persuaded Madhur and Sanford to make the long drive to our house in northern Vermont, and Madhur came armed with a satchel full of the necessary herbs and spices, not trusting me to have stocked everything she might need—and rightly so. We may have managed to do a little book work, but I remember those few days only as sheer pleasure. I loved watching Madhur walk down to our garden before a meal and gather up a few just-ripened items and then produce a tantalizing vegetable dish that didn't taste like anything we'd had before. For weeks after they left, the wooden beams in our country kitchen seemed permeated with the scents of cardamom, cumin, coriander, ginger, mace, cloves—and, of course, garlic.

The complex and mysterious world of Chinese cookery was a particularly tough nut to crack. There were several cookbooks on the subject published in the late sixties and early seventies, but, to my mind, none that penetrated the aesthetic of the Chinese approach to food, making it understandable and workable for the American cook. Finally, I came across a proposal from Irene Kuo, who was the very hands-on proprietor of two good, uncompromising Chinese restaurants in New York, one near Lincoln Center and one in Greenwich Village. When I met and talked with her, I realized she had that same special qualification that Claudia and Madhur had: She had grown up in a household where food was honored, and she felt compelled to recover those food memories—in her case, after her family had had to flee China. As a child, she had always been drawn to the big kitchen where family meals and banquets were prepared, and she learned the secrets not only of their native Shanghai cooking, but also of regions like Fukien, when a chef from that

Irene Kuo

southeastern coastal province joined their kitchen and taught her about making stock in the grand style. She also described to me in colorful detail the meals at a Buddhist monastery where she went every year with her parents on retreat, recalling how the monks would go to such extravagant lengths to satisfy in their vegetarian dishes the carnivorous appetites of their guests. There would be little "birds" in their nests, flying "fish," crouching "piglets" not only looking meaty but simulating fleshy tastes and textures.

I was convinced that, with her keen sense of recall and her dedication to bringing to this country the art of the food she had loved as a child, she was the one to teach Americans how to achieve in their own kitchens the harmony of color, taste, and texture that is so essential to every dish. Moreover, her instinct for conveying the physicality of the act of cooking in explosively vivid language was irresistible. She wrote of specifically Chinese methods of cooking as "stir-frying, red-cooking, pan-sticking, slithering, exploding, plunging, purifying, smothering, mating, nestling, capturing, choking, flavor-potting, light-footing, sizzling, rinsing, scorching, drowning, wine-pasting, and intoxicating." And though she admitted that most of these techniques are ones that only professional cooks need to learn, she was determined to help home cooks become adept in the major procedures. "The key lies in understanding the basic techniques—how and why they are used, what they will do to food," she wrote. By now that had almost become my mantra, but I understood how it was indeed the key to Chinese cooking—which was to become our title. Irene believed firmly that one learned by doing, and each of the five major techniques she introduces in the first chapter of her book is followed by recipes that put into practice the principles. She does cater somewhat to American squeamishness, in that she doesn't offer a recipe for a large oil-rich fish to illustrate the technique of clear simmering, but she does describe what Chinese gourmets see as its virtues—"the fine cheek meat, the melting rich lips, and the luscious silky tongue." Her section on cooking in oil— that is, stir-frying—is a masterpiece on what makes this "dashing, flamboyant technique" so effective. She quotes Ar-chang, another of her family's incomparable cooks, telling her, "Once you toss the ingredients for a sizzling stir, even if the stove catches on fire and the fire is spreading with leaping flames, pick up the pan and let it ride the crest of the heat to completion before you put out the fire."

Soon I found myself at home "matchmaking" my ingredients

to make sure they were compatible, cutting them to uniform size, marinating for flavor and tenderness, "exploding" lamb with scallions, "velveting" pieces of chicken or broccoli to make them "snowy, fluffy, and extremely tender," or "slippery-coating" them for a satiny finish. Then the moment of truth would come, when the ingredients were "tossed, turned, flipped, swept, poked and swished." They should "skid over the oiled hot pan so that they spin, slither, dart and tumble," and when we hear crackling noises we know that the liquid has evaporated. Sometimes I would have to shout down the back stairwell of our apartment building when the fire alarms went off, floor by floor, that it was only me cooking Chinese, but that all added to the drama.

When the book was completed, I celebrated with the Kuos at a little restaurant they knew in Chinatown. By then the book's two pages on the art of holding and using chopsticks, complete with illustrations, had improved my dexterity so that I was able to hold my own. But the crowning moment came when C.C., Irene's husband, honored me by extracting the cheeks from a large fish and popping them into my mouth. I felt somehow as though I had earned my degree in Mastering the Art of Chinese Cooking.

Nela Rubinstein was another amateur cook who found herself uprooted—from her native Poland. As the wife of the world-renowned pianist Arthur Rubinstein, she had to learn to adapt to whatever circumstances might confront her when they were traveling. She would improvise with whatever was at hand. After they had had to leave Paris when the Nazis took over, she cooked for her family on a little portable burner in a hotel room on Manhattan's Upper West Side. She was a loving cook and welcomed any challenge, because it was so important to her that her children experience a sense of continuity by sitting down together to familiar dishes, no matter how shattered their world was.

I first encountered her cooking when I had been sent to Marbella, where the Rubinsteins had a vacation villa, to see if I would be acceptable to the maestro as an editor to work with him on his memoirs. Evan was with me, because it was the firm opinion of Bob Gottlieb, my boss, who was then editor-in-chief at Knopf, that it was necessary to establish from the start that I was a happily married woman—so no hanky-panky. The evening we arrived, the local restaurant that the Rubinsteins had planned to take us to was closed, and Nela improvised, cooking a delectable dinner for us.

Later that year, at Christmastime, after Rubinstein had agreed that he would try working with me, we decided to go to Paris, where the Rubinsteins were living, so that Evan could do research on the book he was writing on cheese, after having done a series of pieces for *Gourmet* on the cheeses of the world (a subject dear to both of us). So, while he was hobnobbing with French cheesemakers in the Normandy countryside, I could sit down with the maestro and go through his manuscript. I had done some sample editing and had sent it on ahead, and I could tell by his greeting at their elegant house in the Square de l'Avenue Foch that Mr. Rubinstein was not pleased. We went over a few pages and talked, and then I was dismissed, not even asked to stay for a Nela lunch, which I had been looking forward to. I went back to our nearby hotel feeling I'd better return to New York quickly and admit my failure to Gottlieb. But the next day, I was asked to come back, and this time was greeted by a smiling author who took my coat and ran kisses from my hand to my elbow, saying, "Thank you, thank you. I certainly don't want to make a fool of myself." Evidently, the day before when we'd talked, I had touched a sensitive nerve when I'd said that I was there to help him sound like himself, not like a boastful, foolish fellow. He had read over the first chapters now and knew exactly what I meant. "Let's get to work," he said.

Accustomed to applause, he didn't take criticism easily, but for the next ten days, we worked together steadily every morning. The only distraction was when we would hear Nela starting up her car in the courtyard below and then tearing off to the market. Soon after she'd returned, we would smell delicious aromas wafting up into Arthur's second-floor study, and he would sniff contentedly and speculate on what she might be making. Only Nela could cook for him. Only she could pick out all the right ingredients, because, of course, that was an integral part of her cooking. So the servants just served while she performed.

It would usually be at least one-thirty before we were called down to lunch, our appetites growing agonizingly as we waited. The vodka would be taken from the freezer and poured into little glasses, and a steaming soup would be ladled from a tureen, served with *pierogi*—those little baked turnovers filled with ground meats or maybe cabbage and mushrooms. A fish or fowl or meat dish would usually follow—maybe carp or monkfish, or a lovely chicken with prunes, or boiled beef, not the usual Paris fare. Once, she made calves' brains *en cocotte,* having learned what a fan I was of those little morsels of *cervelle,* and sometimes she would make a tart for dessert, or a simple rice pudding. Later, when I returned to our hotel near the Etoile, happily sated but never too much so—Nela knew just how to maintain the right balance to keep the maestro's figure trim—I would await Evan, who had gone off into the Normandy countryside with his cheesemakers, to sample the local handmade cheese and probe the mysteries of the microbes that lurked in the rafters of the old farm buildings that gave the cheeses their unique flavor.

The more I talked with Nela and tasted the wonderfully eclectic foods she prepared so effortlessly and with such love, the more I urged her to do her own book. The Rubinsteins had known the Knopfs for years, and though Alfred was the one who first encouraged the maestro to put down the colorful stories of his life with which he would regale guests at the Knopfs' table, I learned that it was Blanche who had tried to persuade Nela years ago to do a cookbook. That was surprising, because Blanche seemed to have nothing but contempt for food and was as thin as a wraith. It was Alfred who was the gourmand and loved to entertain authors at long Sunday lunches at their home in Purchase, New York, sometimes inviting them to help him uncork a rare bottle of wine. But Nela's reputation had spread even to Hollywood, where Cary Grant was one of her great fans. And Blanche had a good nose for what was *au courant*. Nela, though, balked at signing a contract; she had clearly been overawed at the idea of having to write down all those recipes, which existed mostly in her head. So, these many years later, when I offered to help and suggested a good collaborator for her, she relented, and in time *Nela's Cookbook* was a *fait accompli*. I even got a call from Cary Grant telling me in his unmistakable voice how wonderful the book was.

Nela made the point that her cookbook focused on dishes that not only could be made at home but were *better* made at home. In a way, the same was true of all the other recipes that represented recovered memories—Claudia's Middle Eastern dishes, Madhur's Indian, Irene Kuo's Chinese—and the memories always added a context and a richness to the home fare being shared with us.

7

American Cooking

But what about mastering the art of American cooking? I began to think to myself. What, in fact, is American cooking? Evan had done some books about the Western frontier, and was particularly drawn to the American food story as a way of uncovering interesting aspects of our social history. When he signed a contract with Dutton to do a book on the subject, we were both excited by the challenge. But it proved to be more elusive than we'd anticipated, and we found ourselves frustrated trying to track down sources. Clearly historians did not find cookery a serious enough subject to be examined and indexed, and we would search in vain for references to food items and even crops. Our best sources proved to be local records, plantation journals, regional recipe collections, and, most of all, talks with people around the country.

When we began this pursuit, I realized what a snob I was. I was ashamed of American food, and my idea of the American gourmand was a caricature of someone who had to stuff himself to excess. I loved the story that Evan told me about when Alexander Hamilton invited the Count de Moustier to dinner and the titled guest refused to eat what his American hostess served; instead, on the pretext of having a delicate stomach, he sent a servant to bring him food that had been prepared by his own *cuisinier*. And James Fenimore Cooper, after years of living abroad, wrote: "The Americans are the grossest feeders of any nation known. . . . Their food is heavy, coarse, and indigestible."

That was pretty much my view, fueled, of course, by my years in France. To me the average American dinner still meant an overflowing plate of meat and potatoes with side dishes of overcooked vegetables. When I was a child and we were visiting my father's family in Montpelier, Vermont, we often went to the Montpelier Tavern, where half-moon dishes of mushy carrots, peas, boiled or mashed potatoes, and a sweet relish or two were always presented surrounding the main dish. When I asked why there were separate dishes, no one had an answer. But over the years I decided it was a sign of the arrested American palate— that childish need to separate each item so that one wouldn't touch another and the flavors couldn't mingle. But wasn't that the very opposite of what a good meal should do? All those flavors were supposed to come together in one delicious intermingling mouthful. Look at the way that the French, the Italians, all the Europeans I'd encountered would cut a piece of meat or fowl with the fork in the left hand, tines turned downward, then pile up a bit of this and of that skillfully on the meat, patting it all down with the knife for safe transport to the mouth. Not Americans. For them it was strictly one thing at a time, switching the fork from left to right hand so that it could act as a shovel.

Actually, my English grandfather used to eat the European way, and I so admired his careful performance that at about seven or eight years old I started emulating him. When I went off to the Spence School for girls, where a sit-down lunch was served at long tables with a teacher presiding at one end, I persisted in this style of eating. The only trouble was that I was still a bit clumsy (or maybe I greedily tried to pile too much on my fork), so a potato or a piece of meat would fall off en route and leave a greasy splotch on my clean shirt. I noticed the teacher taking in my performance, and it was not long before my mother got a call from the principal's office, complaining that my table manners were atrocious and that I had better learn how to eat properly. Humiliated, I reverted to the American way, but I always felt something was lacking and the pleasures of eating had been compromised.

As Evan and I dug deeper into the history of the American appetite, I began to see another side to our heritage. One need only read about Thomas Jefferson's sojourn in France in 1784, of his passion for what the earth brought forth and his determination to improve the range and quality of produce in the New World, to realize what a great contribution to gastronomy this eighteenth-century gentleman from Virginia gave the world. He was in Europe at a time when the art of cookery had become a respectable subject of discussion, and he pursued it relentlessly. He paid to have his man, James Hemings, taught cooking by the Prince de Condé's chef, and he took a three-month junket through France and Italy in his phaeton with only a driver as companion to learn about new crops he could bring back and vines that could be grown by American grape growers to produce decent wines. It is a revelation to look at Jefferson's notes on that trip—his delight in garlicky dishes like *brandade de morue* and *bouillabaisse*, as well as the kitchen journal he kept back home at Monticello with recipes, records of experiments— such as his attempt to grow sugar maples he imported from Vermont in Virginia soil (it didn't work)—and even a drawing of an Italian macaroni machine.

He loved to entertain, and he fed his guests well. Daniel

Jim Beard teaching a class at Seaside, Oregon.

Webster described a dinner at Monticello, served habitually at half past three o'clock, as "in half Virginian, half French style, in good taste and abundance." But for all Jefferson's gourmandise he himself ate sparingly, indulging in meat primarily as a condiment, and glorying in the variety of fresh vegetables he grew on his own soil.

It was when I really got to know James Beard that I started looking at our own food heritage with a new openness. He had always been so helpful with unknown cookbook authors I was trying to launch that, when I felt there was an urgent need with the back-to-the-earth movement growing for a really good book on bread-making, I turned to him for advice and invited him to lunch. We ate at a fine French restaurant near Knopf, and when the readily recognizable large frame of James Beard was spotted, extra treats were sent our way. And there was no question of my getting a bill. All this was new to me, but Jim advised me to accept graciously and just leave a generous tip. The only trouble was that, though I had a credit card handy, there was very little change floating around in my purse. So Jim had to fork out the tip—something he was not accustomed to doing. I thought, That's it. But when we parted, he said he would think about that bread project. Several extravagant lunches later (for which I was better prepared), he announced that he had reflected and decided that he was the one to do the book and would tackle it as soon as he had finished his American cookery book for Little, Brown. Realizing that his American project had been on the burner for a few years now, I proposed that instead he work on the two simultaneously, and that I would help all I could with the bread book. So I started going down to his kitchen in his new house on West Twelfth Street to bake breads with him. I was determined that we get every step of the process down accurately. I knew that yeast doughs particularly were an anathema to timid home cooks, and I wanted a book that a complete neophyte could use with confidence. Jim did not have a particularly analytical mind, but when I questioned him I found there was a gold mine of information to be tapped, and what he did instinctively as a cook could be readily translated to wonderfully instructive recipes. I even got several Knopfites, who had never baked a loaf in their lives, to follow Jim's basic recipe for a home-style loaf, and then bring in their first effort for inspection. It was quite a revelation to see how different the results were—some loaves sagging, some broken away from the crust, some dense, some overly inflated—all from the same formula. Slicing each one open and studying the breads carefully, Jim came up with a several-page analysis of what could go wrong, which went into the book as "Remedies for the Not-Quite-Perfect Slice." As always, his commentary was gentle, encouraging, and illuminating, and one felt that next time surely one would produce a loaf with the right texture and good "nose" that would win the approval of the master.

Watching Jim knead—he always did it with one hand—as he loomed high above his kitchen counter and put all of his considerable weight into flattening, folding, turning, pushing the dough, was further confirmation for me that it was all in the technique. Perhaps that was what was so particularly satisfying about bread. All the elements are in play. If the skies are overcast one day and the air is damp, you might have heavier bread. So you learn to compensate, and as a result no two loaves are ever quite the same. I think that's what fed my own pleasure in bread-making, which had started with my innocent suggestion that Julia pursue the baguette.

While Jim's bowlsful of dough were rising, he would think about lunch. He'd go over to his large refrigerator, swing open the door, and rock on his heels as he cooked up in his imagination something delicious that could be made from the morsels he had stashed away. Nothing was too ambitious. If the thought of a little savory tart appealed to him, he'd whip up a pie dough using the latest kitchen gadget he was trying out, such as the new food processor, the Robot-Coupe from France, which Carl Sontheimer was fine-tuning for the American market (i.e., making it safer, so we wouldn't slice off our fingertips). Sontheimer himself would often stop by for a quick consultation, and Jim would report on his experiments.

Another frequent visitor was young Larry Forgione, who was just launching his first Manhattan restaurant, An American Place, featuring a melding of regional American dishes with a "nouvelle" twist—a concept that would have been inconceivable a decade earlier. Jim loved the idea and ate there often, so he could give Larry his honest opinion about whether a dish still maintained its authenticity, and whether embellishments went too far.

James Beard has often been criticized for taking money to sponsor various new products and kitchen equipment. But it seemed to me that he was careful to lend his name only to something that he had tried out and was sold on. Before the days when Julia had awakened appetites across the country to the joys of French cooking, Jim was out there trying to spread the word about good American food. So he needed Green Giant and Skotch Grills and Omaha Steaks to foot the expenses. The only quarrel I ever had with him was when he let CorningWare equip his new kitchen with their latest countertop burners. They looked smooth as glass—a novel idea at the time—but they were slow as molasses to heat up. Once, when we were doing a promotional TV spot with Jim, it seemed to take an eternity for the water to boil, with camera and crew there waiting. Even Jim's students complained. But he was determined to give those burners a fair trial before he finally gave up on them.

Curiously, James Beard, although he started out in the theater, was not good in front of the camera. He immediately became the actor, as soon as the lens was focused on him. His effort at a television cooking series in the late fifties, sponsored by Elsie the Cow, was short-lived, and later, when he did some shows with Julia, his self-consciousness contrasted painfully with her spontaneity. He admired Julia and was, of course, envious of her.

But Jim was a naturally gifted teacher, and he managed to fire up enthusiasm among his students about the exciting range and variety of good American regional food. When I visited his beginners' class, I watched how he would start them off making

Me with the two giants—Jim and Julia

pancakes, so they could experience the baking process on top of the stove, seeing the plop of batter spread and take form in the pan, then swell and brown, before flipping it over—with a spat-ula (for the timid) or with fingers (for the more brave). His hap-piest classes were the ones he gave in Seaside, Oregon, where he had spent summers as a boy. When Evan and I went out there one summer, we learned all about salmon cheeks, different kinds of clams and oysters, and, of course, Dungeness crabs. We also sailed on Puget Sound and stopped at an island where a native had nailed to a plank the filleted sides of a large fish he had just caught and set it at an angle over the fire to roast, the way the Indians cooked it. And we feasted on that particularly succulent and smoky fish flesh.

Our own pursuit of native food, both for Evan's book and for a series of later pieces that he did for *Gourmet* on the American scene, led us to church suppers with a Scandinavian accent in Minnesota, and a French-Canadian spread in our own territory of Vermont; to cranberry growers in New England, Wisconsin, and Oregon; to the new ice-cream makers like Charlie Cox of Big Alice's in Rhode Island and Ben & Jerry's in our neck of the woods; to the harvesting of wild rice with the Chippewas in northern Minnesota; to celebrating spring with heirloom dishes of heart and lungs of lamb in a Greek community in Tarpon Springs, Florida, and tasting turtle ragout in the Florida Panhandle. We went foraging with Billy Joe Tatum in the hill country of the Ozarks, bringing home a load of precious morels, and we sampled Cornish pasties and mountain goat in Butte, Montana. It was a time of endless research and surprising discoveries. We felt as though we were really tasting America, or, as one Ozarkian put it, "consuming all those vittles from the well-flavored earth."

Our appreciation of American food deepened the closer we got to folk who clung to their roots and took pride in regional products. But again and again we found that ethnic traditions were too readily abandoned by second-generation Americans eager to embrace the American way—hamburgers and hot dogs that could be eaten on the run, fast foods that just needed to be heated up, sweet soft drinks that could be guzzled out of the bottle. In the spring of 1971, I wrote M.F.K. Fisher, whom we had come to know primarily through her extraordinary letters, to tell her about our feeling of despair after a jaunt we had made to Charleston, Williamsburg, Charlottesville, and Atlanta. "How sad," I reported to her, "that it doesn't seem economically feasible to serve fresh vegetables even in a country inn and again and again one runs into stories of people who tried too hard and cared too much about restoring regional traditions and simply failed." In those days, we couldn't find a single restaurant in Atlanta that served traditional Southern food, and we had to head for the hills, to a farm guest house, where finally we sat down with fellow boarders at a big table spread with fried chicken and country ham, dishes of cymlings, cabbage, and stewed tomatoes, yeast rolls and cornbread, to say nothing of an array of homemade pickles and preserves. We talked to one elderly black woman living in the countryside who told us how saddened she was that her son would no longer eat her chittlins, and her face shone with pleasure as she remembered her childhood and what they ate. She assured us that no one ever got sick from all the good nourishment. And did we know, she asked, about sheep's marrow from the jawbone as a cure for the mumps?

I thought I would never find voices that expressed the pleasures of American food the way Claudia Roden and Madhur Jaffrey had preserved their past by celebrating the cooking of their childhood. Then a treasure came my way at Knopf that restored my faith in the power of rich food memories to evoke a time, a place, and an identity—in this case celebrating Virginia country cooking.

I first met Edna Lewis when she walked into my office in the spring of 1972. It was at the suggestion of Bob Bernstein, the CEO of Random House, which had taken over Knopf in 1960. He wanted me to talk to her and his friend Evangeline Peterson. They had been collaborating on a cookbook based on the dishes served at Café Nicholson, the cozy little restaurant under the Queensboro Bridge, where Edna Lewis was the chef for a faithful clientele that included Tennessee Williams and Truman Capote, and other artists and writers seeking the good Southern foods of their childhood. It developed that the book they had done was already completed and on its way to the printer, so there was little I could do to help out on that score. But I was immediately captivated by Edna. She had such a regal presence, wearing one of the dresses that she designed and made herself—a long colorful skirt and top of African batik material with matching scarf draped loosely around her neck. I became even more entranced when she started talking, with a little prodding from me, about the foods of her childhood in Freetown, Virginia, a farming community that her grandfather, a freed slave, had founded. Her long dangling earrings would swing and glitter when she tossed back her head and her long fingers would play with an idea. Then her face would break into a shy smile as she recalled gathering in the spring wild asparagus along the fence row, or morels in oak forests and shady pastures. She described the many dishes her mother would prepare during Revival Week, culminating in the Sunday Revival Dinner (and the long, agonizing wait before they could taste them). Each season has its special bounty, and although the work on the farm was hard, there was always ample reward for their labors in the dishes her family savored together, and with visiting friends and relatives, throughout the year. I sensed from her pleasure that there was a story to be told—with recipes just as she and her family made them. So I suggested that the book I would be interested in would be made up of the kind of memories she had just described, and the ways in which the people of Freetown raised their food and prepared it throughout the year. I asked if they would give that a try.

They were delighted at the prospect and eager to get going. But when they came back a week or so later with some sample pages in hand, I was disappointed. "This isn't you, Edna," I tried to say gently. "It isn't the voice I heard when you were

Edna Lewis, me, and Edna's niece, Nina Williams, at a picnic in Central Park to celebrate the publication of
The Taste of Country Cooking.

talking to me." At that point, Evangeline Peterson, to her great credit, got up and left, agreeing that Edna should be writing the book herself.

The challenge now was to help Edna recover that voice, and I sensed she was uneasy about going it alone. So we tried talking out a section one afternoon, and then, while we were both still giddy with the pleasures she had evoked and the ease with which the details of each anecdote had surfaced, I suggested she go home right away and put everything down just as she had told it to me. It worked miraculously. The next week, she brought in several pages, handwritten on a long yellow legal pad, and the words flowed. We repeated these sessions every Thursday afternoon, when she had time off from her job working with children at the Museum of Natural History, and as the winter passed, the book took shape. The recipes she wrote had the same natural tone, and when I tried them out, I could feel her presence right there with me as I rendered lard slowly and made cracklings, or listened to the cake I was baking—when the quiet noises it made suddenly stopped, this was a sure sign, Edna said, that the cake was done.

We decided that the book should be arranged according to season, because it was the natural order of the farm year that dictated what was served when. After we had distributed almost all the recipes into their rightful seasons, dealing them out like a stack of cards on my office floor, I realized something was missing among the fall festive events: no Thanksgiving. When I asked why, Edna quietly replied: "Well, we never had Thanksgiving. We celebrated Emancipation Day instead." So I urged her to give us the menu for that feast, and the centerpiece of it turned out to be guinea fowl, which I learned were a part of every barnyard in Freetown because they were such good watchdogs. They were also natural symbols of African-American cooking, and they were eaten only on special occasions.

As I worked closely with Edna over the months, I came to know her more intimately, although there was a part of her story she always held back. She told you just what she wanted you to know about herself, no more, and if you tried to get her to fill in the sequence of events that propelled her to leave Free-town, not yet graduated from high school, and find work in Washington and then New York, where first she was ironing in a laundry, then, suddenly, was designing a window at chic Bon-wit Teller's, to say nothing of becoming the chef at Nicholson's, you would probe for the missing pieces in vain. That's just the way it happened.

I knew how much Evan would appreciate Edna, so I persuaded her to come home for a dinner with us several times after an afternoon of work. There was an immediate affinity, and they would sit together sipping bourbon and listening to Bessie Smith recordings well into the evening. When we admitted to her that we had never tasted squirrel, after dismissing the possibility of snagging a few in Central Park, where, we decided, they would be overindulged and not taste at all like their country cousins, Edna insisted that her brother in Virginia shoot a mealful of real Freetown squirrels and parcel-post them to us. The package arrived, and Edna came quickly to skin the little creatures and stew them gently. Then we all sat down to one of those unforgettable dishes with a tantalizing new taste, surprisingly succulent and just faintly gamy.

When *The Taste of Country Cooking* was published, I sensed that the person who would most appreciate it was M.F.K. Fisher. I'll never forget her letter to me about it:

> *Her book is fresh and pure, the way clear air can be, and water from a deep spring. It is in the best sense* American, *with an innate dignity, and freedom from prejudice and hatred, and it is reassuring to be told again that although we may have lost some of all this simplicity, it still exists here.*

I have a photograph that I cherish of Edna Lewis and Marion Cunningham—the two grandes dames of American cookery in the yeasty final quarter of the twentieth century. They look as though they belong together—two sides of the same gold piece. Marion Cunningham represents the America that went

Edna Lewis and Marion Cunningham

west, and her tastes were partially formed by an Italian grandmother and by the abundance surrounding her in southern
California, where she grew up. Clearly she was born with a
natural palate. But it was not until middle age that she found
her calling. Until then she had been a suburban mother and
housewife, afraid even to leave the house and go shopping by
herself, and gradually she had become far too dependent on
alcohol. But on her forty-ninth birthday, something snapped in
her, and she decided she was missing too much and had to turn
her life around. She drove to the nearest airport, in Oakland,
bought a round-trip ticket to Los Angeles, and made herself get
on the plane, flying there and back the same day. When she
returned home that evening and told her family what she had
done, they were astonished. With her newfound confidence, she
announced that she was starting a new life and as of that
moment giving up drinking.

Cooking had always been Marion's secret love, and she began right away taking cooking classes. Before long she was giving lessons in her own kitchen in Walnut Creek and was part of the burgeoning food network around San Francisco. Inevitably, she heard about James Beard's classes at Seaside, Oregon, and she wrote him to ask if she could attend. She fitted right in, and the next summer Jim asked her to come back as his assistant. From then on she was his right hand, helping him with classes and demonstrations whenever he was on the West Coast, and chauffeuring him around Europe. Jim trusted the pureness of her palate and he admired the surety of her taste as well as her warmth and openness with people. And he loved the way she drove—"faster, faster," he would cry as they spun around the hairpin turns on the Côte d'Azur. So it is not surprising that he recommended Marion Cunningham wholeheartedly to me as the one to assume the persona of Fannie Farmer in the late twentieth century.

I had been sounded out as to whether Knopf might be interested in taking over *The Fannie Farmer Cookbook*, long published by Little, Brown, and I was not interested. *Fannie Farmer* was the book I had grown up on—in fact, an old 1918 edition was the one cookbook we had in our kitchen. We consulted it for basic American recipes, and I learned to make white sauce and many a pudding from its grease-stained pages. But after Fannie's death in 1915, nobody who was a real cook and teacher had been in charge of the book. A nephew inherited the role, then his progeny, not one of them an inspired cook, and the rights were eventually bought by the Fanny Farmer Candy Company. In trying to keep up with the times, subsequent editions read like a collection of box-top recipes, and the book that had been a bible in the American kitchen for decades was easily supplanted by Irma Rombauer's *Joy of Cooking*—a welcome novelty because it was so full of her pleasure in cooking—to say nothing of a spate of new cookbooks in the postwar years generated by *House & Garden* and *Good Housekeeping* (for seekers of the quick and easy) and *The Gourmet Cookbook* (for the more adventurous). So I was happy to let the Fanny Farmer Candy people shop elsewhere. It never occurred to me that they would listen to someone who said the book should be not only revamped from top to bottom but given a new voice. However, that's exactly what Frank Benson, their president, was willing to

Jim and Marion picnicking together
(they both adored picnics).

entertain when I was persuaded to talk to him after he had turned down a number of half-baked proposals from other publishers. His only concern was who would do the job.

Who indeed? Of course, I turned to James Beard, and this time he didn't even hesitate before recommending Marion Cunningham. Hardly a New Englander like Fannie, she was born and raised in California, and she had never done a cookbook, never even written a food piece. But Jim was convinced that she possessed the authentic American taste, and that was the essential ingredient needed. He showed me some letters she had written to him, and I was sold.

Marion came east and, as with Edna, I was immediately struck by her presence when we met—her long-legged easy stride, her blond hair pulled back in a ponytail, her clear blue eyes that pierced right into you. It was such an American look, one that could clearly give the stern-faced New England Fannie a new presence a century later. When we had worked out a plan for the overhaul, I notified Frank Benson that I thought we had the perfect candidate, and he flew down from Boston to look her over. All went smoothly, and after a good talk in my office, Mr. Benson gallantly offered us lunch. When we'd settled in at La Toque Blanche, down the street, he asked if we ladies would like a drink. Marion fixed her blue eyes on him and answered, "Oh no, not for me. I'm an alcoholic." I winced. That won't go down in Boston, I thought. But Frank Benson didn't blanch. In fact, he told me some time later that at that moment he was completely won over.

And Marion turned out to be just what was needed. We found a partner, Jeri Laber, to help with the writing and testing, and Marion proved to have an infallible instinct for what tasted good, what recipes should be thrown out and what could be preserved with some careful fine-tuning. She also had a store of really good-tasting recipes, particularly pies, cakes, cookies, and supper dishes, to draw on. She could take a bite of a recipe for a cake from the dreary eleventh edition and know in a flash what it lacked. I think she was always a little uncomfortable with areas of the book that were not fully her own—and we did have to call in extra help with the candy-making and preserving chapters just to get this monumental job done on time. I even offered to revamp the jellied salads, which no one wanted to tackle, and with good conscience I reduced the number of recipes in that department from about thirty-five, including Ginger Ale Fruit Salad, Perfection Salad, and Avocado Mousse (marked "awful" by me in the margin) to eleven, all made now with fresh ingredients. I had been to too many church suppers where the sickly-sweet, bright-red cherry Jell-O salad would melt and flow into what was otherwise the fine cream sauce of a chicken pot pie not to feel at heart that if Fannie was going to improve the American palate, such recipes had to go.

The second edition of the *new* Fannie Farmer, published fifteen years later in 1990, was fully Marion's, and it carried her name as author. By then she had made a name for herself, and her syndicated column was full of honest, down-to-earth advice for home cooks looking for good made-from-scratch recipes amid a sea of overwrought chefs' creations that were increasingly dominating the food pages. Marion loved the stories about how Fannie went down to the docks in the Boston harbor so that she could talk to the chefs just in from Europe and she would bring home samples of their new dishes in little napkins to try out with students at her Boston Cooking School. Some were quite elaborate, such as lobster timbales baked in molds lined with pasta. I was intrigued, because, the very summer when we came across that recipe, Marian Morash, the wife of Julia's TV producer and a wonderful cook who ran a restaurant on Nantucket during the summer, had phoned me to say that she had just come up with a new creation—lobster timbales baked in pasta-lined molds. All of which indicates that there is really nothing new under the sun—just variations on basic themes.

The only time my close friendship with Marion was tested to the limit was when I insisted that for her second revision of the book she address the microwave. I was appalled at the books that were being published and gobbled up claiming that the microwave could do just about everything, and I thought we had a responsibility to set the record straight and be the first to guide the home cook as to what worked and what didn't. Marion agreed reluctantly, bought herself a state-of-the-art microwave, and in her determined way started microwaving everything in sight. But after twice ruining an expensive roast of beef, she balked and called to tell me that she could not go on wasting good food this way. Only when I disingenuously told her what a service she was performing, sparing her readers such disasters, was she willing to persevere. And the result was the first all-purpose cookbook to give straightforward advice, ingredient by ingredient, on the merits and limitations of this dubious invention. (Julia was once asked by an interviewer what she thought of the microwave, and she answered: "It's good for drying out the newspaper when it's been left in the rain.") Perhaps deep down those of us who love to cook shun it because it takes away one of the most gratifying pleasures—the smell of good food cooking.

To make amends, I persuaded Marion to come to Vermont to work together on a few specialties to be developed for the book. One was a wedding cake, which I had urged her to include.

Effortlessly she put together in our kitchen a three-layered creation, which Evan and I admired. But how on earth would the
three of us do justice to eating it? We all agreed it shouldn't go
to waste—that was something our Depression generation
could not countenance. So Evan, the incorrigible newsman
who'd grown up working on weekly papers, called our local
newspaper and learned that there was a folk fair that day in
nearby Hardwick and, yes, they were having some raffles. Why
not a wedding cake? The only trouble was that the three-tiered
frosted cake was a bit wobbly and might not make the trip down

Marion, with her wedding cake
that was raffled at the fair

our rough mountain road intact. So we carefully inserted tooth-picks at intervals to hold the layers together more securely, and covered up the traces with dabs of icing. The cake traveled suc-cessfully and was raffled off to a prospective bride who was being married the next day. We went home elated, imagining members of the wedding party biting into pieces of that light, moist, rich cake with appreciation. Biting in? Good heavens, we had left the toothpicks inside. After a few desperate calls, we located the bride's family, and I confessed, alerting them to warn their guests. The next day, they phoned back to tell us it was the best-tasting wedding cake anyone had eaten in years—and nobody choked.

During the late seventies and the eighties, everyone seemed to be getting into the act, embracing by the mid-eighties what was called the "new American cooking." In a 1976 *Forbes* mag-azine story, entitled "The Kitchen: America's Playroom," Craig Claiborne pronounced the trend "a beautiful revolution," and the magazine claimed that "cooking, once a demeaning activity fit only for servants, sissies and overweight mothers-in-law, has begun taking on glamour." And naturally the magazine pointed to a lot of celebrities whose hobby was cooking. They cited the booming market for fine kitchenware and appliances, the prolif-eration of good ingredients in our markets, and the fact that men as well as women were taking pride in producing a meal that reflected well on them. They even quoted me as saying, "If you consider yourself creative, it is no longer possible to be a bad cook" (pretty cheeky words as I look back).

Even at Knopf the contagion spread, and several times a year we would have a Knopf picnic to which everyone brought favorite dishes (no take-out permitted), the more ethnic in ori-gin the better. One of our most conscientious copyeditors, Mel

Rosenthal, who lived in one room and often cooked for himself on a glorified Bunsen burner, would always make his special dish: spinach in cream. He would cook the spinach after work for several days, slowly stirring in more heavy cream with each session, and by the time we all tasted it, just a mouthful or two of that ambrosia was enough to sustain one for the rest of the day. Fernand Point, who said, "*Du beurre, du beurre, du beurre*— that's the secret of good cooking," would have loved it.

In August 1985, a *Time* magazine cover story was "The Fun of American Food," and all the new innovative chefs who stressed good American local produce and New World accents in their cooking were featured. Everyone was scrambling to define the new American cooking. Julia, in her no-nonsense way, declared, "As far as I'm concerned it is American food cooked in America by Americans with American ingredients," whereas Paul Prudhomme, the New Orleans food superstar, claimed, "Only the Creole and the Cajun is the most American of American food because it was absolutely created here. You can't find it anywhere else in the world."

But nothing is created out of whole cloth; each wave of immigrants had brought the tastes and techniques they grew up on in their native lands and adapted them to what they found here. They also imposed their attitudes toward eating. The Northeast, where I grew up, had long suffered from a puritan disdain of the enjoyment of food, whereas New Orleans was fortunate enough to get a lusty mix of French and African influences. Evan's *American Food: The Gastronomic Story*, a book that was really ahead of its time, had come out in the mid-seventies, and now it dawned on me that we needed a whole series of books that could tell the American story. Some of the books might be regionally oriented, but others might trace the ways in which a particular food was used in different parts of the country and helped to shape the character of what we call American cooking. So I got the backing of Knopf's new editor-in-chief, Sonny Mehta, who seemed to delight in all aspects of the American character, and in 1990 we launched a series that we called Knopf Cooks American. We started out with Bill Neal's book, titled *Biscuits, Spoonbread, and Sweet Potato Pie*. He was a passionate North Carolina cook who ran a little restaurant called Crook's Corner in Chapel Hill that was everything that Evan and I had been searching for more than a decade earlier. It was in his introduction that I came upon the words that characterized the series, and which we used as our banner headline: "Our food tells us where we come from and who we have become."

What I naïvely didn't anticipate was the reluctance of bookstores to consider the individual titles as part of an ongoing series and to allocate space to promote them that way. As a result, the books with titles like *The Brooklyn Cookbook*, which had a naturally chauvinistic following, and *Jewish Cooking in America*, which also did, as well as having a well-known author in Joan Nathan, found their audiences, and the regional books did well regionally. But a lot of very original, evocative books that approached the American food story in a new way, like *Real Beer and Good Eats* by sausage-maker Bruce Aidells and Denis Kelly, seemed to die a-borning, particularly after the first flush of interest in the series dissipated. The day when I was browsing through a bookstore and saw Nancy Verde Barr's *We Called It Macaroni* on a shelf promoting Italian cookbooks instead of being placed in the American-cookbook section, I realized the series was a lost cause.

One of the factors that helped fuel the new American food was the counterculture movement of the young that gained ground in the 1960s. At first I took a dim view of the flower children's contributing anything palatable to our gastronomy, for at that stage vegetarian cooking was at an all-time low; it not only looked brown and depressing, it tasted ersatz, with everything trying to pretend to be meat—not a surprising development, since we had no tradition of vegetarian cooking in this country. Then, to my surprise, along came a delightful cookbook by Anna Thomas, a young woman who was trying to make her way in Hollywood as a filmmaker and had decided to write the book to support her ambition. She was of Polish origin and had grown up on good cooking, but now, as a convert to vegetarianism, she realized there was nothing available to help those of her persuasion to prepare really good food that tasted of itself and didn't pretend to be something it was not.

Anna Thomas's voice was the most persuasive factor. She knew how to talk to her generation, and I suspect that her nononsense tone in the introduction to *The Vegetarian Epicure*, describing "the screaming munchies" one gets when high on pot, won many a devoted follower. The book was seductive, too, with Julie Moss's fey drawings of the hippie culture, and pages printed on wheat-colored recyclable stock. I wasn't prepared for how readily it took off, and neither was Knopf. Shortly after publication, Kay Sexton of B. Dalton, a major bookseller then, chided us in her newsletter, saying that Knopf didn't know what a best seller it had on its hand, and she repeated the prediction more than once as we kept going back to print to meet the demand.

At the same time, there were the stirrings of a sinister health movement that fastened on all the things that were bad for us and gained frightening strength during the last decades of the twentieth century. No sooner were we being released from all our inhibitions about enjoying the pleasures of food than the pendulum swung and we were being told about all the things that were unhealthy. Julia bemoaned it as "the fear-of-fat mania," and she remained the one sane voice of reason, preaching the gospel of "Eat a little of everything in modest proportions." That certainly was the approach to food that I absorbed during my years in Paris, and it has sustained me ever since. But the naysayers persisted in their crusade, and butter was being banished from the kitchen, to say nothing of animal fats and eggs that Americans had subsisted on throughout our history. Even I fell for a book that promoted safflower oil as an antidote to the dangerous fats. I liked the fact that at least there was an antidote to the threat of cholesterol, a positive approach, and the recipes from Ed Giobbi, a painter by profession and an amateur cook who lived mostly off the land as his Italian antecedents had, were irresistible.

I remember telling Julia about the premise of the book, entitled *Eat Right, Eat Well—the Italian Way,* and she hooted: "I once had some young cuckoo types living in our house when we were away, and they cooked everything in safflower oil. And it took me months to clean off that stuff clogging up my stove. So, if it does that to the stove, who knows what it does to the lining of the stomach." It turns out that she was right, at least to the extent that safflower oil was soon discredited (perhaps not for Julia's reason), and everyone was backtracking. The same happened in time with butter and animal fat: They turned out to be much better for us than those hydrogenated products, or what Julia called "that other spread" (refusing to dignify it with a name), and soon eggs were back in favor.

Only in America! There is something about us that still nurtures a love-hate relationship with food that is hard to dislodge.

8

What Is Taste?

In the late sixties, we suddenly found ourselves the guardians of two children, Chris and Audrey Vandercook, then thirteen and eleven years old. Their parents, who never had much time for family life, had tended to leave the children's upbringing to Giggy, their housekeeper. Giggy wanted to make the little ones feel loved, so she fed them whatever they wanted. And what they wanted amounted to about three things: hamburgers, chicken, and chocolate cake. Now and then Giggy would take them home with her, and they would be part of her loving family at birthday parties and special occasions. So they had at least sampled some home-cooked African-American food, such as ribs and cornbread. But their daily fare was limited, to say the least.

When we made the commitment, their mother had died and their father was terminally ill, so the children soon came to live with us. We looked forward to a happy family table where we could talk and get to know each other better. But we had to establish some ground rules. We explained that we loved food, and that we were given to experimenting with new ingredients and testing out ideas. So they would have to put up with it and not complain, just enjoy. And they did well, pushing aside only those things they really couldn't stomach.

Chris was the more wary, and he had a unique way of scraping the food off his fork with his teeth, oh so carefully, trying to avoid letting it touch his mouth, and we knew what he was telling us: I can eat it, but I don't have to taste it. Some months after we'd all been together, I put down bowls of a savory stewed dish, and I watched with some trepidation as he took his first bite. This time he could not refrain from comment. "May I ask what I just ate?" he inquired, not really wanting to know. We explained that this was a classic dish from Lyon, France, that was made with, well, tripe—that is, the lining of a cow's stomach. He put his hand to his mouth, left the table, and ran down the hall, trying to make it to the bathroom on time.

To compensate for our insensitivity, I offered to make a beautiful French chocolate cake. Chris loved chocolate cake and could devour a substantial one made from a Duncan Hines mix, which Giggy always used, in less than two days. When I presented the Reine de Saba, which I made carefully following Julia's favorite cake recipe and using only the best chocolate, it was dense and rather flat-looking compared with an American cake that rises to impressive heights by the power of baking powder. I did not hear any yums of pleasure when Chris took his first bite. In fact, the queen of French cakes sat around for almost a week with only perfunctory nibbles taken out of it (his weekly chocolate fix augmented, I suspect, by Mars Bars).

Years later, when Audrey and her family were visiting us, I noticed that her eight-year-old stepson, John, was merely toying with his food every night, not liking anything we put in front of him. So after several days I relented, still not violating our no-negative-comments-at-the-table rule, and told him that I wanted to make a special meal just for him. When I asked him what he would like, without hesitation he replied macaroni and cheese. I accepted the challenge happily and prepared a dish reminiscent of the one that Edie used to give me for my Friday lunches, first making a rich cream sauce, carefully cooking the roux so that it would not taste floury. Then I boiled the macaroni until it was done just al dente and folded the pasta and sauce together with layers of freshly grated sharp Vermont Cheddar cheese, and baked it all in a casserole strewn with buttered breadcrumbs until it was all bubbly and crisply golden on top. When we sat down to dinner, John beamed, but after he had his first forkful his pleasure vanished. "That's not macaroni and cheese," he whimpered. I tasted it, and he was right. The boxed version, I discovered when I made myself try it, was a far cry from the real dish. The little spirals of pasta were cooked so long (following the directions on the box) that they were gluey and were coated in a gummy "cheese" that only faintly resembled cheese and left what was to me a slightly unpleasant aftertaste. And, of course, the dish was not baked—that would be too much trouble—so there was no crunchy topping to contrast with a creamy interior.

One has only to read Eric Schlosser's chilling book *Fast Food Nation* to realize what expert manipulation goes into the manufacturing of taste in processed foods. "Those 'comfort foods,' " he writes, "become a source of pleasure and reassurance, a fact that fast food chains work hard to promote. . . . The rise and fall of corporate empires—of soft drink companies, and snack food companies, and fast food chains—is frequently determined by how their product tastes." And it is obviously important for them to ensnare the taste buds of the young. That way, their victims are hooked—once that ersatz flavor is imprinted on the taste memory, the real undiluted flavor no longer attracts. Their taste is corrupted, often for life. Color, too, Schlosser points out, has an effect, bright-colored foods being more appealing. So the orange glop that came out of the macaroni-and-cheese box was far more immediately seductive than the pale-cream-colored contents of my casserole.

When I attended Madrid Fusion, the food conference held in Spain in 2006, I couldn't help but think that there was a disturbing amount of manipulation of food going on these days on the part of the new, highly applauded star chefs. Obviously their goal in the interest of high art is to heighten the flavor of a food so that its natural attributes are enhanced—not to distort its flavor. Nevertheless, as I watched some of the demonstrations, I felt as though I were looking at an operating table, the chef with the skill of a surgeon wielding injectors and dehydrators and bandaging the product in Cryovac. There was no smell of cooking filling the air, and when the poor, overworked piece of flesh was finally arranged on a plate, it was surrounded by three different foams. I thought a foam was a foam, but evidently you can steam it and bake it, too, if you want to. I admit to having an aversion to foam, particularly when it is pale green. It reminds me all too vividly of what happens when one's dog has deliberately eaten a large dose of grass to purge himself.

It seems to me that with all this experimental, high-tech cooking we are creating more distance between what goes on in the professional kitchen and what we do at home. And I feel passionately that we need to lure more young people into the kitchen, so that it becomes a way of life for them.

But why, I often wondered, hadn't our young Audrey been sufficiently seduced by the pleasures of the kitchen? Unlike her brother, she was always eager to eat whatever we produced, and sometimes she would join us on a Sunday afternoon as we rolled out fresh pasta dough on our new toy—the Italian hand-cranked pasta machine. She would also watch me slash loaves of

French bread with a razor, then slip them into a tile-lined oven and cautiously pick up with tongs an old pre-electric iron that I'd heated red hot so that when I dropped it into a pan of water on the oven floor it would create a huge whish of steam. But I wondered if she shared the sense of breathless excitement that I always felt.

But maybe secretly she thought that we were too obsessed. Once, she had come home from school to find her bathroom tub filled with crayfish, some still alive and swimming, but many of them dead, floating on the water and beginning to smell rank. The Baron de Groot had wanted to prove to me how easy it was to obtain live crayfish from Wisconsin and had ordered a shipment to be delivered at our door. But there were no instructions as to what to do with them on arrival, so we improvised. As I look back, I do wonder why we chose Audrey's bathroom rather than Chris's (ours, incidentally, didn't have a bathtub, so we were exonerated).

At one point, she admitted to me that I seemed so confident in the kitchen that I intimidated her, and that she really wanted to learn to cook. So we agreed that once a week she would prepare the dinner. I would write out the instructions for the dishes she wanted to do, and I would keep out of the way—but within calling distance, so she could holler, "What's moderate heat?" or "Tender to the touch—it's too hot to touch." We thought we might even write a beginners' cookbook this way. But it didn't work. She was too insecure, and I was too anxious. And our system violated what had come to be a conviction of mine: You develop a love of cooking by watching, absorbing, licking spoons, and asking questions of someone you want to emulate. The aura that such a person conveys is contagious. But only if you are susceptible—that is, if you were born with the particular genes.

Can taste be acquired? Is there good hunger and bad hunger? The former *New York Times* restaurant critic Mimi Sheraton was as tantalized by this question as I was, and we signed her up for a book that would explore the subject. But after several years she gave up on it and returned the advance, having decided, I suspect, that it was an unanswerable question, and that there was no prescription for acquiring taste. Moreover, those who don't have it probably don't care, which might limit the sales of her book considerably.

It is not so easy today to come by a mentor—a parent or grandparent or, as in my case, an aunt whose happiest moments were cooking for Uncle Doc. How does one attach oneself to someone's apron strings when there's no one in the kitchen? I feel particularly blessed because over time I have had the good fortune to work closely with a succession of great cooks, helping them develop their cookbooks. And I am constantly learning from them.

A few years ago, I was working with Lidia Bastianich on the second book she did for Knopf, *Lidia's Family Table*. A writer new to her, David Nussbaum, was helping her with this book, and because I felt it important that he watch her at work to capture her voice, I suggested we cook together in my kitchen. Lidia can be such an empowering cook, and I wanted her to convey some of her insights, to give us a better understanding of how to cook with all our senses, and to inspire us, when we're alone at our stoves, with ideas as well as the tools for improvisation. At one point, she had finished rolling out and cooking wide strips of her homemade spinach pasta, layering them to make a dish of lasagna, and she had just one long, green and glistening, stocking-shaped strip left over. What would you do with that? I asked. Certainly not throw it out? Heavens, no. In just a few minutes, she had buttered a small, shallow baking

*Working in my New York kitchen
with Lidia Bastianich*

dish and was folding the strip of pasta back and forth into the
dish, spooning on each layer a little of this and that—tomato
sauce, cheese, bits of leftover meat, whatever one might have in
the fridge—to make what she called her "ribbon lasagna." All
that remained was to pop the dish in the oven—a treat to relish
alone on a busy day.

Her risotto also got a second incarnation in Riso Sartù, delicious small molded rice cakes with green peas hiding in the
crevices. But it was watching her carefully tend the cooking of

the risotto later, when we were all together in Vermont, that persuaded David and me that we should try to get her to translate for her readers what she sees, tastes, smells, and listens for in the risotto pan as she tends it. As a result, in the book's risotto recipe, she pauses and inserts with each step a meditation on what we are doing and why, each step of the way. It is an inspirational lesson, and, believe me, you can never feel impatient again as you slowly and attentively stir your pot of creamy rice.

Another revelation for me was watching Lidia sauté ingredients in a large pan. As she added a new component, she would push away what she had just sautéed to create a dry "hot spot" (as she and David dubbed it), into which she would then plop her tomato paste or some other aromatic to "toast" it before incorporating it into the sauce. I had encountered the technique of toasting a paste to intensify its flavor only in Indian cooking; it is essential to building a good foundation, as Madhur Jaffrey had taught me long ago. And now here it was showing up in Italian cooking. The connections are intriguing, and the underlying principle is always the same—the cook's pursuit of better flavor.

That whole experience was heightened for me not only by the fun of having Lidia cook over my big black stove but also by the fact that she brought along her mother, Erminia, and also Mama's boyfriend, Giovanni. And both of them threw themselves into the work at hand. Erminia scrubbed my pots and pans so they shone as they never had before, and Giovanni sat peeling whole cupsful of garlic, which we used almost as fast as he peeled them. The sun went down late in the North at that time of year, so we were just able to catch it sinking behind the mountains as we finally settled on the deck to consume the marvelous dishes Lidia had put together during that day of cooking. As we ate,

Erminia regaled us with stories of her first days in America, the generous welcome she felt and the sense of being cared for. In fact, the immigration office worried that she hadn't spent the full allowance she was given to feed her family the first day. Were they getting enough meat? How little, I thought, we Americans understand of Italian ingenuity when it comes to food.

More recently, I have found myself thoroughly immersed in a form of cooking that was new to me: the world of sushi. The precision, the care, the artistry are all so essential that for a slap-dash cook of Western heritage, like me, it is a transforming experience. You almost have to become Japanese to perform in that world. My teacher-mentor was Hiroko Shimbo when she was writing her all-encompassing book, *The Sushi Experience,* and I realized that her exacting directions and careful balancing, as she put it, "of colors, textures, flavors, and aromas so that they harmonize and complement one another" was what made the huge difference between a mediocre lump of sushi and a masterpiece that explodes with perfection when you pop it whole into your mouth; you can savor each grain of delicately flavored rice, and at the same time all the separate parts melt into a magically transformed taste sensation. The way you line up your ingredients on a tray before you start (even if you have only one ingredient!), the care with which you tie the ribbon on a sushi pouch, the manner in which you put the sushi roll on a plate, and just where you place the dab of wasabi and the orna-mental flower—everything counts.

I realized that it is vital in a book like this to build trust, con-veying to the reader that he is in safe hands; with raw fish, it can be a matter of life and death. So I absorbed from Hiroko the

In safe hands with Hiroko Shimbo

importance of cleanliness, tips about shopping wisely, and how to prepare each ingredient carefully. One Saturday, I went with her across the Hudson to Edgewater, New Jersey, where there is a huge Japanese supermarket. It was particularly jammed that day, because there was a demonstration of a 200-pound tuna being cut up. When it came to auctioning off the choice pieces, the Japanese devotees went wild bidding, no matter the price, for each precious piece of belly meat.

Perhaps Hiroko's greatest gift to me is that I now know, after all these years, how to really sharpen a knife. Forget the expensive electric devices that in time ruin your blades; admit finally that the long butcher's steel, on which Julia nurtured me, is tricky—it's so hard to get the angle right—and really more for honing, not sharpening. It's also frankly scary when you are pulling the blade toward you. The Japanese way is to use a simple rectangular sharpening stone soaked in water, and then to patiently pull or push the blade against it, pressing down with your fingers on the cutting edge to maintain a slight angle (that's a little scary, too, but you get the hang of it). When you've perfected a section at a time, you turn the knife over and repeat the process, going the other way, until the whole blade is razor-sharp from tip to handle. This has now become a weekly ritual for me—and I enjoy it in much the same way as doing my yoga stretches. I even bought myself a good handcrafted knife at a Japanese fair where Hiroko was doing a demonstration, and she had the knife-maker chisel my name in Japanese characters onto the blade. As I see it lying in its sheath, I feel somehow it represents a rite of passage, a feeling that was heightened the first time I nicked myself and the blood flowed. To whom I shall bequeath it one day, when I am gone, I don't know.

Of course, my closest cooking partner over the years was Evan. He worked at home, so he had the fun of improvising dishes for his lunch out of whatever he might find in the fridge. He was fearless as a cook and always inventive, open to trying anything. Sometimes he would leave me a little sample of a dish if he was particularly pleased with what he had wrought. He inspired his own children, too, particularly his older daughter, who clearly inherited the gene. She bears the Welsh name of Bronwyn, and for her sixteenth birthday we delighted her with a Welsh dish to honor her heritage called Love in Disguise— the love part being veal hearts which we stuffed and braised to a delicious tenderness. She loved it. I think she was particularly drawn into our involvement with food because when she came to visit on weekends we would often give a dinner party, and she would get caught up in the sense of excitement that always surfaces as you are trying to get everything in the meal to come together and you greet hungry guests with your *présentation*.

Somehow the talk is always good when the food is, and when the wine flows, and to a young teenager it can seem like a wonderful initiation into the art of living.

Bronwyn tells me that during those years she would sometimes look for a recipe she could surprise us with. One that she found in a magazine she couldn't resist—hot dogs slashed and filled with cheese, then broiled until the molten Velveeta bursts forth (it looked so irresistible in the photograph). But, wanting to be sure it would be appetizing, she tried it first. One bite, she said, and she knew she couldn't make it for us. Her taste was too well honed, and there was no question in her mind but that the concoction was dreadful.

One summer, when she was only about twelve, Bronwyn was taking a course in sculpture at the Museum of Modern Art, and she and her father got to talking about how similar working with clay and with bread dough really were. I came from work on a steamy summer evening to find the two of them elbow-deep in bread dough in our small, hot penthouse kitchen. Neither of them had ever made bread before, but, of course, their dough rose, despite the humidity, and the finished plump loaves were something to write home about. In fact, Evan did just that: He was so carried away by the experience that he wrote about it for *Quest* magazine. A sharp-eyed children's book editor, Betsy Eisele at Crowell, happened to see the piece and asked him if he wouldn't write a bread book for young people. He agreed to if I would be a partner. Thus was born our first joint effort: *Knead It, Punch It, Bake It!*

Knowing nothing about writing for children, we turned to Betsy for advice, and she said to put it all down just as we would if writing for adults. We took her perhaps too literally, for we immersed ourselves so wholeheartedly into the magical world of bread that we ended up with 250 recipes of every description.

Betsy was not daunted and simply declared that we had two books here—one for adults, which Harper, the parent company, would certainly want to publish, and one that we would trim down for young bread-bakers. And that is just what happened.

Another person who helped to hone my own sense of taste was Angus Cameron. He was a legendary editor who at a young age became editor-in-chief at Little, Brown. Before that he had been at Bobbs-Merrill when they acquired *Joy of Cooking,* and he had been instrumental, as I mentioned earlier, in making that book the success it became. He always said, "A good editor has to have a little larceny in his soul"—and he had just the right measure. He had spent a couple of years living with his family in the Alaskan tundra after being blacklisted by McCarthy; not wanting to be a liability to Little, Brown, he had simply taken off. A farm boy from Indiana, he was a hunting-and-fishing man, and he knew how to survive in the wilderness. In the late 1950s, Alfred Knopf was looking for a top editor, and he became convinced that Angus was the best around. That was all that mattered.

Angus and I became good friends, particularly after he lent his support to that book on French cooking by the unknown Smith college woman and her French cohorts. We would often go to lunch together on the day when La Toque Blanche, down the street, served its *tête de veau,* and Angus would regale me with tales about his forty years of cooking game and fish in hunting camps from Maine to Alaska. When he took aim, before he fired his shot, he told me, he always envisioned the meat and just how he would cook it. With game meat, he made clear, flavor depends on how the animal is handled on the spot, how it is transported back home, when it is butchered, and how it is stored. What dish you decide to make depends on knowing all these factors, particularly the age of the animal and, if male, whether he might have run off all his fat during the rutting season.

To prove his points, Angus would bring me samples of older and younger animals and advise me accordingly on what cooking technique would be best. Then we'd swap recipes. Evan and I got to know all kinds of game birds and wild fish and fowl, and to learn what game meats were interchangeable in recipes for raccoon, possum, beaver, and so on. A whole new palette of flavors opened up, and it was exciting to test and adapt and learn. Angus, in turn, was delighted with our experiments.

I kept begging him to write a game-and-game-fish cookbook, since no one had done such a book who had his particular expertise as both a cook and a hunter and fisherman. And clearly the success of game cookery depended on the kind of kitchen knowledge Angus had. But Angus was a Scotsman, and he would argue with me that no game cookbook had ever sold more than a few thousand copies and it wasn't worth the effort. Then came word, via Jason Epstein, the savvy editor (and a passionate cook) at Random House, that L. L. Bean was looking for someone to do an L. L. Bean game-and-fish cookbook, and that caught fire with Angus. The Camerons had been particularly grateful to old Mr. Bean, who headed what was then a small family company, because, when he had heard that Angus and his family were taking off for Alaska, he had personally seen to it that the children were outfitted with the proper outdoor gear, which was not then available in their small sizes. Perhaps it was in honor of that debt, but more likely it was knowing the value of the L. L. Bean name that prompted the Scotsman in Angus to say yes, he would do the book—but only if I would help him.

A Renaissance man, Angus Cameron

After the contract was signed, time went by, and I realized how hard it was to get Angus to sit down at the typewriter. I knew that he had kept careful notebooks over the years, every time he went on a hunting or fishing expedition, but how could we get hold of them? Finally, Jason had an inspiration: He told me to invite myself up to Wilton, Connecticut, where the Camerons lived, to go armed with several large shopping bags and not leave until they were filled with all the notebooks. It worked. I lugged the heavy bags home, and then we turned them over to a typist, who produced about four hundred pages of manuscript. When Angus saw the pile, he exclaimed: "By God, it's done." And I had to bring him down to earth, gently saying that, alas, the work had just begun.

That summer, we had long sessions in Vermont, during which I would mercilessly pin him down to a desk for hours at a time, realizing, of course, that he longed to be out exploring the woods or showing me how to cast my rod in our newly created pond. But gradually, as he absorbed those typed-up pages, he realized what a good book there was in all that material, and he began to enjoy shaping it and sharing his expertise. And he knew so much. He was a Renaissance man, who might suddenly quote from Chaucer as he was skinning a raccoon, or come up with a reference to Shakespeare as he talked about how, in the subtle art of cooking, one ingredient becomes a catalyst for others. He loved everything about food, and he honored nature by treating its gifts with respect—and by eating with gusto.

The book, which came out in 1983, is still in print and remains a favorite among hunters. Up in my neck of the woods, in the Northeast Kingdom of Vermont, where a lot of folk hunt to put away a winter's supply of meat for their families, several hunters I know own a now dog-eared copy jointly (too expensive for each to buy one), which they pass around every hunting season for cooking ideas. I find that I dip into it often just to enjoy the spirit of Angus in his recipes for Crooked Knife Stew or Eggs Hopeful (when there's no fresh meat in camp) or his advice on "Bay Leaves and Other Real or So-called Fighting Herbs and Spices (with comment on some herbs that are bashful)." Food was an integral part of his life, and his delight in it brought him close to simple, earthy people—politics aside—and he could always find a good story.

Just as in real life we come to know someone through his or her connection to food, so in fiction a telling aspect of a character's personality surfaces in his or her feelings about eating—something, after all, that occupies a good part of our lives. In the writers I've worked with, I find that the way in which they use food as a revelation of character can vary greatly. Some don't go near it at all. But Anne Tyler admitted, in answer to a question about why so much of the important action in her novels occurs at meals and celebrations: "I seem to be drawn to scenes involving food, and I think that's because people's attitudes toward food reveal so much about them. Are they feeders, or withholders? Enjoyers, or self-deniers? What exactly is on their plates—or in the saucepans they're eating directly from as they're hunching over the stove? It's all a kind of shortcut to tell my readers whom they're dealing with."

In her poignant novel *Dinner at the Homesick Restaurant,* Ezra Tull, the eldest son in a dysfunctional family, chooses to be a cook in a restaurant. When he was young and his sister was the victim of one of his mother's rages, "he would slip downstairs and fix her a mug of hot milk, sprinkled over with cinnamon. He was always so quick to catch his family's moods and to offer food and drink and unspoken support." His dream is one day to get through a single meal with his family from start to finish—no outbursts, no one running to the powder room, no one saying, as his father declares when, finally, after years of estrangement, he sits down with his family, "I hope you don't serve that kind of food a fellow can't identify . . . a mishmash of food, one thing not separate from another." Of course, Ezra, now chef at his own the Homesick Restaurant, is about to produce a splendid meal for his family, starting with an eggplant soup with bananas as the surprise ingredient.

In her novel *Digging to America,* Anne subtly uses the power of food to show the hold that the past can have on a character. Maryam, after more than twenty years in this country, still relishes the Iranian food she was brought up on, in the same way she finds it hard to let go of her sense of "otherness" in her adopted land.

On the other hand, John Updike, who grew up on heavy Pennsylvania Dutch fare (as did his character Rabbit), would not, I suspect, consider the relationship with food as a particularly telling aspect of behavior. I think it might seem trivial to him. And yet he has written this delicious scene in *Rabbit Redux* about Jill, the flower child who has moved in with Rabbit:

> For supper Jill cooks a filet of sole, lemony, light, simmered in sunshine, skin flaky brown; Nelson [Rabbit's son] gets a hamburger with wheatgerm sprinkled on it to remind him of a Nutburger. Wheatgerm, zucchini, water chestnuts, celery salt, Familia: these are some of the exotic ingredients Jill's shopping brings into the house. Her cooking tastes to him of things he never had: candlelight, saltwater, health fads, wealth, class. . . . Her cooking has renewed his taste for life. They have wine now with supper, a California white in a half-gallon jug. And always a salad: salad in Brewer County cuisine tends to be a brother of sauerkraut, fat with creamy dressing, but Jill's hands toss lettuce in a glowing film invisible as health. . . . Contentment makes Harry motionless; he watches the dishes be skimmed from the table, and resettles expansively in the living room. When the dishwashing machine is fed and chugging contentedly, Jill comes into the living room, sits on the tacky carpet, and plays the guitar.

What could more effectively evoke the transformation of Rabbit than that lemon sole and tossed salad? Even the dishwasher is purring.

But it is not often in novels that food is used in this transforming way. We come from a literary tradition that is predominantly male Anglo-Saxon and not conducive to searching out clues about a character through his or her sense of taste. Food has always been something taken for granted, like sleep and digestion and elimination—not to be dwelt on and, of course, not talked about. Perhaps, with our current unabashed pleasure in the joys of eating well, it may become a more useful tool for novelists. This happened with sex. And certainly there is an appetite now for reading all about the behind-the-scenes workings of a restaurant kitchen where the testosterone flows, the vocabulary consists of four-letter words, and the competition is brutal. But what does that have to do with taste?

It is all the more surprising that a writer like M.F.K. Fisher should have emerged pre–World War II, at a time when America was at a low point gastronomically. Not that her early books were as widely appreciated as they are today, but there was a small, hungry following that cherished her as a writer who dared to embrace food as a part of the sensual life. I ate up her lusty description of how, when living in Dijon as the wife of Al Fisher, at a formal lunch for the wives of academics, she dove into the intact, tough-shelled *écrevisses* with her fingers and sucked out the meat, thus managing with one lusty gesture to break down the stiff formality of the table. I've read again and again her story of the meal she ate alone in a country restaurant in Burgundy, urged on by a food-impassioned young waitress, in which she details course after course so palpably that I always feel myself virtually bursting by the end of the lunch she describes, to say nothing of a little tipsy. And among my favorites is the ritual she evokes of picking peas on a terrace in Vevey overlooking Lake Geneva, shelling them and rushing the peas into the waiting pot of boiling water; then the thrill of their taste, made all the more poignant because they are being shared with the people she loves most in the world. It never occurred to me that this was "food writing." It is simply passionate writing that embraces the fullness of life—and that includes food.

Over the years, I had developed a friendship with M.F.K. Fisher through the letters we exchanged. It started with my sending her the odd book I was publishing, not necessarily about food but something that I sensed would strike a responsive chord. And she invariably gave me her honest reactions. She took vicarious pleasure in Mary Roblee Henry's book about restoring an old farmhouse in Provence (but couldn't help slyly pointing out that Madame Henry never put on just a sweater; it was always a *cashmere* sweater), and she was particularly entranced with Jane Grigson's *The Art of Charcuterie,* which she found very "titillating" (although she didn't think it was for American cooks, "no matter how seriously they took their avocation").

Some years later, when Mary Frances had Parkinson's disease and her eyesight had deteriorated so that she found it difficult to read, I sent her a tape of John Updike reading his short stories. For once she couldn't wait to write. She picked up the phone and, in her wispy, girlish voice, which always seemed to me at odds with her character (but maybe it made one draw close to her and be particularly attentive), she confessed that listening to Updike was almost indecent, he was so sensuously caressing with his own words. But she was mesmerized.

Mary Frances was most comfortable writing letters, and, indeed, she collected a full library of correspondents. I suspect that the written word was the most releasing form of communication for her. She got to know you that way, and, particularly when she was alone in her later years, she lived vicariously through letters.

We had been writing back and forth for a good half-dozen years before we all met. Evan and I were doing some research in the Napa Valley, and she insisted we stop by for lunch. It was a scorching-hot California summer day when we pulled up at the frame house she lived in then, in St. Helena, and she greeted us with an embrace and a slightly enigmatic smile. "It's too hot to eat anywhere but in my cellar pub," she said, "so we're having lunch there." We dutifully followed her down the steep stairs to a dark and deliciously cool, musty-smelling cellar where a table was set with bright pottery and a bottle of wine. We immediately tucked into the good Provençal lunch she had made— a substantial salad, as I remember, cheese, fruit (her food was never fancy, just full of honest flavor), and, of course, the wine—and we talked for hours.

That lunch marked the deepening of a friendship in which we shared just about everything—from identifying mushrooms and the best way to dry them, to the secret life of the trout and how it survived the winter in our frozen pond. We anguished together when Diarmuid Russell, who was her literary agent of long standing, and Henry Volkening, his partner, both died too young, within a year of each other, of lung cancer; and she would tease me for my exhibitionist streak, which she claimed lurked in her, too. This was in reference to my description of flipping pancakes on a Boston TV morning show that Evan and I were on to promote our bread book. "The thought of it makes me laugh aloud," she wrote, "you and he would make a marvelous team with the pan-cake flipping and his deadpan mellifluous patter." She loved Evan and was one of the few people who got away with teasing him. She saw us as an entity, and she believed deeply in partners—"It's my idea of being equal," she wrote me.

One of life's puzzles that had long haunted Mary Frances was old age. As a young woman, she had been drawn inexplicably to a portrait of an ancient Swiss woman that she had stumbled on in a junk shop in Zürich. After she bought it and brought it home, it became what she called a kind of lodestar for her over the years, and she felt compelled to learn more not just about that indomitable woman in the portrait, Ursula von Ott, but about the mystery and the art of aging. Over the years, she had written many stories "about people who were learning it

M.F.K. Fisher at her Last House

and practicing it long before I was," she said, and we agreed that they should be gathered in a book, which she would call *Sister Age*. In her introduction, she wrote:

> St. Francis sang gently of his family: his brother the Sun, his sister the Moon. He talked of Brother Pain, who was as welcome and well-loved as any other visitor in a life filled with birds and beasts and light and dark. It is not always easy for us lesser people to accept gracefully some such presence as Brother Pain or his cousins, or even the inevitable visits of a possibly nagging harpy like Sister Age. But with a saint to guide us, it can be possible.

She particularly wanted me to see the old portrait that she thought would make an interesting cover, and the next time we were visiting her at "Last House," in Sonoma, she brought it out. I remember her so vividly sitting by the fire with the portrait propped up in front of her. It had by now been destroyed by silverfish, but still the image of Ursula remained intact, mesmerizing both of us.

I had told her, in the summer of 1976, that Evan and I were making a trip to France and Italy and we were bringing along my ninety-year-old Aunt Hilda and my mother, who was a mere eighty-two, and it was not surprising that she was intrigued. Mary Frances had rented a flat that year with her sister Nora in Aix-en-Provence, and I wanted to stop and see her to do some book work. When I promised her that my elderly relatives would not be in our way, she not only dismissed that notion but, I could tell, welcomed the idea of their intrusion. She always tended to run away from me when I wanted to go over a manuscript, because she had an almost pathological dislike of looking back over words she had put down on paper.

We met at the Longchamps, where the tables spilled out onto the Cours Mirabeau. As we were sipping a cup of café au lait and I had just pulled out my notes, two furtive figures crept by the terrace in front of us and disappeared. The second time they sneaked by, Mary Frances suspected who they were and, relieved at the distraction, asked if they could join us. For the next four days, she took them over, observing intently, drawing them out, occasionally teasing, and making them feel altogether special.

One day Mary Frances proposed that we drive over to Marseille to have lunch at a restaurant she was particularly fond of. Hilda was thrilled and put on her Kate Greenaway dress for the occasion, leaving the top part half open so she could fan herself and let in a little air as she and Mother settled into the sizzling hot backseat of our rented Fiat. But they were undaunted as we sailed through the dusty streets full of the bustle of Mediterranean life. After we found a parking lot, we walked past the *vieux port*, lined with bistros boasting bouillabaisse where *le patron* stood outside belting out his wares in a raucous voice to try to lure us in. But finally we made it through garbage-strewn streets to the quiet oasis of the Jambon de Parme where the Kennedy sisters, Mary Frances and Nora, were awaiting the Hedley sisters.

When we were seated, Hilda found herself elbow to elbow on the banquette with a gentleman with a well-chiseled profile who was eating alone. His first course was set in front of him—one of those beautiful small pale-green melons accented with dark-green stripes set simply on a leaf with a little decorative cap removed from the top so you could spoon out the luscious, juicy flesh—and Hilda leaned over toward him, exclaiming that it looked just like a Cézanne. Whereupon they struck up a conversation that went on intermittently all through lunch, as Mary Frances eavesdropped in awe and fascination.

For months afterward, Mary Frances remembered that meal, and she would refer often in her letters to Aunt Hilda's conquest. She still worried about the lobster salad they had ordered, which came all gussied up with apple slices and pieces of truffle that Hilda had thought were raisins. We'd all taken a bite and found the lobster meat a bit stringy, too.

"Well," she wrote, "I think the worst but at the same time one of the pleasantest gastronomical points was when your mother and Aunt Hilda decided to order lobster salad at the Jambon de Parme, and were confronted with a French concoction that would KILL any New Englander not raised in international diplomatic circles, Quel désastre! What a weird mess. And we went right on tucking into our pasta."

Signed: "Love neither cautionary nor discretionary to you and Evan . . ."

I secretly rejoiced at how readily the Hedley sisters had embraced that salad and how open they seemed to be to new tastes. It's never too late, I thought.

Even for Chris Vandercook. To my surprise, a few years after Evan had died Chris suggested that for Christmas I visit Hawaii, where he has been living for the past twenty years. He wanted us to explore what Hawaiian food really is—not the fancy fusion cuisine that the star chefs were touting so successfully, but the street food, the hole-in-the-wall ethnic dives, the shacks along the coast, and the kinds of meals that his friends made at home. So, the morning I arrived, we picked up his longtime friend the jazz singer Azure McCall and headed toward a round-the-clock restaurant called the Like Like Drive Inn where we downed fried rice, hot banana cakes, and sampled "loco moto," an enormously generous bowl of rice with eggs, hamburger, and gravy floating on top. Later, we were treated to

A dinner at home with Chris

a taste of suburban entertaining. All the guests brought a pot-luck dish—pupus, they are called—and there were as many ethnic flavors as there were nationalities gathered around: from sushi and sashimi to tortilla pinwheels wrapped around meats to seaweed poke. John Waihee, the ex-governor of Hawaii, when he heard of our quest, came over to talk to us and claimed that the quintessential Hawaiian dish was Spam musubu—a ball of rice wrapped in Spam and seaweed. I didn't know whether he was pulling my leg.

Another evening, Azure put on a very different spread for us, of the good foods that she grew up with. She made a big pot of chicken and gravy, and another of rich deep-brown braised rib-eye stew; there were casseroles of sweet potatoes and macaroni and cheese; and greens cooked with ham hock—and warm rolls to sop up the pot likker. To cap it all off, a Southern-style peach cobbler.

Christmas dinner was had at the home of David Wilson, a Britisher who loves to cook. Together with his Japanese wife, he runs a successful public-relations business, but he far prefers to bring his clients and friends home and give them something he has made than to treat them to yet one more fancy restaurant. Not that he doesn't get good ideas from the pros, as I could see from the *ahi katsu* he was preparing as a first course, based on a recipe in Chef Alan Wong's book. As he confidently dredged the slices of fish in flour, butter, and finally panko (the Japanese breadcrumbs), then slipped them into hot fat briefly, he talked about what a great cook his mother was and how he, growing up in the north of England, inherited his sense of taste from her. The rest of the Christmas dinner was a tribute to her, from the beautifully browned eighteen-pound turkey with sage-and-sausage stuffing, roasted potatoes, and sprouts to the English plum pudding with clotted cream. Another fine example of how through the power of taste we can evoke all the nuances of a perfect traditional Christmas dinner, right in the middle of the Pacific.

The lovely, slim eighteen-year-old daughter of the Wilsons, a graceful blend of her Japanese mother and tall English father, announced at the end of dinner that she was going to have to marry a man who cooks. She confessed that she is so hopeless that she can't even recognize a single flavor in what she is eating. Maybe. But my guess is that if she found herself stranded in a gastronomic wasteland she would be able to call upon her ingrained taste memories and would blossom as a cook.

As for Chris, the last night I was in Hawaii, he suggested we cook together in his galleylike apartment kitchen. His few pots were pretty sorry-looking, but he had recently bought himself an imposing rice-cooker, and he came up with the idea that the fresh mahi mahi that we'd just bought at the fish market could be steamed on top of the rice. Why not? So we scattered some shredded ginger, scallions, and cilantro leaves over the fish, sprinkled on a little soy sauce and toasted-sesame oil, and slipped the fillets on top of the rice for the final five minutes or so of cooking.

The dish was a triumph. Even more so being the invention of one who once prided himself on that telling gesture that said: I can eat it but I don't have to taste it.

9

Treasures of the Good Earth

In the summer of 1980, one of those uncanny happenings occurred for which there is no rational explanation. I think I've had more than my fair share of them in my life, for which I am very grateful.

It had been a bad year for us. Evan had had a series of slight strokes, caused, as it turned out, by a clogged carotid artery that had to be reamed out. Then I underwent a mastectomy. To cheer me up the night before my operation, Evan, who was just recovering from his surgery and still a bit unsteady, made the long trek up to the hospital and appeared in my room laden with a feast—a good *pâté de campagne,* some ripe cheese, a baguette, and a bottle of wine. He even brought a candle, so we could eat in its soft light. When my doctor, a rather conservative type, passed by, he did a double take, then gave us a nod of approval.

But all this is preamble to the story of Bryn Teg.

That summer, we treated ourselves to a six-week vacation, both to recover our spirits and to finish our bread book. We rented a place sight unseen on Stannard Mountain, in the Northeast Kingdom of Vermont, where we could be alone, a good eight miles away from the family enclave in Greensboro where I'd spent my summers. Only daughter Audrey, who'd been visiting my family, had inspected the place, and she reported that we were going to love it because it had a big black commercial stove. The house was the creation of Carlos Montoya, son of the famous Spanish guitarist and a musician himself. He fell in love with this rugged part of Vermont and felt he had to build a house that would make the most of the mountain view and fit in with the landscape. The only trouble was that he ran out of money, and to recoup he tried opening a Spanish restaurant in Montpelier. I'm afraid that he was ahead of his time, and Montpelier was not ready for his noisy jazz bar with Spanish tapas (a word not yet in our culinary vocabulary) to graze on. So he had to sell his house and cut his losses; he took off for Martha's Vineyard, where he has become a very successful landscape designer.

On our way north, we had picked up a twelve-week-old Welsh-terrier puppy. We had just lost a young border terrier to the parvovirus—another blow that unfortunate winter—and the little black-and-tan creature now sitting on Evan's lap seemed like our new lease on life. Of course, she had to have a Welsh name, and from the list of possibilities Evan had thought up, we both fastened on "Teg," meaning "beautiful"—a word we had seen attached to villages and valleys and streams the one time we'd been in Wales. As we drove up the steep dirt road and saw for the first time the house that Carlos built standing tall on the hilltop, the hemlock exterior graying with the weather, we felt that fate had brought us here. There was a lower deck, for outdoor eating, and an upper deck for meditating, both facing the Green Mountains and the western sun. Right away we started calling the place Bryn Teg—Beautiful Hill—and we knew it was meant to be ours. Fortunately, Carlos was eager to sell.

As we settled in, we realized not only that Carlos had brought over the sturdy chef's stove from his restaurant kitchen but that

The first summer at Bryn Teg

the cellar of the house was filled with large commercial tins of ginger, cloves, cinnamon, poppy seeds, and so on, all the spices we needed to test Grandma McLeod's Gingerbread, Pumpkin Bread, Sticky Buns, and Seeded Loaf. He had even left behind cartons of the kind of yeast we liked best for bread-baking, and in the cellar we found a small stash of Mexican tiles, left over from making the rust-colored tile floor in the kitchen, ready and waiting to line the shelf of the brick oven I would improvise.

But more mysterious was the revelation about the name Bryn Teg that occurred a few years later, when Evan was doing a story on Wales and we took our second trip there. This time we stopped at the village of Salem, where his grandfather had grown up before setting out to preach the gospel in the New World. We talked to an old man who remembered Evan's great-grandmother. He had just had his midday meal, and bits of unchewed cabbage would spurt from his mouth as he described how, when she was an old lady, she would walk the long miles from their farm on the hill above to attend chapel every Sunday. As the memory surfaced, he bent over to illustrate the dog walking with her, and demonstrated how she tucked the lantern under her arm. The house was gone, but he pointed out the church graveyard that we must visit. A little later, we were standing among the stones, and as I looked at Evan, I thought he had seen a ghost. I understood why when I read on the slab of granite in front of him *William Jones and Mary Jones* and, under their names, BRYN TEG, their home.

Our own "beautiful hill" opened up an unexpected new dimension in our relationship to food. As we turned the clayey soil for our first vegetable garden, planted a Dutchess apple tree and raspberry bushes, and tried to nurture herbs unaccustomed to this cold climate, we were awakened to the profound differences that soil and climate have on taste. Basil leaves, for instance, turn tough and slightly bitter if they have to endure too many chilly summer nights, and tomatoes will never achieve the same sweetness as those grown in San Marzano soil under an Italian sun. So you have to learn to compensate. We soon realized how much more challenging gardening is than cooking. As a cook, you are in control. But as an amateur gardener, you learn to submit to and respect the whims of nature, particularly in the

Ed Giobbi, my guiding spirit

Northeast Kingdom of Vermont, where the growing season is so short and the rocky soil so unyielding.

Somehow I don't think we would have made it through those first years of trial and error without the sensible and encouraging voice of Ed Giobbi, who seemed to be always at our side as we learned to garden and then to relish what we had wrought in our new country kitchen. In spite of his former weakness for safflower oil, I had come to respect and love him as one of the most gifted cooks I've known, and in the eighties I was helping him develop a book called *Pleasures of the Good Earth*. He was an artist, and he lavished the same creativity on cultivating food and cooking it for his family as he did on his painting. A second-generation Italian, he loved perpetuating the Old World skills and traditions he had learned from his father—foraging for wild mushrooms, hunting for mussels on the rocks of the Connecticut shore (at a time when mussels were considered trash seafood), canning tuna, curing pork, making sausages, and producing fine wine, which he stored in a natural stone cave on his land in Katonah, New York. He developed strategies for extending the growing season and for getting the most out of his garden, including what I considered one of the most pragmatic tips: Don't weed too vigorously; tucked in the soil can be treasures like purslane, dandelions, and lamb's-quarters, which you'll come to relish as nature's treats. I've always taken this advice to heart—and been rewarded.

When the book came out, Alice Waters, a true kindred spirit, whose message about the importance of the quality of good local produce was being heard across the land, wrote: "What is so distinctive about the cooking in this book is that there is flavor and richness here that is the product not of manipulation, but of a profound respect for what comes from the earth and a true connection to nature and the cycle of the seasons." I certainly learned, as I made one inspired dish after another, how, when the seasons dictate what goes together, flavors and colors and textures play off each other and create a natural harmony that is always naturally delicious.

The back-to-the-earth movement that the sixties generation had spawned did put the emphasis in the right place, and the food world soon climbed on the bandwagon. More than ever, we began to focus on the quality of ingredients, emphasizing the importance of whole grains and garden-fresh vegetables untainted by chemicals. I persuaded an English professor, Catherine Osgood Foster, with whom I had studied at Bennington, to do a book on organic gardening after seeing a piece she had written for our alumni magazine. It was full of sensible advice, including a formula for killing bugs the wholesome way, which I promptly put into practice with great success. When I told my mother what the secret was—to use a spray made up of crushed garlic and hot red peppers—her reaction was predictable. "No wonder," she said, "the bugs die."

We also had the good fortune, soon after buying the house, to meet Adele Dawson, an herbalist, a psychic, and a forager, who at the time was gathering material for a cookbook for "Creative, Environment-Concerned People." When she came to pay a visit to Bryn Teg, she walked the land with us and pointed out all the edibles surrounding us, including wild sorrel, milkweed, fairy ring mushrooms, and shaggy manes. Everything had its season, and she sketched out for us what to look for in the early spring, from fiddleheads to wild asparagus and leeks, and what we should gather in before going back to the city in the fall. She carefully explained how best to cook the milkweed growing all around us during its three different seasons: the early shoots, which were so good just steamed in butter; the flowers, before they opened up, dipped in a beer batter and fried; and then the pods, which could be stuffed like zucchini flowers. We tried them all and were seduced.

Adele was also a dowser, as I found out. I had been doing a bread-baking demonstration at a workshop at her place, and when I was ready to go pick up Evan, who had sneaked off to the local library for the day, my car keys were missing. Not wanting to disturb Adele, surrounded as she was by her followers, I walked the mile to the library and then returned with Evan to see if we could hitch a ride with someone. As we approached her house, we could see Adele out in the road, walking in deep concentration and slowly swinging an amulet. Suddenly she stopped, the amulet moving quickly now, and she called out as we approached, "You'll find the keys right here." And, sure enough, we pushed away the brush, and there they were.

Adele Dawson was in truth a flatlander, the term Vermonters use for anyone out of state. She had moved to the little town of Marshfield only during the last quarter of her life, and word of her gifts spread. I had known of Marshfield when I was a child in Montpelier because of my grandmother. She had once lost her diamond wedding ring and was frantic to find it. So she sought out an old farm woman in Marshfield who was known to have the gift of sight and set off to seek her help—a good fifteen miles away, quite a trek in those horse-and-buggy days. It didn't take the old lady long to close her eyes and see a vision of a sparkling stone enwrapped in dark cloth hanging in a dark, enclosed space. Could it be that the ring had fallen into the hem of a dress that was hanging in a closet? As soon as my grandmother returned home, she went to her bedroom closet, and there, hidden in the folds of the hem of a dark dress, was her wedding ring. I always loved this story, and the day Adele was dowsing for my keys it struck me as uncanny that she should have settled in the same village as my grandmother's famous psychic and taken on her mantle.

Adele brought some of that psychic sensibility into her relationship with food. In her introduction to the book she was then working on, and which was published after her death as *A Dollop of This and a Smidgeon of That,* she wrote:

> In working with the recipes in this book, you will notice how archetypal images that come out of past human experiences take on tangible qualities from

our conscious, everyday life. Food becomes symbolic as well as nourishing and delicious. Love, sex, security and adventure tumble in our inner blender with apples, mangoes, carrots and cream.

These recipes will satisfy hunger and dream, wish and memory. Each dish connects us with the world, its history and climate, human relationships and bits and pieces of other people's lives.

Now, I well know that Julia might have a good laugh at what went into that blender, but when you sat at Adele's table, as we did several times, you couldn't help but feel that primal connection to the bounty of the earth.

Many years later at Bryn Teg, I experienced an atavistic impulse that took me by surprise because it surfaced so spontaneously. My stepdaughter Bronwyn's husband, David, had just shot the beaver that for two seasons had been destroying the lovely pond that we had created out of marshlands. I respected the fact that this industrious creature was only doing the work for which he had been programmed and that he had systematically felled all the surrounding birches, poplars, and willows and gnawed away at the laurel and crab-apple trees, not only for his own nourishment but to build a dam and a lodge for the winter. But I also realized it was only matter of weeks before that dam, created out of all the detritus he pulled into the water, would overwhelm our drainage system and flood the surrounding fields and probably the county road. Moreover, his lodge was ready to accommodate a mate, and it wouldn't be long before there was a whole family of sharp-toothed beavers to increase the workforce and compete with me for swimming rights. So I convinced myself that he had to go. Several neighbors offered to shoot him, and one or two even dropped by with their rifles at sundown. But the nocturnal beaver is a wily fellow, and it required persistence and careful observation of his habits to flush him out. Fortunately, David felt challenged, and we purchased a gun in my name at the local country store. David then proceeded to station himself patiently by the pond at dawn and at dusk, throwing sticks into the water to arouse the beaver's curiosity and make him surface. On the fourth day, I woke to the sound of two shots fired, and I looked out to see the victim—a good hefty fifty pounds—lying in the grass, his glossy coat glinting in the sun.

David with the beaver

It was at that moment that something stirred in me. We had to honor that noble creature, not just throw him on the garbage heap. And—unconsciously thinking of Angus Cameron, I'm sure—what better way to celebrate than to eat his liver? So David dutifully extracted the vital organ, and while it was still warm I dredged it in flour and cooked it quickly in sizzling butter. It made a delicious breakfast, and seemed a fitting way of giving thanks.

I told this story to Christopher Hirsheimer, whom I had just come to know as a great food photographer, and who was also at the time executive editor of *Saveur* magazine, and he urged me to write about it. But when the piece was published, I wasn't prepared for the hate mail—the number of sensibilities that were deeply offended by this sadistic, selfish woman from New York City who felt she had to have her revenge on one of God's noble creatures by eating it, moreover relishing it, just because it had mucked up her pond. I realized that I had touched a very sensitive nerve in people, and that the American relationship with food, particularly when it comes to the killing of animals, is complex. One correspondent pointed out that the beaver was an endangered species, but that was hard to believe in northern Vermont, where families of beavers flourish more than ever in pond after pond, moving on after their dams and pavilions are built, and leaving the denuded shores looking like a ghost town. It was also suggested that no one ate this rare species any more, but, as Angus found in *Larousse Gastronomique,* the beaver is hunted in North America, France, Scandinavia, and Germany for its fur as well as its meat, and the Catholic Church accommodatingly classed its meat with that of water fowl so it could be eaten during Lent. "The French were no fools," Angus commented to me.

I think maybe I had another motive for wanting to test beaver meat further. Evan had contributed a recipe to *The L. L. Bean Game and Fish Cookbook* for a rather dubious part of the animal—the tail. Evan, alas, was no longer with us to stand up for his recipe for fried beaver tail, and I had a sneaking suspicion that he had never really tried it out himself, not having had access to the prime ingredient. So to me it was a matter of defending his honor against the skeptics to prove that the fried tail was indeed delicious. Now, the tail is a flat, hairless, scaly appendage, shaped like a paddle. When a beaver wants to assert himself, he slaps that paddle noisily into the water—a tactic that our beaver had used frequently with me, particularly when I entered his territory early in the morning for a swim. I didn't know precisely what kind of meat might be encased inside or how to get at it. The recipe simply said, "Skin the tail," and as I tried to plunge my sharp knife into the rough, leathery surface, I realized it was going to be hard work. But with perseverance, I eventually uncovered a fatty, gristly tissue. Following Evan's recipe, I cut this "flesh" into strips, which I simmered in vinegary water to tenderize them, then drained them, dredged them in breadcrumbs, and fried them in hot oil. When they were ready, I popped a glistening morsel into my mouth and was ravished. It was crisp outside and unctuous within. I quickly offered a taste to David and Bronwyn, only to see the horror on their faces as they bit through the crustiness into what seemed to them like pure fat.

Had tastes really changed so radically in just one generation? In the past, what I would describe as wonderfully *onctueux* (an adjective that in direct translation is considered derogatory these days) was something to savor. But the obsession with fat that has had such a stranglehold on this country has really altered most people's palates. I've seen many an otherwise appreciative eater shun the marrow in an osso buco—that succulent prize bit in the shank bone, which, come to think of it, the beaver tail resembled. I secretly raised my glass to Evan and thanked him for this once-in-a-lifetime taste treat.

The first few years that we were at Bryn Teg, Russ McAllister, the farmer down the road, who had only a few acres left of what had once been a large farm, used our pastures for grazing his relatively small milking herd. In return, he urged us to take as much milk as we needed from the tank in his milk room. The first time we walked down the dirt road at twilight to get the milk, I was immediately brought back to summers when I was a child and we would go to the neighboring farm at the end of the day, swinging our milk pails, which we would fill to the brim. When we got home, the milk was carefully poured into glass bottles, and we would wait for the thick yellowy cream to rise to the top, then stick our fingers in and lick appreciatively. I did the same with the fresh milk from the McAllisters', and it tasted every bit as delectable as it had some fifty years before.

One of the rewards of saving some of that luscious cream was to have enough to make a batch of hand-churned ice cream, flavored purely with fresh berries or fruit ready to burst with ripeness. First we would have to chip enough ice off the huge blocks that were delivered each week to keep our old nonelectric icebox chilly, then there was the endless turning of the crank, each of us taking turns until our arms ached. Finally, our frozen cream would be too thick to churn another round, so we would pry off the top, pull out the paddle, and all dive in to lick the dasher.

Vermont maple syrup and walnuts were also wonderful with that cream, and the secret was using dark Vermont maple syrup, considered an inferior grade in the marketplace but by far the most intense in flavor. Not long after we'd settled into Bryn Teg, we discovered that John Reynolds, a second cousin of mine, one generation removed, lived just on the other side of the woods with his young family and was producing maple syrup, tapping every maple within reach. Now, with his more modern equipment—sleek plastic lines running from tree to tree replacing the old buckets—his reach includes our woods, and every summer I am blessed with gallon Mason jars full of that good dark maple syrup, as much as we can use.

Another gift of nature has been the wild sorrel that creeps into the rock garden, flower beds, and forests. Adele taught us to recognize its tongue-shaped leaf with two small spears protruding at the stem, and as soon as we tasted its acidic bite, memories of *potage St. Germiny*, sorrel omelettes, and sorrel-onion custard, which we'd relished in France, surfaced. Soon we were not only hoarding our weeds but had planted one cultivated variety in the herb garden that produced so prolifically we had all that we could use; we even took home frozen packets to last the winter. I discovered so many new and surprising ways of cooking with these lemonlike leaves that I wondered why they weren't used more in cooking. Perhaps it's because they do turn an unappetizing khaki color when cooked, but don't let that deter you. You can always put an edible flower on top of the drab-looking sauce à la Aunt Marian.

I soon dubbed sorrel, as well as the tart-tasting gooseberry, the lemons of the North. And, indeed, both are used in lemonlike ways. I had never tasted a gooseberry until we went on that trip to Wales where, at the Glen Severn Inn, overlooking the Wye Valley, we were served a fine grilled mackerel with a good plop of gooseberry sauce on top in place of the usual lemon wedge. It was delicious, with the tartness of the green berries cutting through the natural oiliness of the fish. I wanted to experiment more with this sharp fruit, but, although I found that old American cookbooks were full of recipes calling for gooseberries—the Shakers were particularly fond of them in preserves and ketchups—it was hard to get them, even in specialty markets. And then we discovered why when we went to buy a couple of gooseberry bushes from our friend Lewis Hill, who ran a nursery in nearby Greensboro and was a most knowledgeable Yankee. He had the plants, but he cautioned us that we would have to plant them five hundred feet away from any white pines. It developed that those prickly berry plants, along with currants, were responsible for the disease known as white-pine blister rust, which had threatened white pines all over America since the early 1900s.

So, during Franklin D. Roosevelt's presidency, the government sent out the Civilian Conservation Corps to pluck up all the offending bushes. Even as Lewis Hill passed on the official warning to us, it was clear that he took it with a grain of salt. It has become obvious in recent years that only the wild plants are the culprits, and that only a certain variety of pine was affected. Meanwhile, America lost its gooseberries. One more example of the American tendency to overreact when there is a suspicion that food is the enemy. Today too many Americans are wary because of the hidden threat of mad-cow disease in beef, so offal is more shunned than ever. Cheese lovers are struggling to halt the FDA's ban on the importation of raw-milk cheese. Not only are the most delicious cheeses made with unpasteurized milk, but, according to Matteus Kohler in nearby Greensboro, one of the most gifted cheesemakers I know, raw milk is more beneficial, provided the cheese is made under scrupulously sanitary conditions. Now there is a movement afoot in California to outlaw the making of foie gras because it is cruel to overstuff geese in order to fatten their livers.

I confess that I used to buy into that particular nonsense, until the summer that Evan and I were in the Dordogne doing a story on the specialties of that region. We were staying at a country inn, and in the evening, when we took a walk, we would hear what seemed to be the mournful, frightened hawking of geese rising from the neighboring farms. I visualized the birds' feet nailed to a plank as food was being shoved down their throats. Then we visited a goose farm, where the ruddy-faced farmer welcomed us with a glass of his homemade wine and proudly took us out to his barn at feeding time. As we approached, the now familiar cry of the geese rose, and it was clearly in anticipation of supper. The farmer sat down on a stool with a little electric corn-grinder in hand, and one by one the geese waddled up to him and sat on his lap. As he let the freshly ground corn tumble into the open beak, he would stroke the throat of each bird until it had had enough and would contentedly wander off. Is that cruelty? Rather than banning the making of foie gras, it would behoove us to enforce standards in this country for the raising of animals under humane conditions. Read Michael Pollan's revealing book *Omnivore's Dilemma* and you will understand the devastating consequences of the industrialization of our farms today. The way beef cattle and pigs are raised and slaughtered and the appalling factory life of our chickens, as well as in the methods used to increase the production of milk (as Anne Mendelson discovered in her research for *Milky Ways*, her upcoming book on milk)—these atrocities make the techniques for fattening the goose look benign.

If we wait long enough, the pendulum invariably swings, and

we take a more measured position. The gooseberry was exonerated, and now in Vermont we have two thriving gooseberry plants that are so prolific I am forever finding new ways to put them to good use. Family and friends who visit seem to relish the gooseberry fools and flummeries and crumbles and buckles and other old-fashioned desserts we turn out, to say nothing of the little pots of gooseberry jam that have developed such a following it is hard to keep up with the demand. But sometimes, on a hot July day, after I have topped and tailed huge piles of gooseberries, then stood over the seething mass of boiling fruit, uncertainly testing again and again a dab of it on a chilled saucer to try to determine the right jelling point, I wonder if I'm not obsessed.

One summer day, we stopped at a nearby yard sale and I asked the woman presiding over her wares why she was selling all her canning equipment. She replied fiercely, "Because I've had it. I never want to put up another thing in my life." I sympathized—to a degree.

On the other hand, my friends Nova Kim and her partner Leslie Hook would protest; this kind of thinking goes against what they so vigorously advocate. Their mission is to awaken all of us to the abundance around us and to persuade country people, particularly in the depressed rural areas, that one could almost subsist on nature's abundance if we all knew how to recognize wild edibles, and to harvest them, cook them, and preserve them. But it's a hard sell to the native population in northern Vermont. Hunting and fishing are a way of life, and what one brings home is good honest meat. But fiddleheads and milkweed, to say nothing of those mushroom-toadstools that can kill you, they're not real grub.

Nova is an Osage Native American, imbued with the spirit of

*Foragers Nova Kim and Leslie Hook
with Nova's granddaughter*

being part of the Circle of Life. Somehow she made her way to Vermont and found the perfect mate in Les, a true Vermonter, with just the right amount of Yankee skepticism and savvy to serve as a foil. So far they have done wonders establishing wild-mushroom workshops, guiding all-day foraging expeditions, and selling their finds to the best chefs in northern and central Vermont. One can also subscribe as a private customer to their almost weekly home-delivery service, or monthly mailing of dried varieties during the winter. I have been the lucky recipient of their hands-on service for several years now, and it is like having the Good Humor man drive up the road and appear at your door when Nova and Les come by bearing their gifts. Only much, much better. One is left with, perhaps, a basketful of chicken-of-the-woods and pheasant's-back mushrooms, as well as angelica hearts and bracken-fern spears—treats not often had today. Every mouthful is a new experience: Some mushrooms are more woody than others, some more intensely flavored, and wild greens can be slightly grassy or as sweet as young asparagus.

As Wendell Berry wrote in *The Unsettling of America*, "If you take away from food the wholeness of growing it or take away the joy and conviviality of preparing it in your own home, then I believe you are talking about a whole new definition of the human being." Add to that the joy of coming upon a patch of golden chanterelles, as I did one day at the edge of our woods, then carefully plucking them from their beds, and sitting down only moments later to their woodsy, faintly sweet, and musty flavor, and you feel that you have joined the Circle.

Perhaps inspired by this feeling of connection to the earth that the miracle of Bryn Teg brought us, I recently felt impelled to try to raise some grass-fed beef on our land, and together with Bronwyn and David (of beaver fame) we persuaded John Reynolds to undertake the venture. John had for many years nurtured young heifers and then sold them to dairy farmers when they were ready for milking. But in recent years there had been so little market for them, as small dairy farms were being squeezed out by industrial giants, that it was no longer a viable undertaking. However, there was clearly a growing demand for locally grown beef, and it could be done on a small scale. I particularly longed to see cattle grazing again on our pastures, maintaining the farmlands instead of letting them revert to second growth and close in all around us. Whenever I've taken a walk through the surrounding woods and meadows I have been struck at how hard our Yankee forebears worked at creating

One of the "girls" with the house and pond in the background

those pastures, heaving rocks from the soil and building stone fences with their own hands. Raising some beef cattle seemed a way of honoring them and preserving the fruits of their labor and at the same time of joining in with the new crop of Vermonters who were finding alternate ways to survive as farmers.

So in the fall of 2006 John and his son, Travis, started erecting fences and building a shelter. Soon they transported six sturdy Black Angus cows, carefully selected and certified pregnant, to stake their claim on our hilltop. I got acquainted with them only through the computer, as I already returned to the city, and the digital images of those cows assured me they were well padded and weathering the winter (it took a good twelve bales of hay a day to feed them). Then in early March, the day before my birthday, I got an e-mail from John's wife, Carol, describing how the first calf had been born the night before at

39 degrees below zero. When she and John discovered the creature, he was half frozen and they took him home in their Subaru to their warm kitchen to thaw out. "Blankets, towels, a hair dryer, a woodstove, and perseverance did the trick," she wrote. Then, of course, he needed his mother's milk so Carol had to return him, wrapped in her son's warm hunting jacket, to the frigid night and wait while he finally figured out how to get at the milk. By 2 a.m. he was satisfied, but starting to freeze again as the mother persisted in licking him all over, so once again the little calf had to be bundled up and brought back to their warm house for the night.

How I shall feel when this creature is mature and ready to be sent off to market, I am not quite sure. But at least I can rest assured that the meat I am consuming is from an animal that has been raised with tender loving care.

10

The Pleasure That Lasts the Longest

After Evan died, in the winter of 1996, I doubted that I would ever find pleasure in making a nice meal for myself and sitting down to eat it all alone. I was wrong. Instead, I realized that the ritual we had shared together for almost fifty years was a part of the rhythm of my life, and by honoring it I kept alive something that was deeply ingrained in our relationship. In fact, more than ever I found myself, about mid-afternoon, letting my mind drift toward what I was going to conjure up for dinner when I got home. Instead of walking into what might have seemed an empty apartment—actually, I've always had a dog who is hungry to greet me—I gravitate toward the kitchen, as I did as a young girl to bask in Edie's warmth, and I can't wait to bring it to life, to fill it with good smells, to start chopping or whisking or tossing and smelling up my hands with garlic. I turn on some music and have a glass of Campari or wine, and it is for me the best part of the day, a time for relaxation. When, at last, I sit down and light the candles, the place across from me is not empty.

Several summers before he died, Evan had posted on the refrigerator door—a catchall for food notes in our house—this quotation from Alfred North Whitehead: "Cooking is one of those arts which most requires to be done by persons of a religious nature."

He suspected I would love that thought, fancying myself to be of a religious nature. He knew that I have always felt that the preparation of food is one of the most joyous and inwardly satisfying of all activities that we as human beings are peculiarly privileged to indulge in daily. Other creatures receive food simply as fodder. But we take the raw materials of the earth and work with them—touch them, manipulate them, taste them, glory in their heady smells and colors, and then, through a bit of alchemy, transform them into delicious creations. Cooking demands attention, patience, and, above all, respect. It is a way of worship, a way of giving thanks.

Later, when I pursued the root of the word "religious," I found that it is thought to spring from *religare*, meaning "to bind, to tie fast, to reconnect." Isn't that what we do when we cook? We connect again to the earth, to the source of our food, and we bind to one another in the sharing of it, the breaking of bread together, the celebrating of life.

When I make bread with children for the first time, I am particularly aware of the exciting sense they feel of actually giving birth to an inert, big blob of water and flour, watching the yeast become active. As we knead the dough, we can feel it transformed from a sticky, lumpy paste to a cohesive mass that is smooth and resilient and bouncy under the heels of our hands. When we poke it, it springs back at us. It is alive. Sometimes it forms bubbles and blisters in its eagerness to expand. Then, after we put it down for a nap with a towel laid over it, we return an hour or so later and find that it has doubled or tripled in volume. Now it's time to tame it and punch it down (the kids always love the punching part). Later, when it goes into the oven, it responds to the heat, rising again, settling into the shape we have given it, and sends forth the most tantalizing aroma as

*Making bread with Audrey's stepchildren and friends
in our Vermont kitchen*

*Preparing pizza with my grand-niece and -nephew,
Josy and her brother Tayo*

it bakes. No wonder that through the ages we have endowed bread with symbolic meaning: the staff of life, the bread of heaven, the body of Christ.

As I look at the carts at the supermarket laden with frozen dinners and other quickie foods that need only to be heated in the sterile microwave, I often feel sorry for the people who are missing out on the endlessly rewarding experience of cooking, even if just for oneself.

How different strolling through the farmers' market in a big city can be. You can feel the camaraderie that springs up when people of like minds are in pursuit of an old-fashioned-tasting peach or locally grown heirloom tomatoes or an artisan cheese made with whole, unpasteurized milk. When such markets were a novelty, some thirty years ago, that pulse was even more strongly felt, because the experience was so new to everyone there and somehow releasing. It was not unusual for Evan and me to be asked by a fellow shopper what we were going to do with a big bunch of basil we'd bought, and soon I was giving out Marcella's recipe for pesto. Someone once asked what that weird vegetable was that looked like a space-ship with antennae sticking out of it, and when we said kohlrabi, she remembered that her German mother used to cook it. Brussels sprouts were never so delicious as when we brought them home still clinging to their tall stalks. Once, we tucked some live eels into our shopping cart. The fisherman from Long Island said he didn't have time to kill them (or was he testing us?). Fortunately, by the time we got home, they had smothered in the plastic bag, so we didn't have to nail them up and whack them on their heads.

But what about all the time it takes? That's the complaint I constantly hear—all the shopping, tracking down of special ingredients, then the cooking and washing up, for something that is devoured in a matter of minutes. Is it really worth it? The English food writer Jane Grigson regarded this quick consumption as a blessing. In her lovely book *Good Things* she wrote:

> Cooking something delicious is really much more satisfactory than painting pictures or making pottery. At least for most of us. Food has the tact to disappear, leaving room and opportunity for masterpieces to come. The mistakes don't hang on the wall or on shelves to reproach you forever. It follows from this that the kitchen should be thought of as the center of the house. It needs above all space for talking, playing, bringing up children, sewing, having a meal, reading, sitting, and thinking. . . . It's in this kind of place that good food has flourished. It's from this secure retreat that the exploration of man's curious relationship with food, beyond the point of nourishment, can start.

Another complaint I hear, particularly from young people, is that they can't afford to cook because it is so expensive. One recipe alone will call for three different kinds of fresh herbs, so the cook has to buy three plastic packets at about $1.99 each in order to snip off a few leaves (while the rest, not very fresh to begin with, wither away); then there's that expensive aged balsamic vinegar or truffle oil or crème fraîche, of which they'll use only a few spoonfuls to enrich the dish. They're right. Too many cookbooks today are written by chefs who have no patience with such mundane concerns. Their mission is to create dazzling dishes to impress their clientele. Moreover, they have all those luxuries at their fingertips. So it is hard for them to think like home cooks. For us, cooking should be an ongoing process; we should be planning through the week, dreaming up new ways to use what is on hand, finding substitutes, if necessary, and improvising, maybe creating our own crème fraîche. All of this is both creative and challenging, particularly so for the lone cook because we constantly have to struggle in the supermarkets to find single portions, and we're forced to make compromises. Is it really worth buying a huge bouquet of parsley just to have a little to sprinkle on the fish? One feels frustrated. But maybe frustration encourages creativity. I sometimes find it so.

Though I am perfectly content cooking alone, I welcome having another body in the kitchen. We all do things a little differently, and we learn from each other. It's also nice to feel that we are passing on our pleasure in cooking to a younger generation, particularly at a time when most kitchens seem to be empty places.

The winter that Evan died, we had already booked an apartment in Paris for our spring jaunt there. It was a yearly pilgrimage that we always made, just to immerse ourselves again in French life, to go to the markets and to cook and eat good, simple French food again, and spend time with our friends the Roths. Instead of canceling, I asked my grand-niece Josy, then fifteen years old, if she wanted to come along, and, of course, she fell in love with Paris just as we had fifty years before. Certainly that latent food gene was awakened. Our *pied à terre* was very close to the rue de la Huchette, where Evan had been bludgeoned with a *matraque* by the angry restaurant proprietor, and when we walked down the narrow street to find a cozy place to eat, she was invariably whistled at and wasn't ashamed to enjoy it. The next year, when she was choosing a college, she settled on Barnard, so we spent many happy weekends cooking together in my ninth-floor kitchen. Once, when her boyfriend called from Michigan, she blithely informed him that he would have to call back, because we were in the middle of the cheese course (he married her a few years later and has been eating well ever since). Not long ago they came east from California, where they now live and teach, and I got a touching note from Josy saying how much the weekend in New York brought back memories of the times we spent together in the apartment.

"I think I learned how to be a woman then," she wrote, "relaxing with you after I'd had an energizing and exciting day of classes and you'd come home from a long day at work, and

Josy in Paris

we'd create a simple meal together. I remember once it was a beautiful little pasta dish of cream, ham, and peas improvised from what was in those plastic containers in your refrigerator. Through the years I've cherished those evenings and I've carried the same ritual over into my own family today. Thank you."

Cooking with a chef, on the other hand, is a learning experience, particularly if you can lure the pro into your own kitchen so that he has to translate what he is doing in a professional setup to your inevitably less efficient home kitchen. One summer recently, I had the chef Scott Peacock, Edna Lewis's devoted partner, who took care of her during the last years of her life, up to Bryn Teg for a visit so we could talk through some of the challenges he was up against writing a memoir of his relationship with Miss Lewis, as he always called her. I suggested to Scott (in part because I wanted to play sous-chef with him) that we invite the poet Galway Kinnell and his wife, Bobbie, a former fellow editor at Knopf, who live on the next mountain north, for dinner, since I know they are unabashed lovers of good food.

Scott wanted particularly to do things with local produce and was delighted to find green tomatoes and some very sharp, ready-to-bolt arugula in my garden. And then there was the mint I had carried back from Georgia, which Scott had given as mementos to those who'd participated in the memorial service for Edna that past May. He had carefully planted each seedling in an empty eggshell, as Edna in *The Taste of Country Cooking* described her mother doing every spring, lining up the shells on the kitchen windowsill until the soil was warm enough to receive them. My plant had flourished when I transferred it, shell and all, to the Vermont earth. Together these three finds formed the foil for a deliciously inventive combination that Scott had just come up with for the *Today* show: a salad of big juicy watermelon chunks, slivers of green tomatoes, and torn arugula leaves tossed with lots of mint and a sweet-sour dressing. When he asked me if I had liquid honey for the dressing, I was found wanting. But I quickly responded with the suggestion that some of that dark maple syrup would do the trick. And it did, splendidly.

We had managed to find a whole bone-in shoulder of pork at a not-too-distant farm that raised its own organic meats, and we planned on the bay-studded, slow-braised roast that was in the book that Scott and Edna did together, *The Gift of Southern Cooking*. They had developed this special recipe when they were visiting friends in the Georgia countryside and discovered during a morning walk not only a patch of wild mushrooms but several wild blackberry bushes with ripe berries ready for the picking. As firm believers in "What grows together goes together," they added these treasures to the braising liquid of tawny port and meat juices and created an unbelievably sumptuous sauce.

Well, Edna was certainly looking down on us that day, because, when we took a break and had a walk, we stumbled almost immediately on a spot I had not noticed before where just enough small golden chanterelles were thrusting their heads up through the loamy soil to give us several handfuls, all we needed for the sauce. Then, around the house, I inspected the wild blackberry bushes that had been almost dormant for several years and saw that they were sprouting juicy dark berries as they had never done before. Only the peaches for the shortcake

Scott Peacock with Edna Lewis

were from foreign soil, and, of course, the stone-ground grits that Scott usually carries with him.

As a pot of those grits simmered slowly on the back of the stove all afternoon, and we mixed and rolled out the biscuit dough for the shortcake, I got Scott to talk about the art of creating a recipe and where his own innate talent came from. He had started out as a musician but lacked the gift, so he said, to be a great one, and unconsciously some of that sense of harmony crept into his cooking—the need for balance, dominant chords against the flights of fancy. At one point he tasted something and muttered for my benefit, "A little more Schubert than Mahler?"

Later, at dinner with the Kinnells, we talked about how careful cooking is like writing. You have to find the exact word (or ingredient), to pare down (to get the essence of a flavor), to make seamless transitions (the compatible movement from one course to another). And then there is the focusing, knowing what you are doing. One big difference is that Galway can put away a poem and go back to it again and again, sometimes for years, refining and perfecting it, whereas the chef is not allowed that indulgence. He has to get dinner on.

Fortunately, at Bryn Teg the dining table is right in the middle of the kitchen, so, after we had consumed our luscious watermelon salad, we had the fun of watching, out of the corner of our eyes, Scott making the sauce at the last moment, reducing, tasting, balancing, tasting again, and correcting, in Zen-like concentration, until it was exactly to his liking.

We dedicated the meal to Miss Edna Lewis. She would have particularly appreciated how every element of it had a story, a past, a connection to the earth.

After Scott went back, I was left with a considerable amount of braised pork, and now it was my turn to be inventive. As I searched the crammed fridge for what might give new life to yesterday's meat, I couldn't help but think, It's not fair, chefs don't have to do this. They start with everything new, fresh, and top-quality, and they would have tossed out long ago that precious bit of leftover pan drippings I tucked away in a jar last week, and those wilted leeks and limp bunch of carrots in the vegetable drawer. But do I really have to get rid of that pure pork fat from last year? And that packet of sumac I brought back from Israel—well, let's not count how many years ago? I can feel Scott looking sternly over my shoulder. Yes, out. So, instead of cooking, I end up nervously housecleaning. The refrigerator suddenly becomes my worst enemy instead of my best friend, and when I have removed a mold-covered Bolognese sauce that I'd spent a whole afternoon cooking, and washed out the veggie bin, where a bit of slime has collected, it takes me a while to get my appetite back. Maybe that's why more people don't cook.

But I recover and whip up some sauce Gribiche, a favorite dressing, tart with chopped cornichons and capers, and thickened with sieved (or finely chopped) hard-boiled egg, always so delicious over cold meats. For another dish, I mince some of the meat and mix it with rice and a little leftover pesto sauce (that I refrained from throwing out) and stuff the prolific male zucchini flowers that don't bear fruit. Another night, I make a hash for supper, from the pork meat cut very fine, mixed with garden potatoes, peppers, and scallions.

A lot of the dishes I make for myself today are scaled-down versions of recipes that I can't resist as I come upon them in whatever cookbook I am working on. Of course, the author usually claims it cannot be done for one, but don't believe it. Lidia Bastianich has a beautiful dish in her *Lidia's Family Table* in which she first cooks slices of zucchini or eggplant, then browns scallops of pork, veal, chicken, or turkey breast, layers the meat and the vegetable in the big skillet, and finally creates a little pan sauce, sprinkling on cheese before the whole thing finishes cooking briefly in the oven. When I asked why I couldn't make just one serving of it in my small, trusty iron skillet, she looked doubtful. But I tried it, making sure that my pan was well filled, that there was enough liquid, and doing a little arithmetic to reduce the amounts. It worked perfectly—in fact, it gets better every time. And there's only one pan to clean up!

Of course, the other important learning experience when it comes to food is travel. I loved traveling with Evan to do stories, because, inevitably when the subject of food came up, it would form a bond, and people would let us into their hearth and home. He was a wonderful listener and could coax memories and stories out of the most reticent, even getting them to share their secret recipes. I would take notes, knowing instinctively what he wanted recorded. So there was a hole in my life when we could no longer make these trips together, and I welcomed going on a few adventures with some of my authors.

Joan Nathan persuaded me and my stepdaughter Bronwyn to come with her to Israel when we were doing the illustrations for her book *The Foods of Israel*. We traveled with Nelli Sheffer, the gifted photographer, who knew every inch of the land and was sensitive to all the nuances. Once, we stayed at a kibbutz so close to the Lebanese border that we could hear the rumble of gunfire in the distance. We even brought home rocks from the Sea of Galilee after we had watched an Israeli woman, who was

With Joan Nathan (left) *and my stepdaughter Bronwyn Dunne in Israel*

living off the land nearby, bake her loaves of bread by tossing them on sizzling-hot rocks that she had gathered by the shore. I must admit that when I got home I never succeeded in producing a palatable bread using this method. But I still cherish my Galilean stones. Recently Hiroko Shimbo gave a superb Japanese dinner, and for one of the courses a bowlful of very hot rocks was placed before each diner, with stern warnings not to touch. Alongside were thin slivers of raw fish, which we were told to slap on the rocks for just a few seconds on each side

In Luang Prabang with Nina Simonds (left)
and her friend Susan Bang (right)
before the welcoming ceremony

before dipping them into a sauce and popping them into our mouths. Maybe my Galilean stones could be put to use the same way—Middle East meeting Far East in a happy fusion.

I took my first trip to the Far East with Nina Simonds and her husband. I particularly wanted to get a better understanding of the naturally healthy diet that most Asian countries subscribe to, which was the subject of her new book, *A Spoonful of Ginger*. The night we arrived in Singapore, we went to the Herbal Restaurant in the Imperial Hotel and were greeted by the herbalist Li Lian Xing dressed in a doctor's white coat. After he took each of our pulses and examined our tongues, he prescribed what we should be having for dinner. We ordered accordingly, and as we consumed all the light, flavorful dishes, I thought what a different attitude people can have toward their food when they know it is health-*giving*, not threatening.

Later, in the lovely town of Luang Prabang, in northern Laos, the inn where we were staying offered to put on a welcoming ceremony for us. Women in the neighborhood brought dishes for us to savor together, and I was particularly moved when one very old woman came across the stone floor of the pavilion on her knees, holding out a bowl for me. She bowed a thank-you several times, and her eyes filled with tears as she expressed her gratitude that such an elderly American woman as I was would have come all this way to honor them with a visit.

As to the yearly pilgrimage to Paris, I found that there is nothing like having the irrepressible food writer Jeffrey Steingarten in the city at the same time, along with Claudia Roden, an equally passionate lover of Paris. Together we have roamed the streets as Jeffrey sniffed out new bistros and brasseries to write about or went in search of the best croissant or the most perfect baguette *à l'ancienne* (he was even appointed one of the fifteen judges for the annual competition for the Grand Prix de la Baguette de la Ville de Paris in 1998), or delved into the cellar of Pierre Hermé's shop on the rue Bonaparte to sample his latest pastry and chocolate creations. We also consumed the best vegetarian cuisine we'd ever tasted at Alain Pasard's lovely restaurant L'Arpège and were all dazzled by his creativity at coaxing out such intense and satisfying flavors from various often neglected vegetables and marrying their different essences to perfection.

I always like to stay in an apartment or, if possible, arrange an apartment exchange when I go to Paris. That way I can bring home some of the fresh herbs, greens, vegetables, and fruits spilling out of the fabulous markets all around. As long as I have a small kitchen, I can re-create the sautéed daurade with the glistening fish I picked up in the market, or make a *boeuf bourguignon* with the cut of meat the butcher recommended. Above all, I can wallow in all my favorite cheeses—a lusty Epoisses, Livarot, Langres, or hard-to-get Sousmaintrain, a Vacherin Mont d'Or (best eaten with a spoon), a farmhouse Camembert, a mountain Cantal, or a Muenster from Alsace. A good *fromager* will always tell me what's good to eat right away and what should ripen for another several days or a week or so. Slowly savoring those cheeses, washed down by a sturdy wine from the region, convinces me that, as M.F.K. Fisher suggested about herself, there must be some French genes deep within me.

Another rewarding trip was with Lidia Bastianich to research material for her book *Lidia's Italy*. After several days in Naples, where we immersed ourselves in the noisy, throbbing markets and sampled street foods and Neapolitan pizzas and pastries, we took off for the mountains east of Naples to visit an *agriturismo* near Caserta where they made their own cheese. After tasting the delicate fresh goat's-milk cheese that Liliana Lambert made, as well as the assertive aged kind steeped in herbs and spices, I felt her old father eyeing me. He wanted to know how old I was, and he seemed puzzled that at my age I would venture so far from home, sampling local fare, snapping photographs, and hopping over rugged terrain to visit the sheep. Wasn't it time for me to stay home? Maybe. But I still have so much to learn.

Moreover, I always take home new tastes and new challenges, so my table for one is constantly changing. And friends and family who partake of my fare are, I hope, never bored. There is an old Italian saying, *A tavola non s'invecchia*—"At the table one never grows old." Isn't that reason enough to come home at the end of the day, roll up one's sleeves, fire up the stove, and start smashing the garlic?

As Brillat-Savarin wrote: "The pleasures of the table are for every man, of every land, and no matter of what place in history or society; they can be part of all his other pleasures, and they last the longest to console him when he has outlived the rest."

The pleasure of a freshly grilled sausage on a hilltop in Vermont

Recipes

 *This symbol at the end of a recipe signals some comments, suggestions, and variations or culinary tips I have learned from my mentors, or improvements I have arrived at through trial and error. Every recipe continues to evolve, and I trust that all who make these dishes will come up with their own improvisations.*

From the Past

Aunt Marian's Ham Timbales

Spaghetti and Cheese

Shepherd's Pie

Croquettes

Bitki

Variation: Middle Eastern Bitki

Sauté of Chicken with Vegetables

Frenchified Meatloaf

Butternut Squash in Cream and Cinnamon

Bread Pudding

Summer Berry Pudding

Schrafft's Butterscotch Cookies

Mrs. Cooney's Hermits

French—and Other—Influences

Céléri Rémoulade
Boudin Blanc
Jacques's Version: Boudin Blanc
A Good Hash
French Bread (Baguettes)
Individual Pizza
Evan's Lamb Curry
The Versatile Stir-Fry
Sweetbreads Sautéed with Morels and Cream
Brains with a Mustard Coating
Braised Veal Shanks with Gremolata
Martha's Paprikash with Little Dumplings

A Taste of Bryn Teg

Sorrel Soup
Stuffed Zucchini Blossoms and/or Milkweed
Pods Fried in Beer Batter
Sorrel and Leek Pancakes
Shad and Shad Roe in Sorrel Sauce
Gooseberry Sauce for Grilled Trout or Salmon
Rabbit in a Sweet-Sour Chocolate-Accented Sauce
Gooseberry Fool
Variation: Gooseberry Flummery
Tart Dough
Gooseberry Tart
Rhubarb and Strawberry Tart
Freeform Apple Tarts

Variation: A Large Freeform Apple Tart
Frozen Maple Mousse

Cooking for One

Broiled Bluefish or Mackerel over a Bed of
Fennel and New Potatoes
James Beard's Swordfish-Olive Pasta
A Cornish Hen with Herbal Stuffing Under the Skin, Broiled
Lidia's Gratinate of Cutlet with Eggplant or Zucchini Slices

Wanna Buy a Duck?:
Duck Stock
Cracklings
Jacques's Duck Giblet Salad
Sautéed Duck Breast with Madeira à la Julia
Skillet Duck Legs with Parsnips à la Jacques
Variation: Skillet Duck with Celeriac, Fennel, and Peppers
Mini-Cassoulet

The Nine Lives of a Leg of Lamb:
Sauce Gribiche for Cold Lamb or Other Meats
Evan's Lamb Curry*
Shepherd's Pie*
Casserole of Lamb, Mushrooms, and Bulgur or Barley
Eggplant Stuffed with Lamb, Red Pepper, and Rice
Lamb Hash*
Lamb Croquettes*
Minced Lamb on Toast
Lamb Soup with Leeks and Flageolets

*See cross-references for recipes

From the Past

Aunt Marian's Ham Timbales

The first edition of *The Fannie Farmer Cookbook* had seven different timbale recipes, including a Swedish sweet version. By the mid-forties, the number had climbed to twenty entries—that's how popular they were in that era. This recipe is based on the memory of my Aunt Marian's timbales.

Serves 4

3 tablespoons butter, plus more for greasing molds
1 cup milk
½ cup fresh breadcrumbs
1½ cups ground country ham
3 eggs, lightly beaten
1 tablespoon chopped fresh parsley
1–2 teaspoons chopped fresh sage, or ½ teaspoon dried
Salt to taste

Melt the butter in a saucepan, then stir in the milk and breadcrumbs.

Cook gently over low heat 5 minutes. Stir in the ham, eggs, and seasoning, going easy on the salt if your ham is quite salty. Pour the mixture into eight well-buttered muffin tins or Pyrex dishes, and set them in a pan of hot water that comes about two-thirds of the way up the sides of the mold. Bake in a preheated 350-degree oven for 20 minutes. Let stand out of the water for 5 minutes before unmolding. Serve with a mushroom sauce, if you like.

Timbales can be made with chicken, turkey, lamb, fish. It's a good way to use leftovers—in fact, plan on leftovers with timbales in mind. Vary the seasonings, and choose an herb that goes well with your ground meat: tarragon, for instance, with chicken, or a little dill if you're using fish. And if it's summertime, don't forget to snip off a few edible flowers to decorate the plate, the way my Aunt Marian always did.

. . .

Spaghetti and Cheese

I made this recently, thinking that, after all these years of tasting the wide world of Italian pasta, I would find spaghetti in a creamy cheese sauce rather passé. But instead that taste memory surfaced, and I was right back in my middle-school years slurping down the spaghetti strands dripping with that creamy sauce, so rich with aged Vermont Cheddar cheese that it was like a pudding, and I loved it. I realized that in a way this dish had been an initiation into territory I was yet to discover. All the component parts, though simple, were basic and authentic— and not un-Italian, sort of a preamble. Your children will adore it—that is, if they haven't been corrupted by the packaged macaroni and cheese, and even then, maybe you can wean them.

This recipe is about right for two. You can also halve it to make it just for yourself, or do the whole amount and freeze half of it for a rainy day. Or double or triple it.

Serves 2

Salt
3 ounces spaghetti
2 tablespoons butter
2 tablespoons all-purpose flour
1 cup milk
Freshly ground pepper
Gratings of nutmeg
6 ounces Cheddar cheese, coarsely grated or cut in small, thin pieces

Topping
¼ cup breadcrumbs
2 teaspoons melted butter
2 tablespoons grated Parmesan cheese or Cheddar

Bring to a boil a big pot of salted water. Break the spaghetti strands in half (forgive me, Marcella and Lidia, but that's what we did in those days), and drop them into the boiling water.

Meanwhile, melt the butter in a small heavy pan, stir in the flour, and let cook gently a minute or two, stirring. Remove from the heat, and when the bubbling has ceased, pour in the milk all at once, and whisk constantly over low heat until the sauce thickens, scraping the bottom and sides of the pan. Season to taste with salt and pepper and a few gratings of nutmeg. Off heat, add the cheese, a little at a time, stirring until it is all melted.

By now the spaghetti should be done al dente. Taste, and when it is ready, drain and toss it into a 1-quart or slightly smaller baking dish, not too shallow. Pour the sauce over, and fold it into the spaghetti. Sprinkle the breadcrumbs on top, drizzle the butter over, and cover with the grated cheese. Bake in a preheated 375-degree oven until lightly browned on top and bubbling below—about 20 minutes if it's warm when it goes in.

It was Julia who taught me in making a béchamel *or white sauce that trick of pouring in the milk cold after the bubbling of the roux has ceased, and whisking vigorously when you put the pan back over low heat. That way, you don't have to go to the bother of heating the milk.*

It may seem like heresy to use Parmigiano-Reggiano for the topping, but it adds an Italian touch and it is awfully good.

· · ·

Shepherd's Pie

This was a dish we often had when there was leftover lamb, and it can also be made with rare roast beef. It can be pretty dreary if the lamb or beef is overcooked to begin with and there's not much juice or gravy to moisten it. But it can be delicious made with rosy meat, well seasoned, and gravy (or an improvised gravy if there's none left). I noticed that Jane Grigson in her *English Food* adds three chopped garlic cloves to the meat. Our cook Edie wouldn't have been allowed that liberty, but that's the way I would do it today.

Serves 4

2 pounds all-purpose or baking potatoes
4 tablespoons butter
Milk or light cream as needed
Salt and freshly ground pepper
1 medium onion, chopped
2 tablespoons light olive oil or vegetable oil
2 or 3 garlic cloves, chopped
2 or 3 tablespoons red wine
2 cups finely chopped lamb or beef left over from
    a roast, cut close to the bone, and preferably
    rare
1 teaspoon chopped fresh rosemary, or ½ teaspoon dried
    rosemary or *herbes de Provence*
1 cup leftover gravy (or see alternative below)
2–3 tablespoons grated Cheddar cheese

Boil the potatoes in their skins until tender. Peel and mash them well, stirring in the butter and as much milk or cream as you like, then season.

Meanwhile, sauté the onion in the oil for 3 or 4 minutes, add the garlic, and continue to sauté gently until soft. Splash in a little wine and cook down, then add the lamb, herbs, and salt and pepper, mixing well. Stir in the gravy (or make the improvised gravy below, right in the pan).

Spread the meat into one large casserole or four individual pots, and top with the mashed potatoes. Fork the potatoes up to make a hilly surface, and sprinkle on the cheese. Bake in a preheated 400-degree oven for 10 minutes, then turn the heat down to 350 and bake another 10 minutes, if all the elements were warm when they went in, or 20 minutes if cold.

🥣 *The meat is much better if you mince it fine by hand rather than submit it to the rigors of a grinder; it's worth the extra effort. For an improvised gravy before putting the meat in the pan, sprinkle 2 tablespoons instant-blending flour over the onions and garlic, cook a minute or so, then gradually add 1 cup light beef or veal or chicken broth and ½ teaspoon tomato paste, stirring until smooth. Season, and cook down until thickened, then add the meat. When I make a small Shepherd's Pie just for myself, I usually find enough leftover pan juice mixed with a little water or broth and/or wine to make about ¼ cup of juice—enough to moisten ½ cup minced lamb or beef.*

· · ·

Croquettes

As a child I used to love croquettes—the way the crusty fried coating would give way to the creamy inside, exploding in the mouth with tantalizing flavor. In old American cookbooks there were plenty of croquette recipes, using game-bird meat, sweet potatoes and peanuts, even tripe, but the fear of frying that took over in the latter part of the twentieth century made the croquette a relic of the past. Which is ridiculous, because if your croquettes are well coated they are sealed, so the fat doesn't penetrate. So let's bring back the croquette to the place of honor it deserves. They aren't hard to make, but you do need to get started ahead of time so they can chill at least four hours before frying. Or better, prepare them the night before.

Makes 4 croquettes, serving 2 to 4

3 tablespoons butter

⅓ cup flour

1 cup chicken broth

2 cups finely minced cooked meat (turkey, chicken, lamb, ham)

3 scallions, finely chopped

2–3 tablespoons chopped fresh parsley, chives, marjoram, or mint, or a combination (see below)

Salt and freshly ground pepper

Flour for dredging

1 beaten egg

¾ cup fresh breadcrumbs

1 quart or more oil for deep-frying

Melt the butter in a small saucepan, stir in the flour, and cook gently 2 to 3 minutes, stirring frequently. Off heat, pour in the chicken broth and whisk vigorously. Return the sauce to the heat, bring to a simmer, stirring constantly to eliminate any lumps, and cook gently about 5 minutes. Stir in the meat, scallions, and the seasonings and let cool, then refrigerate for at least 1 hour. Shape the cold meat mixture into four cylindrical croquettes; roll them first in flour, then in egg, and finally in breadcrumbs, making sure that they are coated all over. Chill at least 4 hours or overnight.

Heat the oil to about 380 degrees, or until a crumb of bread dropped in the oil sizzles immediately but doesn't turn dark quickly, and lower the croquettes into the hot fat. After about 2 minutes, when browned on the bottom, turn them and fry for 1 or 2 minutes more. Remove them with a slotted spoon and drain on paper towels. Keep warm in the oven until ready to serve, but they are best eaten right away.

⚗ *Use whatever meat you have left over—chicken, turkey, duck, seafoods—or vegetables. And vary the seasonings. Cheese (about 2 cups grated) can be very good, particularly in ham or vegetable croquettes. And if you like things a little hot, add 2 or 3 drops of Tabasco or a dash of cayenne pepper. Choose an herb that marries well with the flavor of the meat—tarragon, for example, with poultry, sage with pork, rosemary with lamb.*

. . .

Bitki

Here is the dish that I used to make in my college days when I was trying to lure guests with what I thought an impressive main course, yet one that could be done ahead and was quite inexpensive. I'm not sure where the recipe came from or how it got its Russian name, but that added to its appeal. In the forties, sour cream suddenly flooded the supermarkets, all packaged in neat cartons, and it was quite the popular item. Over the years, I've played with the basic recipe and under the influence of Claudia Roden have made what I think of as a Middle Eastern version, with lamb instead of ground beef and yogurt instead of sour cream (see variation that follows).

Serves 4

6 slices yesterday's white bread, crusts removed
1 cup milk
3 very large white onions, sliced
3 tablespoons butter
1½ pounds ground beef
1 teaspoon mustard
Several drops Worcestershire sauce
2–3 tablespoons chopped fresh parsley
Salt and freshly ground pepper
1 cup sour cream, at room temperature
A sprinkling of paprika

Tear the bread into rough pieces into a bowl, and pour the milk over. Let soak while you sauté the onions slowly in the butter in a large skillet. After a few minutes, cover the pan, and continue to sauté over low heat, shaking the pan occasionally so the onions don't stick, until they are soft and golden-colored.

When the bread is soft, squeeze out the milk and discard it. Mix the bread with the ground beef, add the mustard, Worcestershire, and parsley, season liberally with salt and pepper, and with your fingers blend well. Shape the meat into balls the size of a golf ball, and tuck them into the pan with the onions. Cook slowly, covered, turning them now and then, for about 20 minutes.

Stir the sour cream into the onions and meatballs, and cook gently until heated through. Taste, and add more salt and pepper if needed. Sprinkle paprika on top, and serve with rice or noodles or mashed potatoes.

VARIATION   This is my Middle Eastern–style version, made with lamb. It's a little lighter, with the elusive flavor of cinnamon and allspice.

6 slices yesterday's white bread, crusts removed
1 cup milk
3 very large white onions, sliced
3 tablespoons butter or vegetable oil, or a combination
1½ pounds ground lamb
1 teaspoon cinnamon
½ teaspoon allspice
Salt and freshly ground pepper
½ cup pine nuts (optional)
1 cup plain whole-milk yogurt
1 teaspoon cornstarch mixed with 1½ teaspoons water
A sprinkling of crushed dried mint

As done above, soak the bread and sauté the onions. Mix the ground lamb well with the well-squeezed bread, and the spices, salt and pepper, then form into balls a little smaller than a golf ball. If you want to use the pine nuts, make an indentation in each lamb ball and insert a few pine nuts inside. Cook as described above. When done, whisk the yogurt and cornstarch together in a saucepan over low heat until thoroughly blended, and let the mixture boil as slowly as possible, stirring in one direction, for about 10 minutes. Now stir that in with the lamb balls and onions, and sprinkle just a little dried mint on top.

A trick I learned recently from Claudia is to add a little cornstarch to the yogurt so it won't curdle when it goes into the hot meatballs.

Sauté of Chicken with Vegetables

This is another dish that I often made for small dinner parties and served with rice or noodles for a complete main course. In the forties, I wouldn't have thought beyond mushrooms and onions for the veggies, but today I'd be more apt to surround the chicken with fennel, and/or artichoke hearts, celeriac, or parsnips and red pepper. They're all good, so I mix and match according to what looks appealing in the market.

Serves 4 (and can be easily doubled, using 2 pans)

One 2½-to-3-pound chicken, cut into 2 legs, 2 thighs,
  2 wings, 2 breasts
Salt and freshly ground pepper
2 tablespoons vegetable oil or light olive oil
2 tablespoons butter
1 large sweet onion, halved and cut in ¼-inch slices
1 large red pepper, halved, seeded, and cut in strips
1 good-size fennel bulb, trimmed and cut in ¼-inch slices,
  stem end to root
¾ cup chicken broth
3 tablespoons white wine
Garnish: 2 tablespoons each chopped fennel leaves and
  parsley

Wash and dry the chicken pieces. Sprinkle lightly with salt and pepper. Heat the oil in a large sauté pan that will accommodate the chicken in one layer comfortably. Drop in all the pieces—they should sizzle in the hot oil—and cook, turning frequently, over moderately high heat for about 10 minutes. When they are browned all over, lower the heat, put on a cover slightly askew, and cook another 5 minutes for the breast meat, 10 minutes for the rest.

Remove all the chicken pieces to a plate and keep warm. Pour off all but a light film of the fat from the pan, toss in the butter, and, when melted, scatter in the onion, pepper, and fennel slices. Salt lightly, and cook over moderate heat, tossing frequently, then cover the pan for the last 5 minutes to let the vegetables soften. If the pan becomes too dry, add a little of the broth. Now return the chicken pieces, laying them on top of the vegetables, and let everything cook together about 5 minutes, or until the chicken is done; insert the point of a knife in one of the thigh pieces, and be sure the meat is no longer rosy close to the bone. Remove everything to a warm platter, and correct seasoning. Pour the wine into the pan, and let it almost evaporate over medium heat, then pour in the broth, and cook down until almost syrupy. Pour this sauce over the chicken, and sprinkle fennel and parsley leaves on top.

VARIATIONS

- 9-ounce package frozen artichoke hearts blanched (or equivalent amount of fresh) with two or three leeks cut in 1-inch pieces
- a medium eggplant cut in 1-inch chunks, with one or two tomatoes cut in chunks and 8 small mushrooms
- ¾ pound celeriac, peeled and cut in chunks, with red-pepper slices
- three or four large parsnips, peeled and cut in equal-size chunks, with red-pepper slices

In the old days, I would have just tossed all the veggies in with the chicken after the initial browning, but I learned from Julia that that way the chicken stews, so the meat tastes boiled and the skin loses its slight crispness. So I developed the above method to avoid those problems. She also alerted me to the fact that the breast cooks faster and should be removed from the pan sooner.

. . .

Frenchified Meatloaf

When I was in Paris, I sent this recipe that I had developed to my parents, hoping they would try it for a more *pâté-de-campagne*–like version of our standard meatloaf that I had developed. Knowing my mother's aversion to garlic, I suggested that the two fat garlic cloves called for could be sliced and spread on the top and removed before serving, to get just a whiff of that garlic flavor, but it is really much better when they are mashed into the ground meats.

Serves 6 with leftovers

3 slices homemade-type white bread, crusts removed
3 pounds ground beef, veal, and pork (about ½ beef portion
     and ½ each of veal and pork)
1 large onion, finely chopped
1 large egg
1 tablespoon Dijon mustard
2 teaspoons salt
2 fat garlic cloves, peeled, chopped, and mashed with
     ½ teaspoon salt (or see below)
Several grindings of black pepper
¼ cup chopped fresh parsley
2–3 tablespoons chopped fresh herbs (basil, tarragon,
     marjoram), or 1 teaspoon *herbes de Provence*

2 bay leaves
2 strips bacon
½ cup red wine

Spin the bread in a blender to make crumbs; you should have
1½ cups. Dump everything except the bay leaves, bacon, and
wine into a big bowl, and blend well, preferably with your hands.

Arrange the bay leaves on the bottom of a large loaf pan, and
pack the meat mixture in. Place the strips of bacon on top, then
pour the wine over, punching a few holes into the meat with
your fingers so it will seep down a little. Let marinate for an hour
or so, then bake in a preheated 325-degree oven for 1½ hours.
Turn out of the pan, and remove the bay leaves. And pour any
pan juices on top.

*If veal is too expensive or hard to get, use about ¾ beef to ¼ pork,
ground.*

*If you prefer, slice the peeled garlic instead and press into the
top of the meatloaf, then remove the slices before you turn the
meatloaf out. I also noted to my parents that I served this with a
winter squash, split in half, with some butter smeared over and a
teaspoon or so of some maple syrup they'd sent me in their care
package to Paris. If you do this, put the squash in about ½ hour
before the meatloaf, then let it continue to bake alongside.*

· · ·

Butternut Squash in Cream and Cinnamon

We first came upon this recipe in an artists' and writers' cookbook published in the forties, and I'd say that it was probably

the vegetable dish that we served the most frequently at dinner parties, and always for Thanksgiving and Christmas feasts, over the years. Everyone seems to love it—and it couldn't be simpler, particularly after the food processor came along to make the grating a snap.

Serves 6

1 large butternut squash (at least 2 pounds)
Salt
1 teaspoon cinnamon
1 cup heavy cream

Cut the squash into quarters, remove the seeds, and peel it (a sharp vegetable peeler is the best tool). Grate the squash through the coarse holes of the grating blade of the food processor. Spread half of the grated squash over the bottom of a shallow 1- or ½-quart baking dish, sprinkle salt over lightly, then dust with half of the cinnamon. Repeat with the rest. Pour the cream over slowly, letting it seep down. Bake, covered loosely with foil, in a preheated 350-degree oven for 40 minutes, then uncover and bake another 10 to 15 minutes, until the squash is very tender.

. . .

Bread Pudding

At a country inn in Wales, I had one of those taste-memory moments that made me realize how a simple pudding of eggs, bread, and milk could in a flash call up a flood of memory so acute that for an instant I was right back in childhood. The baked dish was brought in, wrapped in a white linen napkin, the way Edie would have served it, and as it was spooned onto the plate I had my first whiff. Then, when I took a taste, the hot raisins bursting in my mouth, the sensation was so powerful that the tears rolled down my cheeks (adding a little salty flavor).

Serves 4 to 6

2½ cups milk

2 tablespoons butter, plus a little for buttering the dish

3 slices homemade-type bread, crusts removed, crumbled to make 1½ cups

½ cup raisins

Grated rind of ½ lemon

½ teaspoon lemon juice

3 large eggs

3 tablespoons sugar

About 4 gratings of nutmeg (about ⅛ teaspoon)

Topping: crushed sugar cubes, to make about 2 tablespoons

For serving: heavy cream

Heat the milk with the butter, stirring until melted. Remove from the heat, stir in the crumbled bread, the raisins, grated lemon rind, and lemon juice, and let cool to lukewarm. Separate the eggs, and beat the yolks into the milk and butter along with the sugar. Beat the whites in a clean bowl until they form soft peaks, and fold them into the pudding mixture. Season with nutmeg, and turn into a lightly buttered shallow baking dish. Sprinkle the crushed sugar cubes on top. Set the dish in a pan of simmering water, and bake in a preheated 325-degree oven for 1 hour. Serve warm with a pitcher of heavy cream.

I discovered from Edna Lewis how much better crushed sugar cubes are than plain granulated sugar as a topping. They're particularly good if you've stored them in a jar with a vanilla bean.

Bread pudding is best warm, but it can be very good cold, too. I've even had it for breakfast straight from the fridge.

. . .

Summer Berry Pudding

This is a favorite family dish that we made throughout the summer, as the succession of berries ripened—blueberries, raspberries, currants, blackberries. You can use more than one kind of berry when their seasons overlap. I used to love lining the bowl with slices of good white bread and then pouring on the hot berries and watching the juice seep into the bread, transforming it all into a beautiful blue or red or purplish dome. The first bite seems like the essence of summer, and anyone tasting it for the first time invariably makes a little gasp of pleasure.

Serves 6

1 quart fresh berries (blueberries, raspberries, currants, blackberries, or a combination)
¾ cup water
⅔–¾ cups sugar, depending on the sweetness of the berries
9 slices homemade-type white bread, crusts removed
Soft unsalted butter, less than 1 teaspoon
For serving: heavy cream

Pick over the berries and rinse them. Put them in a nonreactive saucepan with the water and the sugar, and cook over medium heat, stirring often, until they soften but have not started to burst. Line the bottom and sides of a round bowl with the bread slices, buttering *very* lightly only the pieces that have to stick to the sides of the bowl, and cutting triangles and trimming as necessary to cover completely the inside of the bowl. Pour the berries and their juice over the lined bowl, then fold over any overlapping pieces and put an unbuttered slice on top, trimming as necessary to fit. Place on top a plate that will fit into the bowl, and press down so that the juices ooze around the top. Put a small weight, such as a couple of tuna-fish cans, on the plate, and refrigerate for several hours or overnight. The pudding can be served from the bowl, but it makes a more handsome presentation if it is turned out onto a round platter. Serve with a pitcher of heavy cream.

. . .

Schrafft's Butterscotch Cookies

When I was a child growing up in Manhattan, one of the great treats was to go to Schrafft's for one of their wonderful ice-cream sodas or a milkshake. Their butterscotch sundaes were particularly delicious, with the warm butterscotch sauce hitting the cold ice cream and turning slightly brittle at the edges, and there was a scattering of pecans on top. We'd always take home a dozen of their large butterscotch cookies, and the flavor was reminiscent of that sundae. It was my favorite cookie for many years. Then Schrafft's disappeared, and I despaired of ever tasting them again. But when we were working on the revised *Fannie Farmer Cookbook,* I asked Jim Beard if he remembered those butterscotch cookies so we could include them, and not only did he remember them with the same affection, but he called up the president of what remained of the Schrafft's company and got them to give him their recipe.

Makes about thirty 3-inch cookies
(a lot, but you can freeze them)

14 tablespoons unsalted butter, at room temperature
1¼ cups dark-brown sugar
1 egg
2 tablespoons nonfat dry milk
1 tablespoon vanilla extract
1¾ cups all-purpose flour
½ teaspoon baking soda
½ teaspoon salt
1 cup finely chopped pecans

Cream the butter and sugar in a bowl. Beat in the egg, dry milk, and vanilla. Mix and toss the flour, baking soda, and salt, then mix in the dry ingredients with the creamed mixture. Fold in the pecans. Drop the batter by heaping tablespoonsful onto greased cookie sheets, leaving 2 inches between. With your lightly floured fingers, press out each mound into a circle about 3 inches in diameter. Bake in a preheated 375-degree oven 8 to 10 minutes, until lightly browned. Remove from the oven, then carefully scrape up the cookies with a spatula, and place on racks to cool.

When Jim Beard gave me the recipe, it was really a formula geared for turning out about two hundred cookies. And there were several unfamiliar, chemical-sounding ingredients called for. When I asked Jim to translate, he said just to use Crisco. So I reduced the amounts and substituted Crisco, and we both agreed the cookies were as good as we had remembered. Now, since hydrogenated products have fallen into such disrepute in recent years, I make the batter with all butter, and I think the cookies are even better. But if you're wedded to Crisco, use ¾ cup of it, and only 2 tablespoons butter.

Today you can use Silpat mats to line your baking sheets instead of greasing them (they are much easier to clean).

. . .

Mrs. Cooney's Hermits

My grandmother's cook used to make these old-fashioned New England cookies in a large shallow baking pan and cut them in squares, but this method—given me by Marian Morash, who wrote *The Victory Garden*—combines something of both the drop cookie and the pan method, and they're the best hermits you'll ever taste.

Makes 36 bars

12 tablespoons unsalted butter, at room temperature
⅔ cup granulated sugar
¾ cup dark-brown sugar
2 eggs, beaten
3 cups all-purpose flour
½ teaspoon salt
1 teaspoon baking powder
1 teaspoon cinnamon
1 teaspoon ground cloves
½ teaspoon ground ginger
¼ cup molasses mixed with 2 tablespoons warm water
1 cup raisins

1 cup chopped walnuts
Glaze: 1 beaten egg

Cream the butter with the two sugars, then beat in the eggs. Toss together the flour, salt, baking powder, and spices, and add them to the butter-sugar mixture along with the molasses. When well mixed, fold in the raisins and nuts. Divide the batter in fourths, and plop two mounds each, with space between them, onto two greased baking sheets. Shape each mound, using your floured hands to push and pat the dough down into a strip about 10 by 3 inches. You should have two strips on each baking sheet, placed several inches apart. Paint the tops of each with the egg glaze, and bake in a preheated 350-degree oven for 15 to 20 minutes, depending on how crisp you like yours. While still warm, cut each strip into nine bars.

I've tried using dark maple syrup instead of molasses (6 tablespoons of it, with no water), and it was good, but the bar didn't have that unmistakable hermit flavor. These keep well, and you can also freeze them, but I like them when they're a little stale, dunked in coffee like biscotti.

French—and Other—Influences

Céléri Rémoulade

Here is my version of an old standby of French bistros and charcuteries which I make often because it is always such a poignant reminder of our Paris in the late forties, particularly eaten with a few slices of French *saucisson sec* alongside.

Serves 4

½ large celery root, or a small whole one (about 10 ounces
    to make 2 cups julienned)
6 tablespoons mayonnaise
2 teaspoons Dijon mustard, or more to taste
2 tablespoons plain whole-milk yogurt
Salt and freshly ground pepper to taste
About 2 tablespoons chopped fresh parsley

Peel the celery root, and cut it into very thin slices. Stack several slices, and cut into thin julienne strips. Do the same with the rest of the slices. Mix together in a bowl the mayonnaise, mustard, and yogurt. Toss the strips into the dressing, and add a little salt and pepper. Mix well, then taste, and adjust the seasonings to your liking. It should have a slightly tart and mustardy flavor. Try to let it sit several hours or overnight in the fridge, and add the chopped parsley just before serving.

🥣 *The yogurt is my touch. It thins the mayonnaise and gives a slightly tart accent. You can, of course, use a little lemon juice instead.*

. . .

Boudin Blanc

When Ray Sokolov was the food editor for the *New York Times*, in the early seventies, over lunch one day, I told him of Evan's and my yearly ritual making *boudin blanc*. In spite of my protest that *Times* food-page readers wouldn't be interested in spending Sunday afternoon stuffing hogs' casings, he wanted to do a story. And so I gave in (I did want a book from him), and we demonstrated for him and his photographer—Evan plunging the delicate filling through a hand-held sausage stuffer, with me catching it below in the casings as they swelled in my hands. Ray thought the whole performance highly scatological, and he loved it. And in 1976 Knopf published his book *The Saucier's Apprentice,* a one-of-a-kind classic on the great French sauces. (It is still in print.)

This recipe is based on the one in Jane Grigson's *The Art of Charcuterie* and seemed to us to make a white sausage closest to the one we tasted at our first lunch together. But over the years we played with the recipe, sometimes making it more creamy, and recently I've succumbed to Jacques Pépin's formula (see the variation), because it is particularly delicious.

Makes about 2½ pounds sausages

Hog casings
¾ cup fresh breadcrumbs
¼ cup heavy cream
½ pound chicken breast
½ pound pork loin or tenderloin
1 pound leaf lard
1 tablespoon coarse salt
1 teaspoon freshly, finely ground white pepper
1 teaspoon *quatre-épices*
3 medium onions, finely chopped (about 2½ cups)
3 eggs

For cooking
5 cups water
2½ cups milk
Melted butter

Rinse the casings, running water through the inside, and soak in cold water about 1 hour.

Soak the breadcrumbs in the cream. Skin and bone the chicken, and put with the pork and fat through the fine blade of the meat grinder. Season with the salt and pepper and the spices, then grind again. Mix in the onions, breadcrumbs and cream, and the eggs, beating thoroughly, preferably with an electric mixer. Using a hand-held sausage stuffer or the attachment on a standing electric mixer, fill the casings, not too tightly, tying them with strong string every 6 inches.

Bring the water and milk to a boil in a large pan. Put the sausages in a basket or strainer tray and lower them into the hot liquid. Once the water returns to a boil, quickly turn the heat down and keep it at a very slow simmer for 20 minutes. As the

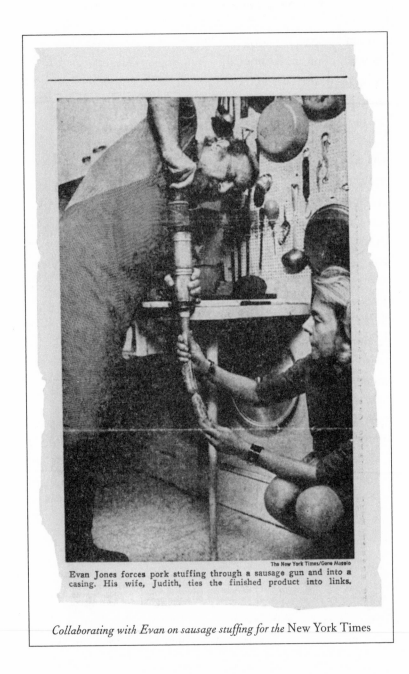

Evan Jones forces pork stuffing through a sausage gun and into a casing. His wife, Judith, ties the finished product into links.

Collaborating with Evan on sausage stuffing for the New York Times

sausages rise to the surface, prick them gently with a needle so they won't burst. Remove the strainer tray carefully, and let the sausages drain; then refrigerate overnight. The next day, prick them, brush them with melted butter, and either grill, broil, or fry them gently until heated through.

JACQUES'S VERSION   Jacques uses all chicken breast for the meat—1½ pounds of it—with 1 large onion, finely chopped; 2 cups heavy cream; a scant 2 teaspoons salt; a generous teaspoon freshly ground pepper; 2 slices white bread, processed to crumbs; and ¼ ounce dried black chanterelles, coarsely chopped. He cuts the breast meat into 1-inch pieces and refrigerates them, meanwhile sautéing the onion in about 2 tablespoons butter and ½ cup water until all moisture is gone. Then he puts the cold chicken in the food processor, adding ½ cup of the cream, slowly adding more while processing and seasoning with salt and pepper. Finally he mixes everything together and fills the casings.

The secret ingredient in Jacques's boudin is the dried chanterelles. The little black pieces look just like truffles, and their flavor is intense, because it hasn't been leached out by soaking them beforehand. Jacques also suggests that, instead of piping the filling into hog casings, you can encase it in plastic wrap, roll it into a tube, then tie it off at intervals. A good alternative if the casings are hard to come by, but to my mind you miss half the fun.

A Good Hash

I love hash, but it has to be well made—moist and beautifully glazed on the bottom—and it's important to use the right-size pan for the amount you are making, to get it just right.

Serves 2

2 tablespoons butter
2 fat shallots or 1 medium onion, chopped
1 rib celery, chopped
½ large red or green bell pepper, chopped
2 or 3 mushrooms (optional), chopped
2 medium or small potatoes, boiled until just tender
        and skinned, then chopped
About 6 ounces cooked beef, lamb, pork, corned beef,
        or poultry, cut into small dice
Salt and freshly ground pepper
¼ cup lamb, beef, veal, or chicken stock
2 tablespoons chopped fresh parsley

Melt the butter in an 8-to-9-inch skillet, and sauté the shallots, celery, bell pepper, and mushrooms (if using) until almost soft, about 5 minutes. Stir in the potatoes and the meat, and season with salt and pepper to taste. When everything is beginning to sizzle, pour in the stock, and cook over low heat, partially covered, about 10 minutes. Turn the hash over with a spatula, cover, and cook, uncovered, another 5 minutes or so. By now the liquid will have evaporated, and a crust should be forming on the bottom. When it is browned to your liking, turn the hash over again and brown the other side. Serve with parsley sprinkled on top.

🥣 *It is always important to include some aromatic vegetables, to lend moisture and just a touch of sweetness, which helps to encourage the glazing. I sometimes include a little finely chopped carrot or parsnip or white turnip—whatever I may have on hand. It came as a surprise to me to learn from Julia that a good hash needs some stock or even gravy, if you have it, not only to keep it from drying out but, as with the vegetables, to form the slightly crusty glaze.*

. . .

French Bread (Baguettes)

My love affair with the French baguette goes back to the days when I was in Paris, and Evan and I would buy one fresh every day. Then Julia finally worked out a formula (see page 84) so that we could all duplicate the real thing in our home kitchens. This recipe is based on Julia's, although over the years I've tinkered with it a bit, and now I usually start the dough the night before. I've always liked making baguettes on a Saturday or Sunday, so that we could tear off a hunk to make pizzas for lunch, and I still do the same thing for myself.

Makes 3 loaves plus 1 small pizza

2 cups warm water
1½ teaspoons instant yeast
3 tablespoons whole-wheat flour
About 5 cups unbleached white flour (I use King Arthur)
2 teaspoons kosher salt

To make the starter: Pour 1 cup warm water into the bowl of a standing electric mixer. Stir in 1 teaspoon of the yeast, the whole-wheat flour, and 1 cup of the white flour. Mix well, cover with plastic wrap and a kitchen towel, and let sit 12 to 18 hours at about 70 degrees. The starter will be nice and bubbly and smelly when you are ready to use it the next day.

Stir into the starter the remaining cup of warm water and ½ teaspoon yeast, the salt, and about 3½ cups white flour, and mix well, using the dough hook. Continue to knead briskly with the dough hook, adding more flour until you have used up the remaining ½ cup and the dough starts to come away from the sides of the bowl. Turn the dough out onto a floured surface, and knead lightly for a few minutes. Clean out the bowl, and return the dough to it. (If you are making a pizza, set aside the necessary amount of dough; see below.) Cover the bowl, and let dough rise at room temperature for about 1½ hours, until it has more than doubled in volume.

Turn the dough out onto a floured surface, and divide it in thirds. Pat one piece of the dough into an oval about 6 inches long. Fold in thirds. Now with the side of your hand, punch a trench down the center lengthwise and fold over lengthwise. Pinch the ends of the fold together. Flour the work surface again, and roll the dough out as if you were making a clay snake, starting with your two floured hands in the center and moving them outward as the roll stretches to a length of about 15 inches. Pick up the dough (it will stretch a little more as you do so), and arrange on a floured kitchen towel. Pleat the edge up on the long side nearest you, to separate this loaf from the next one; continue to form the remaining 2 loaves. When all 3 are in place on the towel, to prevent the loaves from spreading out, prop the long sides with something the length of the loaves; the back of your counter can serve as one prop, some loaf pans as the other.

Cover loosely with a towel, and let rise until doubled—about 40 minutes.

Meanwhile, place a baking stone on a rack in the oven, and preheat to 450 degrees. (At this point, I heat up an old hand-held iron directly over the gas; when the loaves go into the oven, I pick up the iron with tongs and plop it into a pan of cold water to create a great whoosh of steam. See below for other, possibly easier methods.)

When the loaves have risen, flip them over one at a time onto a tray or a piece of stiff cardboard the length of the loaves, sprinkled with cornmeal, and slash each loaf diagonally three times. Slip 1 loaf onto the hot oven baking stone. Do the same with the remaining 2 loaves, shutting the oven door behind you quickly after each goes in. Now apply your steam-creating device.

Bake 15 minutes at 450 degrees, then turn the heat down to 400 and bake another 10 minutes, until the loaves are crusty and golden. Let cool on racks propped up so the air circulates.

Other possibilities for creating steam are to throw a handful of ice cubes on the oven floor or to spray the loaves with water just before they go into the oven and again a few minutes later.

Of course the baguettes are best eaten the same day, but what you don't finish, freeze, tightly wrapped in plastic. I even cut the remaining loaves in thirds and wrap each piece individually to defrost for a single meal. Let the frozen bread defrost at room temperature, then recrisp briefly in a hot oven.

INDIVIDUAL PIZZA   For 1 pizza, you'll need a piece of dough slightly smaller than a baseball. Put it in a small bowl with 1 teaspoon olive oil, turning to coat all sides, then cover with plastic wrap and let rise until doubled—about 1 hour. Sprinkle some cornmeal on a paddle or rimless baking sheet, turn the dough out on top of it, and with the palm of your hand push and stretch the dough all around to make a circle 6½ to 7 inches in diameter. Fill the circle almost to the edge with whatever ingredients you have on hand that strike your fancy. Here's a topping I often use: a shallot, very thinly sliced and scattered evenly over the dough; 6 tablespoons goat cheese crumbled over; and a dozen cherry tomatoes, sliced in half, arranged on top. I slide the pizza onto my hot baking stone and bake in a preheated oven 450 degrees for 15 to 20 minutes, until crusty, lightly browned around the edge, and bubbling on top.

A few minutes before baking time is up, I scatter about 2 tablespoons grated Parmesan on top.

The above is just one of many fillings that I've found particularly good, and you can use the amounts as a guide for your own improvisations. Mushrooms are always welcome, as are preroasted eggplant or zucchini slices and red peppers, and, of course, your own tomato sauce, with or without bits of meat or sausage. Anything goes. As James Beard said, "We're Americans and we can do what we please."

·   ·   ·

Evan's Lamb Curry

Evan always loved to play around with curry flavors, even before Madhur Jaffrey came into our lives and taught us that curry was not a single bottled spice. Nevertheless, I loved this improvised curry he made.

Serves 5 to 6

3 tablespoons vegetable oil

2 large onions, chopped

3 garlic cloves, chopped

1½ green peppers, seeded, ribs removed, and chopped

4 cups lamb cut into 1½-inch pieces (either raw or cooked rare)

2 cups lamb, veal, or chicken broth

1 teaspoon fennel seeds

2 tablespoons good madras curry powder, or more to taste

2 tablespoons turmeric

Salt

2 tart green apples, peeled, cored, and cut in eighths

¼ cup unsweetened shredded coconut

1 tablespoon fresh lemon juice

Heat the oil in a large skillet, add the onions, garlic, and green peppers, and sauté gently about 10 minutes, stirring frequently. Stir in the lamb pieces, then add the broth, fennel seeds, curry, turmeric, and a sprinkling of salt. Cover the skillet, and simmer gently for about 1 hour. Add the apples, coconut, and lemon juice, and cook about 8 minutes, until the apples are tender. Taste, and correct seasoning; you may want more salt, and a bit more curry if you like it spicy.

If you are using cooked lamb, reduce the cooking time to 30 minutes, and if the sauce seems too loose, remove the meat with a slotted spoon and cook it down until syrupy.

It is sometimes hard to find unsweetened coconut, and if the sweetened kind was all that there was in the larder, Evan would soak it in hot water to lessen the sweetness and, perhaps, use a bit less of it.

The Versatile Stir-Fry

What a new world opens up when you start thinking Chinese—or Asian—style for those scant 2 or 3 ounces of meat or poultry you may have when you've bought a slightly too-big steak or are portioning a tenderloin of pork for different meals or have half of a chicken breast. I'm talking about stir-fries, and there are many ways to go—spicy with maybe peanuts or cashews, sweet and sour, or velveted and tossed with a variety of stir-fried vegetables. I learned the basics from Irene Kuo, who is unequaled in her ability to explain the techniques of Chinese cooking to Westerners so that we can readily perform in our own kitchens. The secret, of course, is fast heat and having all your ingredients lined up and ready to go. There's usually an initial 30-minute marinade for the meat, so I get that going, prep the vegetables, mix the sauce, and put on the rice. Then I can relax and watch the news before the last-minute fireworks.

About rice, incidentally: I am constantly told that you cannot successfully cook less than 1 cup of rice. Nonsense. All you need is a small, heavy pot with a tight-fitting cover (I have a 5-cup Le Creuset with a bottom diameter of 4½ inches, and it is perfect). I throw in ½ cup long-grain rice, pour in 1 cup water, bring it to a boil, cover, then turn down the heat to low and cook 15 minutes. Another 5 minutes of resting off heat and it's done. It has never failed, and gives me an ample portion with some leftover to use in soup or a rice salad. I do the salting and buttering after cooking, because how I want to season depends on how I'm going to use the rice. For Chinese stir-fries it should always be plain.

About the vegetables, whatever Chinese recipe you consult

will give you specifics: bamboo shoots, snow peas, wood ears, etc. The only basic essentials are ginger and garlic—and very often scallions—all of which should always be in the larder or fridge. For the rest, I find I can improvise with what's available: For example, broccoli stems, peeled and cut thin, make a fine substitute for bamboo shoots; zucchini or even frozen peas can take the place of snow peas; dried mushrooms and black beans always add distinctive flavor. Hoisin sauce as well as oyster sauce are good condiments, which you can always have on hand.

The list of ingredients in the recipe below may look daunting, but don't forget, you don't have to go out and buy each item; you look in the fridge or, perhaps in summer, in your garden, and work with what you have. There is a bit of chopping and slicing involved, but the more you use a sharp knife, the better you get at it, and you can have everything lined up in a very short time. (I hate giving exact prep times, as they do in recipes these days, because it all depends on who is doing the chopping.)

But the beauty of the stir-fry is that you have a complete meal with more than about three times the amount of vegetables to meat. And the final fast, heady stir-frying takes only minutes, executed just as the rice is ready. Here is an example of a typical stir-fry from my kitchen these days.

Serves 2

4 ounces pork loin or tenderloin, cut in sticks approximately
    1½ inches long and less than ½ inch wide

Marinade
2 teaspoons soy sauce
2 teaspoons dry sherry
2 teaspoons cornstarch
2 teaspoons vegetable oil

1½ tablespoons vegetable oil
1 fat garlic clove, peeled, sliced, and smashed
2 quarter-size pieces peeled ginger
4 ribs celery, cut in sticks (about 1 cup)
1 medium white turnip, peeled and cut in sticks (about ½ cup)
1 medium carrot, peeled and finely julienned
Splash of dry sherry
⅔ cup chicken broth
6–8 scallions, trimmed and split in half lengthwise

Sauce
Pinch of salt
Pinch of sugar
1 tablespoon soy sauce
2 teaspoons oyster sauce
2 teaspoons cornstarch dissolved in 2 tablespoons water

A light sprinkling of sesame oil (about 8–10 drops)
12 blanched almonds (optional)

Mix the marinade ingredients together, and toss in the pork.
Refrigerate for 30 minutes.

Heat the wok, then pour in a tablespoon of the oil, and when it is good and hot, toss in the garlic and ginger. Toss and stir for about 15 seconds, then dump in the pork, reserving what little marinade may be left. Stir-fry vigorously over high heat for 2 minutes. Remove the pork to a plate, pour the remaining oil into the wok, and toss in the celery, turnip, and carrot. Stir-fry over high heat for about 30 seconds, then add the sherry and the broth, and cook until the vegetables are crisp-tender—maybe 2 minutes, but you have to taste to determine just how you like your stir-fry vegetables. Now toss in the scallions, stir-fry 30 seconds, then add the reserved pork along with any remaining marinade liquid and the sauce ingredients, and give everything a quick turn. Sprinkle on the sesame oil and almonds, if you like. Serve with rice.

Other good combinations are beef with peppers and black bean sauce, shrimp with bean sprouts, chicken with snow peas and water chestnuts.

·   ·   ·

Sweetbreads Sautéed with Morels and Cream

In the spring in Paris, fresh morels are proudly displayed in every outdoor market, their little brainlike heads piled high for all to admire. And a favorite dish in almost every good bistro is a mating of meltingly tender sweetbreads with the wild, earthy flavor of fresh morels. These little treasures are much harder to come by in America, although there are patches of them all over, from the Ozarks to the woods of Oregon. But I always bring home a bagful of dried morels from Paris so I can indulge year-round in what is perhaps my favorite dish.

Serves 4

About 1¼ pounds sweetbreads
1 lemon
Salt
About 8 grams dried morels (a scant ½ cup)
3 tablespoons butter
Flour for dredging
2 fat shallots, finely diced
¼ pound fresh button mushrooms
2 tablespoons dry sherry
¼ cup or more chicken broth
½ cup heavy cream

To prepare the sweetbreads (or brains): Put them in a bowl of cold water in the sink, and let cold water drip over them for 1 hour. Remove the sweetbreads to a saucepan, and cover them by 2 inches with fresh cold water. Squeeze the lemon over them and sprinkle on 1 teaspoon salt. Bring slowly to a boil, then turn the heat to very low, so they simmer gently, cover askew, for 20 minutes. Immediately plunge into ice water, and when they are thoroughly chilled, gently remove some of the skin and any tough connective tissues. Separate each piece of sweetbread where it comes apart naturally to get at some of the tough inner tissues, but don't overdo so that the delicate meats fall apart. Don't worry, they will cook to a melting tenderness. Now put the meat on a plate in a single layer, put another plate on top, and weigh it down with a can. Refrigerate for at least an hour or overnight.

While the sweetbreads are firming up in the refrigerator,

soak the morels in ½ cup water. After 30 minutes, melt the butter in a good-size skillet, dredge the sweetbread pieces in lightly
salted flour, shaking off excess, and sauté them in the butter for
about 1 minute each side; they should be barely golden, not
browned. Toss in the shallots and the fresh mushrooms, sprinkle with a little salt, and let cook a minute. Splash in the sherry,
and reduce by half. Add the morels and their soaking liquid and
half of the chicken broth. Cook gently with cover askew 10 to
15 minutes, adding more chicken broth as needed. Add the
cream and heat, then scoop out the solids to a warm platter, and
turn up the heat, if necessary, to let the sauce reduce slightly.
Taste and correct the seasoning, then pour the sauce over the
sweetbreads.

· · ·

Brains with a Mustard Coating

I first tasted this delightful dish at the Four Seasons, when I was
having lunch there one day with Jim Beard. Chef Seppi Renggli
was always most solicitous whenever Jim was on a special diet
(which he almost always was, alas, the last years of his life), and
he would prepare a special low-fat and/or low-salt entrée that
was always quite tasty. But when I ordered these crusty morsels
of brains and couldn't help but smack my lips with pleasure as I
tasted them, Jim took a bite and insisted that Seppi make him a
small portion. That very night, I couldn't rest until I had found
some calves' brains and tried to duplicate the chef's creation,
which I think I did very successfully.

Serves 2 or 3

1½ pounds calves' brains
1 lemon
Salt and freshly ground pepper
¼ cup Dijon mustard
1 cup fresh breadcrumbs
¾ cup panko (Japanese breadcrumbs)
Canola oil for frying
Garnish: lemon wedges

Soak and poach the brains as described for the sweetbreads in the preceding recipe. Brains are more delicate than sweetbreads, so don't try to remove any veins or coarse fibers until after they have been poached and cooled. And don't overdo it; you don't need to get every vein out—they will melt away anyway. The brains will naturally break up into about six equal pieces. After they have chilled, salt and pepper them lightly, then paint them generously on all sides with the mustard. Dip them into a combination of breadcrumbs and panko. Heat ¾ inch of oil in a heavy pot. When a breadcrumb dropped in sizzles and turns golden, you'll know the oil is hot enough. Lower the brains into the oil gently, and fry about 2 minutes on each side, until golden. Serve with lemon wedges.

I started the Japanese breadcrumbs, called panko, as part of the crusty coating when they became widely available. They make this dish even more scrumptious.

If you're lucky to have any brains left over, try them with Sauce Gribiche, page 277.

Braised Veal Shanks with Gremolata

A favorite dish that Evan and I would often make for the two of us. Some purists think that the garlicky gremolata is too strong for the delicate veal, but we always loved its pungent accent.

Serves 2

Salt and freshly ground pepper
2 veal shanks, cut into 2-inch pieces across the bone
3 tablespoons light olive oil
2 medium onions, chopped
1 medium carrot, scraped and chopped
½ cup dry white wine
1 sprig fresh oregano (8–10 leaves), or ½ teaspoon dried
1 cup peeled, seeded, and chopped tomatoes
1 cup veal or chicken broth

Gremolata
2 garlic cloves, minced
1 tablespoon finely chopped lemon rind
2 tablespoons finely chopped fresh parsley

Salt and pepper the shanks lightly on both sides. Heat the oil in a heavy casserole, and brown the veal on all sides. Push them aside, add the onions and carrot, and cook 1 minute, stirring them into the oil. Splash in the wine, and cook to reduce, then stir in the oregano, tomatoes, and broth. Reduce the heat to a simmer. Cover, and cook gently for 1½ hours. If the sauce seems too liquid, remove the shanks when tender and boil down to reduce the juices, mashing the vegetables into them. Return the shanks to the casserole, and heat through.

Mix the ingredients for the gremolata, and put in a small bowl to sprinkle on at the table.

🥣 *Canned tomatoes, preferably San Marzano, are fine when fresh tomatoes are out of season.*
   I like to put out little coffee spoons, so we could dig out the delicious marrow embedded in the shanks.

. . .

Martha's Paprikash with Little Dumplings

Chicken paprikash became very popular in our household after my brother-in-law, Russ, brought his Hungarian wife to America for the first time. It was in 1957, and Russ had just been awarded the Pulitzer Prize for his coverage of the Hungarian Revolution. He was expected to do a whirlwind tour with his lovely wife, Martha, the former Countess Sennyey. But that didn't stop her from first ferreting out all the special Hungarian food shops in Manhattan's Yorkville so she could fill our kitchen with fragrant Hungarian accents. Evan's daughters were entranced by her, and soon dubbed the romantic couple Uncle Famous and the Baroness (which became the title of a delightful story that Evan wrote for *Gourmet* on our introduction to Hungarian cuisine).

I particularly remember Martha, impeccably dressed, standing at our stove with a glob of dumpling dough on a wet wooden board, rapidly cutting and sliding pieces of the dough directly into a large pot of boiling water. Meanwhile, Russ was saying to the girls, "If you want to keep a man happy when you grow up, be sure to learn to make *csirkepaprikás*," and he told them to get a pencil and paper so they could write down *his* recipe for paprika chicken. Here it is, along with my attempt at Martha's little dumplings.

Serves 4

For the dumplings
2 eggs
1 cup water
½ teaspoon salt
1½ cups flour, plus 1 or 2 tablespoons more, if needed

For the paprikash
1 chicken, about 3½ pounds
Salt
4 tablespoons chicken fat or combination of chicken fat
    and butter
4 medium onions, finely chopped
2 tablespoons sweet Hungarian paprika
Chicken broth as needed
1 tablespoon cornstarch
1½ cups sour cream
Freshly ground pepper

Garnish: butter, chopped parsley

Make the dumpling dough first, so that it can rest for about an hour. Mix the eggs, water, and salt together in a bowl until smooth. Beat in most of the flour, and keep mixing until you have a smooth mass. The dough should start to come away from the sides of the bowl and drop from the spoon in lumps. It will thicken a little while it rests. Cover the bowl, and set aside for about 1 hour or overnight. Test just before cooking, and work in a little more flour if necessary.

Cut the chicken into 8 pieces—2 drumsticks, 2 thighs, 2 wings with some breast meat attached, and the remaining 2 breasts (Russ called for only quartering the bird, but I find our chickens considerably larger than what you get in Europe, so I prefer 8 pieces)—and soak them in a bowl of cold water with 1 teaspoon salt. Meanwhile, heat the fat in a skillet large enough to accommodate the chicken, and sauté the onions very slowly until soft and golden. Push the onions aside, and sprinkle in the paprika, mixing in with the onions. Tuck the chicken pieces into the pan with a little water still clinging to them. Cover, and cook the chicken very slowly, turning it once, for about 30 minutes. Check to see if the skillet is getting dry, and add a little chicken broth if it is. Meanwhile, bring a large pot of salted water to the boil.

Mix the cornstarch with the sour cream, and stir that evenly into the pan. When all is heated through, taste and correct seasoning, adding several grinds of pepper. Cover, and turn off the heat, but keep in a warm place.

To cook the dumplings, bring a large pot to the boil and quickly dip a small wooden chopping board or paddle into and out of the boiling water. Plop one-sixth of the dough onto the center of the wet board. Holding the board above the boiling water at a slight angle and propped on the rim of the pot, with a smallish, sharp knife, cut off a ⅓-inch strip of the dough and push it toward the end of your board positioned over the pot of boiling water. Now, first dipping the knife into the boiling water, at an angle, chop off 5 to 6 small, narrow pieces of the strip, scraping them into the boiling water. Quickly repeat the process with the rest of that piece of dough, and then with the remaining dough. You have to work quickly; the dumpling pieces will rise to the surface of the water and should then cook only about 1 minute. Taste to make sure they are just tender, then drain and toss in a warm bowl with a little salt, as much butter as you like, and chopped parsley.

The chicken may need reheating. If so, do it very carefully, not letting the sauce boil.

Making these dumplings is simply a matter of practice and patience. It looked so easy when I first watched Martha doing it, but the several times when I first tried them, my slices of dough were uneven and I didn't work fast enough, so the first dumplings were cooked before I could drop the next batch in. If you want, try doing them in two or three stages, fishing out the first batch before you drop in the second. You'll find that you get better at it as you go along. I've also found that if I leave the dough in the refrigerator overnight, covered, it is a little easier to handle.

I like to use at least some chicken fat for the sautéing, and if I haven't any on hand, I remove all the fat I can find on the chicken and render it. It's usually not enough, but I augment it with butter. Goose fat is good, too.

An important technique that I learned from my Hungarian sister-in-law is to make sure when you add the paprika not to expose it to high heat or it will become bitter. And, above all, make sure your paprika is fresh. Martha, who lives in Vienna now, replenishes my supply every year with fresh paprika from Hungary. She has taught me to keep it in a cool place, and if it is in a bottle, to wrap it up (I use foil) so that the light doesn't penetrate and fade its dazzling color.

A Taste of Bryn Teg

Sorrel Soup

Serves 6

2 tablespoons butter
2 medium onions, chopped
2 small potatoes, peeled and chopped
4 cups chicken stock
5 cups sorrel leaves, washed, stemmed, and cut into strips
1 cup heavy cream
Salt and freshly ground pepper

Melt the butter in a heavy, medium-size pot, over moderate heat. Add the onions and potatoes, and cook, stirring, for about 5 minutes. Add the chicken stock and 4 cups of the sorrel. Bring to a boil, then reduce the heat to medium-low, and continue to simmer until the vegetables are very tender, about 30 minutes.

Working in batches, transfer the soup to the blender, and pulse to a well-blended but still slightly chunky consistency. Return the soup to the pot over medium-low heat, pour in the cream, and add the remaining strips of sorrel. Taste, and add salt and pepper as needed. Heat until the sorrel is just wilted. Serve warm, or chill and serve cold.

For a richer, truer potage Germiny, use 2 or 3 egg yolks, and mix well with ¼ cup of the cream (in this instance, you'll only need

¾ cup cream total). Ladle some of the hot soup into the egg yolks to temper, then stir them into the soup at the very last. Yum.

.   .   .

Stuffed Zucchini Blossoms and/or Milkweed Pods Fried in Beer Batter

The beer batter for this recipe came from Albert Stockli years ago. He was the creative, temperamental chef of the Four Seasons restaurant when it opened in the sixties in New York, and later he had his own place in Stonehenge, Connecticut. It was there that I worked with him developing recipes for his book *Splendid Fare*. It was the first time I had experienced how a professional chef operated, and I was appalled at the difference between the pro's performance and the way a home cook operated, as I watched him dip a ladle into a hollandaise or a *fond de veau* or put something into a blazing-hot oven and pronounce it done in ten minutes. When I complained that the poor cook at home would be at a loss trying to follow such instructions, to his great credit he installed an ordinary stove in his lakeside vacation house and did most of the recipes over just as a home cook would do them.

Serves 4 as an hors d'oeuvre

Beer batter
One 12-ounce can light domestic beer
1½ cups all-purpose flour
½ teaspoon salt
1 tablespoon paprika

Stuffing
¼ cup minced country ham
¼ cup minced mushrooms
½ cup fresh breadcrumbs
1 egg, lightly beaten
2 tablespoons minced fresh parsley
1 or 2 tablespoons minced fresh herbs (sage, tarragon, dill)
Salt and freshly ground pepper

About 12 zucchini flowers or 18 milkweed pods or a
    combination of both
Vegetable oil for frying

To make the batter: Pour the beer into a large bowl. Sift the flour, salt, and paprika into the beer, whisking until the mixture is light and frothy.

Mix all the stuffing ingredients together, adding salt and pepper to taste. Fill the zucchini flowers with the stuffing, gluing the seams together as best you can. Heat about 2 inches oil in a heavy pot until a breadcrumb dropped in sizzles and turns golden. When it is hot, lower half the stuffed flowers into the oil, and fry until golden on both sides. Drain on paper towels, and repeat with the rest.

You probably won't use up all the beer batter, but it is good for frying so many things. Try shrimp, as Stockli does. If you are picking blossoms from your own garden, take only the male ones—that is, those without the fruit beginning to swell on the stem end. And be sure if you are using milkweed pods to gather them when they are young and tender; otherwise they will be tough and stringy.

. . .

Sorrel and Leek Pancakes

I learned how to make these vegetable pancakes from Marian Morash. It is a great way to use vegetables from your own Victory Garden.

Serves 4 to 5

3 good-size leeks
1 large bunch of sorrel (about 2 cups)
2 tablespoons butter
2 eggs
¼ cup flour
Salt and freshly ground pepper
Vegetable oil or light olive oil

Discard any coarse outer leaves of the leeks, and cut off the tops where the leaves turn darkish green. Quarter the leeks lengthwise, and wash carefully. Drain, pat dry, and cut into small pieces. Remove any coarse stems from the sorrel, then rinse the leaves, dry them, and cut into strips. Heat the butter in a large sauté pan, and cook the leeks, covered, over low heat until tender, about 7 minutes. Add the sorrel leaves, and cook, covered, 2 minutes. Remove to a bowl, and let cool slightly.

Beat the eggs in a separate bowl, and whisk in the flour and

¼ teaspoon salt until smooth. Combine with the leeks and sorrel; taste, and add a few grindings of pepper and more salt if necessary.

Film the bottom of a large frying pan with enough oil to cover, and set over medium-high heat. When hot, drop the leek-sorrel batter in, by the large spoonful. Press down lightly to flatten each pancake into a circle about 2½ inches in diameter. Cook them, adding a little more oil as needed, in two or three batches, over medium heat, for 3 to 4 minutes on each side.

Other possibilities that Marian Morash offers in her Victory Garden Fish and Vegetable Cookbook *are parsnip or Jerusalem-artichoke pancakes, as well as grated zucchini. It's fun to play with these pancakes. I once tried working into the sorrel-and-leek mix some small pieces of salmon that I had left over, and it was delicious.*

If you are serving these as an accompaniment, they don't need a garnish, but alone, they could benefit from a dollop of crème fraîche or sour cream or a wedge of lemon.

·   ·   ·

Shad and Shad Roe in Sorrel Sauce

When we were doing our *L. L. Bean Book of* New *New England Cookery,* attempting to marry old recipes with the new, more eclectic cooking style that emerged in New England in the last quarter of the twentieth century, we came across a recipe for sorrel sauce from Mrs. N.K.M. Lee, who signed herself "A Boston Housewife." It appeared in 1832 in her *The Cook's Own Book,* and she recommended serving it in an omelette. In Vermont the first

tender leaves of sorrel appear in the spring, when the shad is running, and we thought, what better way to celebrate spring than to
marry sorrel, shad, and its roe. So we devised this recipe. The first
time we made it, M.F.K. Fisher happened to be coming for dinner,
and she proclaimed it almost indecent, it was so rich and good.

Serves 6

1 large onion, chopped
1 cup water
1 pair shad roe
Salt
2 tablespoons soft butter
2 sides shad (about 1½ pounds)
Freshly ground pepper
Bunch of sorrel leaves, stems removed and leaves torn in
      shreds (about 1½ cups)
⅓ cup heavy cream

Put the onion and the water in a medium-size saucepan, and
simmer for 5 minutes. Add the shad roe, and sprinkle lightly
with salt. Cover, and simmer very gently for 8 minutes, turning
once. Remove the roe, reserving the cooking liquid. Smear
1 tablespoon of the butter over the bottom of a shallow baking
dish just large enough to accommodate the fish in one layer.

Separate the two halves of the roe and, opening the flaps,
place one half in the center of each side of shad in the prepared
baking dish. Press the roe down, and bring the flaps back over to
just about cover the roe. Smear the remaining butter on top, and
season with salt and pepper. Place the dish under a preheated
broiler, and cook 10 to 12 minutes, until the fish is opaque—be
careful not to overcook it.

Meanwhile, add the torn sorrel leaves to the cooking liquid,
and boil about 5 minutes. Pour in the cream, and simmer

another minute, then purée in the blender or food processor, or, better still, use that handy new device, the immersion blender, if you have one. Spoon the sauce over the broiled fish just before serving.

·   ·   ·

Gooseberry Sauce for Grilled Trout or Salmon

1 cup gooseberries
½ cup water
2–3 tablespoons sugar

Top and tail the gooseberries, and put them in a small saucepan. Cook gently in the water for about 20 minutes, until they are soft. Mix in 2 tablespoons sugar, then taste. If they are too tart, add another tablespoonful of sugar. But remember, the sauce should have the kind of acidity a lemon would have. Serve slightly warm with the fish.

Be sure to use green gooseberries, not the ones that have developed a blush and are perhaps sweeter but less tart and flavorful.

·   ·   ·

Rabbit in a Sweet-Sour Chocolate-Accented Sauce

Not far from our place in Vermont is a commune called The Circle of Angels, whose members follow the principles of the

Middle Eastern philosopher Gurdjieff. We were delighted to find one summer that they were selling freshly killed rabbits, an animal that is not often raised in New England for human consumption. No doubt it is because there is a resistance to eating cute bunnies—what Angus Cameron called "the Bambi syndrome." But Evan and I have always loved rabbit, ever since eating rabbit ragouts and rabbit terrines in bistros in Paris, and we purchased many a lovingly raised, meaty rabbit from the Angels, not only to enjoy ourselves but to convert wary friends. This Mexican-inspired recipe always won them over, partly because the surprise element of chocolate in the sauce and the sweet-sour flavor provide a distraction.

Serves 4

3 tablespoons butter

1 rabbit (about 2½–3 pounds), cut in 8 pieces, plus backbone and ribs

1 large onion, sliced

2 ounces ham or prosciutto, chopped

1 tablespoon sugar

6 tablespoons cider vinegar

1¼ cups red wine

1¼ cups rabbit broth (see below) or chicken broth

Salt and freshly ground pepper

2 teaspoons chopped fresh rosemary, or ½ teaspoon dried, crumbled

1 tablespoon coarsely grated bitter chocolate

3 tablespoons raisins

3 tablespoons slivered almonds

Melt the butter in a large skillet, then add the rabbit pieces, the onion, and the ham. Sauté gently for 10 minutes, turning the rabbit pieces after the first 5 minutes. Dissolve the sugar in the vinegar, and pour it into the skillet along with the wine and broth. Transfer the contents of the skillet to a shallow earthenware dish or other heatproof casserole, salt and pepper to taste, and bake, uncovered, 40 minutes in a preheated 350-degree oven. Spread the chocolate, raisins, and almonds over and around the rabbit pieces, and return the dish to the oven for a final 10 minutes of cooking. When the rabbit is ready, give the sauce a good stir, and if it seems too thin, pour it off into a small saucepan and boil it down to thicken slightly. Return the sauce to the dish and serve.

If you have reserved the backbone and ribs, you can make a small amount of broth by simmering them in 2 cups of water along with a small onion and a few sprigs of parsley for about 40 minutes, then season with salt and pepper.

Try grilling the liver and kidneys on small skewers, and serve them as an amuse-gueule *before the main event. Or, if you have squeamish company, save them for yourself. They are scrumptious.*

. . .

Gooseberry Fool

These are both old English desserts that can be made with almost any kind of berries, wild or cultivated—currants, raspberries, elderberries. The name "fool" is derived from the French *fouler,* to crush, and according to Jane Grigson, that's just the way the gooseberries should be prepared, not over-cooked and blended to a smooth slop. The fool is finished with whipped cream folded in, whereas the flummery is simply thickened with cornstarch, and served with cream or custard on the side. The word "flummery" is used as a slight pejorative, meaning "nonsense" or "humbug." How that is connected with this ancient dessert remains a mystery. I'm giving the recipe for the fool first, the flummery as a variation.

Serves 4

2 cups gooseberries
2 cups water
½–¾ cup sugar
¾ cup heavy cream

Top and tail the gooseberries, and put them in a nonreactive saucepan with the water. Bring to a boil, then simmer until they are tender. Stir in ½ cup sugar, and mash the berries. Taste, and see if you want the full amount of sugar. Let cool thoroughly. Whip the cream until it forms soft mounds, then fold it into the gooseberries. Spoon into six sherbet glasses and serve well chilled.

VARIATION: *Gooseberry Flummery*   Cook the gooseberries as above. Dissolve 3 tablespoons cornstarch in ¼ cup water, and stir that in along with the sugar. Serve in chilled in sherbet glasses, and pass around a pitcher of heavy cream.

I always pick my gooseberries for cooking when they have reached full size but are still green. They have a much tarter flavor at this stage, but they do need a fair amount of sugar. So be sure to taste and make your own judgment.

Tart Dough

I've found the food processor such a blessing in making pie doughs, particularly those that are rich with butter, that I would never go back to using my fingers for the initial mixing, although the final *fraisage* with the palms of the hands is still an essential step in making these doughs.

Enough for 8-inch tart pan

1 cup all-purpose flour
¼ teaspoon salt
1 tablespoon sugar (only for a sweet tart)
8 tablespoons cold unsalted butter
3 tablespoons ice water

Mix the flour, salt, and sugar, if using, in the bowl of a food processor. Cut the butter into small pieces, drop them through the tube of the processor, and pulse long enough to say "alligator" fifteen times. Pour in the ice water and process long enough to say "alligator" ten times. Transfer the dough to a work surface, preferably marble, and smear it out in small increments with the heel of your hand, then gather the dough together into a round. Sprinkle with flour, wrap in waxed paper, and refrigerate at least 20 minutes or until ready to use.

It was the inspired French cooking teacher Lydie Marshall who taught me the trick of saying "alligator" so one knows just how long to pulse the dough. Of course you can mix by hand if you are skilled at it, but this method is infallible.

Gooseberry Tart

Serves 6

1 sweet Tart Dough (recipe above)
¼ cup gooseberry jam or currant jelly
2 cups gooseberries, topped and tailed
⅔ cup sugar

Roll the dough out into a circle approximately 9 or 10 inches in diameter. If the dough is very cold before rolling out, let it warm up slightly at room temperature. Transfer the dough to an 8-inch tart pan with removable bottom, tucking it into the inside rim firmly. Trim the dough all around, leaving enough on the rim so you can fold it over inward, then crimp it all around. Paint the bottom of the dough with the gooseberry jam. Arrange the gooseberries on top, and sprinkle the sugar over them. Bake in a preheated 425-degree oven 10 minutes, then lower the heat to 350 degrees and bake an additional 45 minutes.

· · ·

Rhubarb and Strawberry Tart

Rhubarb is another tart accent of the North Country. Just one plant will furnish a small family all it needs to make some of the good desserts and condiments that grace the Yankee table. Here's a tart to celebrate the spring, when the first strawberries appear.

Serves 6

1 pound fresh rhubarb
½ cup sugar
1 sweet Tart Dough (page 256)
½ cup currant jelly or gooseberry jam
1 pint fresh strawberries
Whipped cream (optional)

Cut the rhubarb into 1-inch pieces, and toss in a bowl with the sugar. Cover, and set aside for a few hours or refrigerate overnight. Transfer the rhubarb and accumulated juices to a saucepan, and cook them down slowly, uncovered, for about 20 minutes. Remove the rhubarb with a slotted spoon, reserving any remaining liquid in the saucepan for the currant or gooseberry glaze.

Sprinkle some flour on your rolling pin and on your work surface, preferably marble, and roll the dough out to about a 10-inch circle. Press it into an 8-inch tart pan with removable bottom, and crimp all around. Prick the bottom all over with a fork, and line the shell with aluminum foil, then fill it with small weights, such as dried beans or pebbles. Bake for 15 minutes at 425 degrees, then remove the foil and weights, and bake at 350 degrees for another 10 minutes. Remove from the oven, and let cool slightly.

Meanwhile, as the crust is baking, make the glaze. Mix the reserved rhubarb juice with the jelly, and cook down briefly, until thick and syrupy. When the crust is ready, smear the bottom with about half of the glaze, then spoon on the rhubarb. Hull the strawberries, split them in half if they are quite large, and place them in concentric circles on top of the rhubarb. Paint the strawberries with the remaining glaze. Serve, if you like, with whipped cream.

I worked this recipe out because I never much liked the way cooking the rhubarb in the pie made the crust soggy. I also don't like the taste of cooked strawberries, and when you have just picked beautiful little berries, you want to make the most of them.

. . .

Freeform Apple Tarts

The beautiful Dutchess apple tree in front of our house gives us just about all the apples we can eat during the fall, and often we have hauled bags full of them back to New York so we can freeze them, simply peeled and cut in wedges. That way, we can make several quick little tarts, or a larger freeform one, and savor the delight of our own really flavorful apples during the winter months. I like to bake these small rounds while we're having dinner so that they can be eaten hot from the oven.

Makes 4

1 sweet Tart Dough (page 256)
4 generous tablespoons apricot or gooseberry jam
3 small-to-medium-size tart apples, peeled, cored, and cut in thin slices
4 tablespoons sugar, or more, depending on the tartness of the apples

Roll out the Tart Dough, and cut four circles about 5½ inches in diameter. Transfer to a baking sheet, and curl just a little the edges of the circles of dough all around, so juices won't run off. Paint the bottoms with the jam, and arrange slices of the apple all around, overlapping them. Sprinkle a tablespoon of sugar over each, and pop them into a preheated 425-degree oven. Check after 15 minutes, and if they are lightly browned at the edges and the apples are soft, they're ready; if not, bake 2 or 3 more minutes. Serve hot.

VARIATION: *A Large Freeform Apple Tart*   To make a large tart, use one and a half times the amounts called for in the sweet Tart Dough on page 256, and roll it out into an oval about 14 inches long and 10 inches wide. Transfer it to a baking sheet and paint the bottom with ⅓ cup jam, leaving a 1½-inch border all around. Toss slim wedges from 4 small-to-medium-size apples with ⅓–½ cup sugar, depending on their tartness, and then distribute them over the painted area of the dough. Fold the 1½-inch border of dough over onto the filling, pleating at intervals to make it fit. Sprinkle a little more sugar over the edges, and bake in a preheated 425-degree oven for 10 minutes, then turn the heat down to 375 degrees and bake another 45 to 50 minutes. Paint a little more jam, melted this time, on top.

🥣 *When Julia and Jacques made their freeform tart in the TV series they did together, they didn't agree about much, which only goes to show that there is no one way to bake a tart. So take liberties. Julia wanted to cook down the apricot glaze with sugar and Grand Marnier, then strain it to make her glaze; Jacques was content simply to mix together apricot jam with a little Calvados or cognac. I'm flexible. If I'm in a hurry, I simply use a good preserve from the jar for the glaze. They also suggest adding currants, dried apricot, and cinnamon to the filling, but I feel that if the apples are as good as our Dutchess, I don't want to interfere with their wonderful flavor.*

One tip: If you have a Silpat mat, line the baking tray with it and you won't have a messy cleanup.

Frozen Maple Mousse

This is a dish Evan and I created when we were thinking of new ways to use good Vermont maple syrup in recipes for *The New New England Cookbook*. It is deliciously rich.

Serves 6

1 cup maple syrup
2 egg whites
Pinch of salt
1 cup heavy cream

Pour the maple syrup into a 1-quart pan and set over medium heat. Meanwhile, put the egg whites in the bowl of a standing electric mixer with the salt, and beat until they form firm peaks. Watch the syrup carefully now; as the large bubbles start to become smaller bubbles, scoop up a spoonful of syrup about 8 inches above the pan and let it fall back in; if the falling syrup spins a thread, remove the pan immediately from the heat (it should be about 260 degrees). With the electric mixer going, pour the hot syrup in a thin, steady stream into the egg whites.

Pour the cream into a separate bowl, preferably over a panful of ice to get greater volume, and beat until soft mounds form. Fold the beaten cream into the maple-egg mixture, turn into a serving bowl or individual sherbet glasses, and freeze for 2 hours or more before serving.

Cooking for One

Here are some of the things I love to cook for myself.

Broiled Bluefish or Mackerel over a Bed of Fennel and New Potatoes

This is one of those simple, delicious dishes I often make for myself. It's all ready in half an hour, and there's only one cooking pan to wash up. I love fatty fish like bluefish and mackerel, with their assertive flavor, and the sweet fennel and young potatoes create a perfect balance here.

Serves 1

1 small bulb fennel, or ½ large bulb
2 or 3 small new potatoes
2 tablespoons olive oil
Salt and freshly ground pepper
1 bluefish or mackerel fillet

Trim the fennel bulb, removing the tough outer pieces and cutting off the stalk. Reserve the fennel leaves. Slice the bulb horizontally in ¼-inch slices. Don't peel the potatoes; just trim the ends and cut them into ¼-inch slices. Toss both with the olive oil in a skillet, and heat it up. When hot, add water just to cover, and cook covered for 15 to 20 minutes, until the vegetables are soft, adding more water as needed so they don't scorch. Transfer to a shallow, preferably oval baking dish, salt and pepper lightly, and lay the fish on top, skin side down. Rub a little olive oil on the fillet, and salt and pepper it. Slip the dish about 6 inches under a preheated broiler, and cook 5 to 6 minutes, until just done. Sprinkle some chopped fennel leaves on top.

. . .

James Beard's Swordfish-Olive Pasta

One day when I went down to Jim's West Twelfth Street house to work with him on his pasta book, he greeted me with the happy news that the evening before he had just tasted a fabulous pasta dish with swordfish that he was going to make for me for lunch. It has become one of my favorite pastas, and I often make it for myself after I've enjoyed a big slice of broiled swordfish and set aside a piece for this dish.

Serves 1 as a main course, 2 as a beginning pasta course;
can be easily multiplied

3 ounces swordfish, at least 1 inch thick
⅓ cup finely chopped Italian black olives
Salt and freshly ground pepper
3 ounces fusilli, penne, or ziti pasta
1 large shallot, sliced thin
1 fat garlic clove, sliced thin
2 tablespoons olive oil
½ teaspoon dried oregano or *herbes de Provence*
2 teaspoons capers
Chopped fresh parsley

If your swordfish hasn't been cooked, line the broiler rack with aluminum wrap, rub on a little oil, set the fish on top, and broil 4 minutes on one side. Turn, top with the olives, and broil 2 to 3 minutes longer. If you are using precooked swordfish, just heat it briefly under the broiler with the olives strewn on top.

Bring a large pot of salted water to a boil, and drop in the pasta. While it cooks, sauté the shallot and garlic in the olive oil over low heat until they are soft; don't let them brown. Add the herb and capers. Slice the swordfish in thin strips, and spoon it and the olives into the shallot-caper mixture. When the pasta is done al dente, drain it, reserving ½ cup of the cooking water, and mix the pasta in with the swordfish, adding pasta water as needed to moisten the pasta and make a few tablespoonsful of sauce. Salt and pepper everything, then toss into a warm bowl and sprinkle parsley on top.

I've departed a bit from Jim's recipe as I learned new, invaluable tricks about the subtle art of Italian cooking from Lidia Bastianich. Most important, save some of that pasta water, because you do need some moisture in that swordfish-olive sauce. And slicing garlic cloves thin, instead of chopping them, makes them soften more easily without burning.

A Cornish Hen with Herbal Stuffing Under the Skin, Broiled

Serves 1 or 2

1 Cornish game hen

Stuffing
2 garlic cloves, peeled and smashed lightly
Salt
2 shallots, chopped fine
2 strips lemon zest, chopped fine
1 tablespoon finely chopped fresh tarragon, or ½ teaspoon
    dried
6–8 branches fresh Italian parsley, chopped fine
Freshly ground pepper
1 tablespoon olive oil, plus more for rubbing

Rinse the hen, and dry thoroughly. Cut along the breastbone from head to tail, using a sharp knife to cut through the skin and flesh, then cutting through the bone with poultry shears. Open the bird up like a book, and flatten.

Chop the garlic cloves with ½ teaspoon salt, then mash to a paste with the flat of your knife. Mix with all the other stuffing ingredients, grinding a generous amount of pepper in with them. With your fingers, loosen the skin from the breast side, then thrust a finger farther down to reach the thigh and leg meat, loosening that as much as you can. Spoon the stuffing into both sides, pushing some of it down as far as possible over the legs. Rub a little more oil over the surface on both sides, and salt lightly. Place the bird, skin side down, in a broiler pan and set it on a rack 8 inches below a preheated broiler. Broil 15 minutes on the first side, then turn and broil about 10 minutes skin side up. The skin should be well browned. Watch carefully that it isn't broiling too rapidly; if it is, lower the broiler rack a notch. Let sit 3 or 4 minutes at room temperature before eating, then spoon any collected juices on top.

🥣 *You can also grill the butterflied hen; just be sure your fire isn't too hot; you don't want it to blacken before it is done inside. Or you can also roast the hen whole, in which case skip the step of cutting the breast in half. Vary the herb, too, depending on the season and what may be in your garden. I like to scatter some vegetables around the Cornish hen while it is broiling or roasting; red pepper, mushrooms, parsnips, young turnips, fennel are all good—and you'll have a complete meal. They're growing Cornish hens bigger these days, and you may find a whole one too much to consume at one sitting. But it's always good cold for lunch.*

Or you can buy a smaller poussin; just reduce the cooking times by about 5 or 10 minutes.

· · ·

Lidia's Gratinate of Cutlet with Eggplant or Zucchini Slices

I think Lidia was a bit skeptical when I suggested that this was a dish that could easily be made for one, which only made me want to go home and prove that I could do it. Since then it's become one of my favorite solo dishes—a complete meal in itself, and not difficult to prepare, particularly if you have some

good tomato sauce on hand (which every good cook should, of
course, have).

Serves 1

1 small eggplant, about 6 inches, or a small zucchini
Salt and freshly ground pepper
Flour for dredging
1–2 tablespoons light olive oil
3 ounces scaloppini, veal, pork tenderloin, or chicken breast
1 tablespoon butter
1 shallot, minced
Splash of white wine
About 6 fresh basil leaves
3–4 tablespoons tomato sauce
3 tablespoons freshly grated Parmesan
¼ cup veal, beef, or chicken stock

Trim the stem off the eggplant. Slice a wide strip of skin off
lengthwise on either side, then slice lengthwise in ¼-inch slices.
Salt and pepper them, and dredge lightly in flour. If you are
using zucchini, cut it in diagonal ¼-inch slices. Heat 1 tablespoon
of the olive oil in a 6-inch frying pan, and lightly brown the eggplant slices on both sides, adding a little more oil if necessary.
Remove to paper towels. Cut scallop-size pieces of whatever
meat you are using, and flatten them between waxed paper, then
salt and pepper lightly and dredge in flour. Add butter to the pan,
and sauté the meat a minute or two on each side. Remove from
the pan and set aside with the eggplant. Toss in the shallot and
sauté briefly, then splash in the wine, and let it almost boil away.
Put the pieces of meat back in the skillet in one layer with leaves
of basil laid over them, then arrange the strips of vegetable on

top, and spoon about 1 tablespoon of the tomato sauce over each piece. Sprinkle the cheese over, and drizzle just a little tomato sauce in the bottom of the pan, along with the stock. Bake in a preheated 400-degree oven for 8 to 10 minutes, or until the meat is tender when poked and there is still a little sauce left in the pan.

If you are using chicken breast, you should split it in half, open it up like a book, and cut it into 2 pieces (more than 3 ounces but it doesn't hurt to have a little left over). Pork tenderloin will yield pieces that are small in dimension, but you can cut them on the diagonal; you will probably need 4 slices for this dish. You can also use pork loin, but it is not as tender.

Wanna Buy a Duck?

What an absurd idea to buy a whole duck for one person, you might think. A lot of work, expensive, and probably wasteful. But I was tempted recently by an organic five-pounder in the supermarket case, and I thought, Yes, I do wanna buy a duck— just for me. Visions of confits and cassoulet danced in my head, to say nothing of a good duck stock, which is like gold in the freezer. So I brought one home, remembering, as I dreamed up dishes, some of the delights that Julia and Jacques created when we were doing a show on duck for their TV series *Julia and Jacques Cooking at Home*. The one thing I didn't want to do was to simply roast it and then have cold duck on hand, getting drier every day. So cutting up the bird was the first order of the day—not the easiest task, because ducks seem to have very stiff, hard-to-find joints, but a sharp boning knife, poultry shears, and patience all help.

Here is what I got out of that duck in a week of delicious eating:

Duck Stock
Cracklings
Jacques's Duck Giblet Salad
Sautéed Duck Breast with Madeira à la Julia
Skillet Duck Legs with Parsnips à la Jacques
Skillet Duck with Celeriac, Fennel, and Peppers
Mini-Cassoulet

· · ·

Duck Stock

After cutting up the duck into 2 leg-thigh pieces, 2 wings, and 2 breasts (the latter with skin and bones removed—be sure to save both), I trimmed the carcass of its skin and fat (again, save) and put the bones, including the breastbones, in a soup pot along with the neck and wings. I added 1 large peeled carrot and an onion, plus 6 to 8 good-size parsley stems, and poured in about 3 quarts of water. I brought all this to a boil, then skimmed off the scum several times, lowered the heat, and cooked the broth at a lively simmer, partially covered, for about 3 hours. I added about a teaspoon of salt halfway through the cooking, to bring out the flavors, but I always leave the stock purposely undersalted, in case I want to reduce it. This made about 1½ quarts stock.

Cracklings

Cut the more tender, fatty pieces of the reserved skin into ¼-inch slices, and spread them out in a good-size skillet. Fry them very slowly, for 25 to 30 minutes, turning occasionally, until the pieces have released all their fat and are brown and crackling. Lift from the skillet with a slotted spoon, and drain the cracklings on paper towels. Pour the fat through a strainer into a heatproof jar, and keep refrigerated. It is wonderful for cooking, particularly when making pan-fried potatoes. Keep the cracklings in a tightly sealed jar in the fridge.

. . .

Jacques's Duck Giblet Salad

I consider one of the best cook's treats the packet of giblets that one finds tucked into a roasting bird—and if you don't find it, complain loudly and never buy from that source again.

So I was delighted at Jacques's recipe for a duck-giblet salad. He says it will serve two, but I found it so good that I ate the whole thing.

Serves 1

1 packet duck giblets (gizzard, heart, and liver)
2 tablespoons butter
2 teaspoons duck fat
Salt and freshly ground pepper

Dressing
½ teaspoon salt
1 shallot, finely chopped
2 teaspoons Dijon mustard
1 tablespoon red-wine vinegar
1 tablespoon duck fat
1½ tablespoons olive oil

Escarole, endive, watercress, or any mix of more assertive
    salad greens
1 tablespoon or more duck Cracklings (recipe above)

Trim the membrane from the side of the gizzard, and slice it and
the heart into thin strips. After discarding any fat and membrane from the liver, cut it up into somewhat thicker pieces.
Melt the butter and duck fat in a small skillet, and sauté gizzard
and heart strips over medium-high heat for about 2½ minutes,
tossing frequently and adding the liver for the final minute. Salt
and pepper the meats, and remove them from the pan. Mix the
dressing ingredients together, then pour them into the pan and
scrape up all the juices. Heap the greens onto a plate or bowl,
and toss with a couple of tablespoons of the dressing. Mix the
giblets with most of the remaining dressing, taste, and arrange
them on top of the greens. Toss cracklings over all.

Sautéed Duck Breast
with Madeira à la Julia

I used just one of the duck breasts to transform Julia's recipe into a dish for one, freezing the other breast for another day. But this is such a particularly *soigné* Julia creation that it's worth inviting a friend or two to share it. If your duck is a plump one, the two breasts can easily serve three. Wild rice cooked in duck stock makes a splendid accompaniment, but plain rice is good, too.

Serves 1

1 tablespoon butter
2 teaspoons duck fat
Salt and freshly ground pepper
½ whole duck breast, skinned and boned
Flour for dredging
1 tablespoon finely chopped shallots
2 tablespoons Madeira
¼ cup Duck Stock (page 269)
Garnish: chopped parsley

Melt the butter and the duck fat in a small pan just big enough to accommodate the duck breast (I use a 4-inch sauté pan). Salt and pepper the breast, then dredge it in flour, shaking off excess, and slip it into the sizzling pan. Sauté quite vigorously, but not so much that the butter burns, for 2 to 3 minutes on each side (depending on the plumpness of the breast), until the flesh is soft. Remove from the pan, add the shallots and sauté them a minute, then splash in the Madeira. When it's burned off slightly, then add the stock and reduce until syrupy. Cut the breast into 3 or 4 diagonal slices, and return them to the pan to heat through. If you find they are too bloody or even rosy for your taste, just cook them a little longer in the sauce. Remove to a warm plate, surround the duck slices with rice, pour the sauce over all, and sprinkle on parsley.

· · ·

Skillet Duck Legs with Parsnips à la Jacques

To cook the drumstick and thigh, I used Jacques's delicious recipe and adapted it for one. But I did cook the second leg and thigh pieces alongside, so I would have them and some of the seasonings ready to go into my improvised mini-cassoulet (see recipe that follows).

Serves 1, plus leftovers

1 teaspoon duck fat
Salt and freshly ground pepper
2 duck legs and 2 thighs
1 dozen smallish shallots, or halves of very large shallots
1 dozen garlic cloves, peeled
2 medium parsnips, peeled and cut into 1-inch pieces
½ teaspoon dried rosemary
1 bay leaf
½ cup Duck Stock (page 269) or water

Film with duck fat the bottom of a smallish sauté pan (I use my trusty 9-inch cast-iron skillet), and heat it up. After salting and peppering the leg and thigh pieces on both sides, lay them in the pan, skin side down for the thighs, and let them brown over moderate heat, turning the drumsticks once so the skin on both sides browns and crusts. Watch carefully, because the browning can become blackening very quickly. If there's a sign of that, remove the pan from the heat and let cool off, then return it to a lower heat. After 30 minutes for large pieces, 25 minutes for a smaller duck, scatter the shallots, garlic, and parsnips into the pan, tucking them snugly among the thighs and legs; salt and pepper again, lightly; sprinkle on the rosemary and bay leaf; cover, and cook over low heat for a good 30 minutes, until the meat and vegetables are fork-tender. Remove one thigh and leg to a warm plate, and put the other two in a refrigerator container. With a slotted spoon, transfer all the parsnips and half the shallots and garlic to the duck on the plate, discarding the bay leaf (the rest of the garlic and shallots should go in the fridge container). Pour off the considerable amount of fat you will have (it can be used again), and then pour the duck stock or water into the pan. Scrape up any browned bits, and reduce the stock until almost syrupy. Pour over the duck and vegetables on the plate.

VARIATION: *Skillet Duck with Celeriac, Fennel, and Peppers*
Another time, instead of parsnips, I used about a quarter of a medium celeriac, peeled and cut in 1-inch chunks, a third of a fennel bulb in ¼-inch slices, and 3 strips red bell pepper. I used only 3 or 4 shallots and no garlic, and after browning the duck about 10 minutes, I poured off the fat, added ¼ cup white wine and 3 sage leaves, then put the skillet in a preheated 325-degree oven to bake for 40 to 45 minutes, until tender.

Mini-Cassoulet

This little cassoulet would serve two if you included some slices of garlicky sausage. Frankly, it's even better that way.

Serves 1 or 2

½ cup dried Great Northern beans
1 medium onion, in chunks
3 or 4 garlic cloves
1 small carrot, peeled and cut in chunks
Salt and freshly ground pepper
Reserved cooked duck leg and thigh (see preceding recipe)
Reserved garlic and shallots (see preceding recipe)
About ¼ pound garlic sausage, sliced fairly thick and lightly
    browned (optional)
⅓ cup Cracklings (page 270)
1 cup or more Duck Stock (page 269)
⅓ cup buttered breadcrumbs
2 tablespoons chopped fresh parsley

Soak the beans overnight in water to cover by 2 inches.

Bring the beans and their soaking water to a boil, along with the onion, garlic, and carrot, and cook gently for at least 1 hour. Beans are unpredictable, and older ones that have been on the shelf too long can take as much as 2 hours. So taste—it's your only guide. When the beans are tender and the water is absorbed, season them well with salt and pepper, then turn half of them into a small casserole, lay the duck leg and thigh on top, along with the reserved garlic and shallots and the optional sausage slices and the cracklings. Cover with the remaining beans, and pour in enough duck stock so liquid comes about halfway up. Mix the breadcrumbs and parsley together, and scatter them on top. Drizzle just a little duck fat over, and bake the cassoulet in a preheated 350-degree oven for 1 hour.

An alternative way to soften the beans that I learned from Julia, in case you forget to soak them the night before, is to cover them with 2 inches water in a cooking pot, bring to a boil, and let them boil 2 minutes. Remove from the heat and let soak 1 hour before cooking them.

The Nine Lives of a Leg of Lamb

Not long ago, when I had made a roast lamb for a couple of friends, I was left with a considerable amount of leftover roast—fortunately nice and rare. So I had a series of Suppers of the Lamb all through the next week, some dishes dredged out of my childhood, some improvised, some borrowed—all delicious, and so varied that each one tasted different, with its own character. Here's what I came up with:

Cold Lamb with Sauce Gribiche

Evan's Lamb Curry

Shepherd's Pie

Casserole of Lamb, Mushrooms, and Bulgur or Barley

Eggplant or Green Peppers Stuffed with Lamb, Red Pepper, and Rice

Lamb Hash

Lamb Croquettes

Minced Lamb on Toast

Lamb Soup with Leeks and Flageolets

Sauce Gribiche for Cold Lamb
or Other Meats

The first time I had this sauce—in a little Left Bank bistro off the rue de la Seine, simply spread over slices of cold meat—I thought, What a great way of bringing new life to yesterday's roast. I looked for recipes for the sauce, and they varied greatly—some are much more mayonnaise-based—so over the years I have developed a version I like. It tastes delicious with lamb, pork, beef, veal, and is especially good with poached brains and sweetbreads and tongue.

Makes about ¾ cup, enough to dress cold meats for 3 or 4

½ teaspoon salt
1 tablespoon Dijon mustard
1 tablespoon wine vinegar
3 tablespoons olive oil
1 tablespoon capers
2 cornichons, chopped in small pieces
1 hard-boiled egg, chopped fine
Freshly ground pepper
1 tablespoon chopped fresh parsley

Mix all the ingredients together. If you're not using the sauce right away, hold back on the parsley, and mix that in at the last. This is a sauce you have to taste so you can adjust the seasonings to get the balance right. Adjust according to what your palate tells you.

You can cut the meat in strips and marinate them in the sauce for several hours, or you can cut slices and serve the sauce over them. Use as much of it as suits your fancy.

Evan's Lamb Curry

Follow the recipe on page 232, using one-quarter of the amounts called for. Since you'll be using already cooked lamb, it should simmer only about 20 to 30 minutes.

. . .

Shepherd's Pie

Follow the recipe on page 205, using about one-quarter the amounts called for, and arrange the meat and mashed potato in a small casserole dish or one of those ceramic onion-soup pots for a comforting, old-fashioned meal.

. . .

Casserole of Lamb, Mushrooms, and Bulgur or Barley

A simple dish that makes a complete meal with a little salad on the side. Bring ¾ cup water to a boil, and slowly drizzle in ¼ cup bulgur or barley. Add ¼ teaspoon salt, and simmer, covered, for 10 minutes. Turn off the heat and let stand 30 minutes. Meanwhile, sauté about 5 medium mushrooms in a little olive oil with

3 or 4 slivers of garlic for a few minutes, then add chunks of cooked lamb, preferably on the rare side, along with any *jus* or gravy from the roast. If you haven't any left, use about ¼ cup beef stock. Season with salt and pepper and a teaspoon of fresh rosemary leaves or ½ teaspoon dried and crumbled. Bring just to the simmer to heat through, and when the bulgur or barley is ready, toss the two together in a warm bowl and sprinkle some parsley on top.

. . .

Eggplant Stuffed with Lamb, Red Pepper, and Rice

1 small eggplant, 6–7 inches
1 medium onion, chopped
1 or 2 garlic cloves, chopped
½ red bell pepper, seeded, ribs removed, and chopped
1½ tablespoons olive oil
¼ cup cooked rice
⅔ cup cooked lamb, cut in smallish pieces
Salt and freshly ground pepper to taste
1 teaspoon roughly cut fresh rosemary leaves, or ½ teaspoon dried
3 tablespoons toasted pine nuts (optional)
¼ cup fresh breadcrumbs

Prick the eggplant all over, and bake in a preheated 400-degree oven for 40 minutes. Meanwhile, sauté the onion, garlic, and red pepper in 1 tablespoon of the olive oil over low heat until soft. Add the rice, meat, salt and pepper to taste, rosemary, and optional pine nuts. When cool enough to handle, split the eggplant lengthwise, and scrape out most of the flesh, leaving the shell intact. Chop up the eggplant flesh and add it to the pan with the rest of the filling. Let everything cook together a few minutes, check seasoning, and then fill the eggplant halves with this stuffing. Sprinkle the breadcrumbs on top, and drizzle on remaining olive oil. Bake in a preheated 400-degree oven for 25 minutes, until nicely browned on top.

This makes an ample supper for one person, and if it's too much, you'll find that whatever is left is very good cold for lunch the next day. It's a recipe to play with: You can stuff summer squash this way, or green peppers (in which case, use some chopped tomato instead of red pepper in the stuffing), and you can vary with different nuts and a sprinkling of raisins or currants.

Lamb Hash

Just follow the recipe on page 228, using half the ingredients called for and a smaller skillet.

·   ·   ·

Lamb Croquettes

It may seem like a lot of fuss for one person, but I get cravings, and this is one of them. Follow the recipe on page 207, using half the ingredients called for.

Minced Lamb on Toast

Minces, which were very common in old American cookbooks, were simply a way of using yesterday's roast. They don't even warrant a spelled-out recipe, they are so uncomplicated. For one person, remove any gristle and simply chop very fine enough cooked lamb to make about ¾ cup. Sauté a chopped shallot or small onion in a small sauté pan with a tablespoon of butter; add, if you like, a good-size mushroom finely chopped. Cook until soft, then splash in some dry sherry or Madeira to give a good flavor; let it cook down. Add the meat with a bit of gravy, if you still have some (otherwise, broth will do). Stir in ¼ cup heavy cream, and bring to a simmer, reducing the liquids slightly. Salt and pepper to taste, and serve on toast or a toasted English muffin with a little parsley scattered over the top. Simple and delicious.

· · ·

Lamb Soup with Leeks and Flageolets

When you've finally gotten down to the bone of your leftover lamb roast, it's time to make a soup. You're not going to get a very meaty broth from a cooked lamb bone, but it will have flavor, enough to yield one or two servings. Root vegetables are always good, and you can use rice or other grains instead of flageolets. But I like this particular combination. The night before making it, put a handful of flageolets or other beans to soak.

Next day, cover your lamb bone with water, and bring to a boil. Skim, and simmer for about 30 minutes, then add a chopped onion, 1 or 2 leeks including some of the tender green, a chopped carrot, and the soaked and drained flageolets. Simmer about 1 hour, checking to see that there's enough water to cover, until the beans are soft and the liquid is considerably reduced. Season with salt and pepper to taste, and ladle into a soup bowl. Discard the bone, but be sure to scrape off and include any bits of lamb clinging to it.

Index

Page references in *italic* refer to illustrations.
Recipe titles are in SMALL CAPS.

African-American food, 118–19
aging, 153–4
Aidells, Bruce, 129
Aix-en-Provence, 154–5
Allen, Sanford, 98, 99
allergies, 10, 75
All Manner of Food (Field), 79
Alstead, N.H., 52–3
American food, 54–5, 106–31
   American way of eating and, 107–8
   cooking of different cultures and,
     90–105
   fast and simple recipes and, 50–1
   Joneses' research on, 106–7, 108–9,
     113–14
   Knopf series on, 128–9
   "new American cooking" and, 127–8
   Southern cooking and, 115–19, 129
American Food: The Gastronomic Story
   (E. Jones), 106, 108, 113–14, 128
American Place, An (New York),
   111–12
animals, raising under humane conditions,
   175, 178–80
Anne Frank: The Diary of a Young Girl,
   45–6, 53–4
APPLE TARTS, FREEFORM, 259–60
Art of Charcuterie, The (Grigson), 151,
   224
Atlantic Monthly, 62

back-to-the-earth movement, 109, 163–6
baguettes, 25–6, 49, 196
   Child's recipe for, 83–4, 111
   Judith's version of, 229–32
Bailey, Fannie (grandmother), 10–12, 167
Bailey, Phyllis Hedley (mother), 3–6, *5*,
   7–11, 13, 14, 25, 51, 108, 154–6, 166
   Judith's letters to, 18, 19–20, 22–3, 27,
     30–1, 35–6, 39
   Paris trip of, 41–2, *43*
Bailey, Charles (Monty; father), 4, 7–8, 10,
   13, 42
   Judith's letters to, 18, 19–20, 22–3, 25,
     27, 30–1, 35–6
Balthus, 28
Bang, Susan, *194*
Barr, Nancy Verde, 129
Bastianich, Lidia, 137–40, *138*, 192, 196–7,
   245, 264
   GRATINATE OF CUTLET WITH EGGPLANT
     OR ZUCCHINI SLICES, 266–8
Beard, James, 50–1, 54, 69, 80, 89, 93, 96,
   98, 109–13, *113*, *122*, 123, 219–20,
   232, 239
   bread book by, 109–11
   SWORDFISH-OLIVE PASTA, 263–4
   as teacher, *109*, 112–13, 121
beaver, 168–72, *169*
béchamel, 37, 205
Beck, Jean, 86–9

Beck, Simone (Simca), 60–2, 63, 66–7, 70–1, 81, 83–9
beef, 175
  BITKI, 209–10
  boeuf bourguignon, 60–1
  FRENCHIFIED MEATLOAF, 214–15
  grass-fed, raised at Bryn Teg, 178–80, *179*
  SHEPHERD'S PIE, 205–7
BEER BATTER, 247–9
Bennington College, 6–7
Benson, Frank, 122–3
Bernstein, Bob, 115
Berry, Wendell, 178
BERRY PUDDING, SUMMER, 218–19
Bertholle, Louisette, 60–2, 63, 81
Biscuits, Spoonbread, and Sweet Potato Pie (Neal), 129
BITKI, 209–11
BLUEFISH, BROILED, OVER A BED OF FENNEL AND NEW POTATOES, 262–3
Blues (Hersey), 56–8
Bobbs-Merrill, 64, 144
boeuf bourguignon, 60–1
Book of Middle Eastern Food, A (Roden), 91–3
Book of New *New England Cookery, The* (E. Jones and J. Jones), 250, 261
boudin blanc, 35, *226*
  recipe for, 224–7
Bowen, Elizabeth, 55–6
BRAINS WITH A MUSTARD COATING, 239–40
bread, 49, 162, 182–4
  Beard's book on, 109–11
  French, *see* baguettes
  Italian, Hazan's recipe for, 95–6
  Joneses' books on, 143–4, 152, 160
  making, with children, 143–4, 182, *183*
  pudding (recipe), 216–18
Brearley School, 14
Brillat-Savarin, Jean Anthelme, 197
Brown, Helen Evans, 50–1
Bryn Teg (Vt.), 160–78, *162*, 188–92
  beaver at, 168–72, *169*
  gardening at, 163–6, 188–9
  gifts of nature at, 172–4, 176–8, 189–90

  grass-fed beef at, 178–80, *179*
  revelation about name of, 162–3
Burack, David, 168–70, *169*, 171, 178
Burke, Kenneth, 6
butter, 128, 131
BUTTERNUT SQUASH IN CREAM AND CINNAMON, 215–16
BUTTERSCOTCH COOKIES, SCHRAFFT'S, 219–21

Caetani, Princess, 27, 31
Café Nicholson (New York), 115, 118
Calvel, Professor, 84
Cameron, Angus, 64, 144–7, *146*, 170, 253
Camus, Albert, 18, 20, 55
Capote, Truman, 45, 115
CASSEROLE OF LAMB, MUSHROOMS, AND BULGUR OR BARLEY, 278–9
cassoulet, 66–7, 80
  MINI-CASSOULET, 275–6
CÉLÉRI RÉMOULADE, 223–4
Cercle du Cirque, Le (Paris), 28–31, 49
Ceria, Pierre, 20–2, *21*, 28–30, 31, 49
Chamberlain, Samuel, 59
Chambord, Le (New York), 76
Chapin, Paul, 27–32, 39
character, food as revelation of, 147–50
charcuterie, 81–2, 151
cheese, 48, 104–5, 196
  Evan's book on, 103, 104–5
  raw-milk, 174–5
  Spaghetti and (recipe), 203–5
chicken, 175
  BOUDIN BLANC, 224–7
  LIDIA'S GRATINATE OF CUTLET WITH EGGPLANT OR ZUCCHINI SLICES, 266–8
  MARTHA'S PAPRIKASH WITH LITTLE DUMPLINGS, 242–5
  SAUTÉ OF, WITH VEGETABLES, 212–14
Child, Julia, 60–72, 74, 75, 77–8, 81–9, *83*, 91, 94, *113*, 125, 128, 133, 141, 144, 168, 205, 213–14, 229, 260, 268
  baguette recipe and, 83–4, 111
  "fear-of-fat mania" and, 131
  Joneses' visit in Provence with, 86–8

Judith's collaboration with, 64–8, 81–5,
  83
Judith's first meeting with, 68–9
SAUTÉED DUCK BREAST WITH
  MADEIRA, 272–3
television and, 70, 71–2, 112
Child, Paul, 62, 64, 65, 68, 69, 71, 81, 83–7
children:
  making bread with, 143–4, 182, *183*
  shaping tastes of, 76–7, 132–6
Chinese food, 85–6, 90, 99–102, 105
  THE VERSATILE STIR-FRY, 234–7
chopsticks, 85–6
The Circle of Angels, 252–3
Claiborne, Craig, 54, 69–70, 93–4, 127
Classic French Cuisine, The (Donon),
  59–60, 64
Classic Italian Cookbook, The (Hazan),
  94, 95
cookies:
  MRS. COONEY'S HERMITS, 221–2
  SCHRAFFT'S BUTTERSCOTCH, 219–21
cooking:
  developing love for, 135–6
  Judith's childhood memories of, 3–16
  for one, 181, 192, 272–82
  with other people, 186–91
  religious nature of, 181–4
  taking pleasure in, 181–8
  time spent on, 184–5
Cook's Own Book, The (Lee), 250
Cooney, Mrs. (housekeeper), 12, 221
Cooper, James Fenimore, 106–7
copyrighting of recipes, 74
Cordon Bleu (Paris), 62
CORNISH HEN WITH HERBAL STUFFING
  UNDER THE SKIN, BROILED, 265–6
counterculture movement, 129–30
Cowles, Fleur, 33
CRACKLINGS, 270
Crook's Corner (Chapel Hill, N.C.), 129
CROQUETTES, 207–9, 280
Crowell, 143–4
Culinary Classics and Improvisations
  (Field), 80
Cunningham, Marion, 67, 119–27, *120,
  122, 126*
CURRY, LAMB, EVAN'S, 232–3, 278

Damianos, Madame, 42–3, 44
David, Elizabeth, 58–9
Dawson, Adele, 166–8, 173
de Groot, Baron Roy, 75–9, *77*, 136
de Santillana, Dorothy, 63
desserts, 8
  BREAD PUDDING, 216–18
  FROZEN MAPLE MOUSSE, 261
  GOOSEBERRY FLUMMERY, 255
  GOOSEBERRY FOOL, 254–5
  SUMMER BERRY PUDDING, 218–19
  see also tart(s)
De Voto, Avis, 58, 62, 63
De Voto, Bernard, 62
Digging to America (Tyler), 148
Dinner at the Homesick Restaurant (Tyler),
  148
*Dione Lucas Meat and Poultry Cook Book,
  The*, 50
Dollop of This and a Smidgeon of That, A
  (Dawson), 167–8
Donon, Joseph, 59–60, 64
Doubleday, 17, 23, 27, 45–6, 53
dowsing, 166–7
duck:
  BREAST, SAUTÉED, WITH MADEIRA À
    LA JULIA, 272–3
  CRACKLINGS, 270
  GIBLET SALAD, JACQUES'S, 270–1
  LEGS WITH PARSNIPS, SKILLET, À LA
    JACQUES, 273–4
  MINI-CASSOULET, 275–6
  STOCK, 269
  Wanna Buy a Duck?, 268–76
DUMPLINGS, LITTLE, 242–5
Dunne, Bronwyn (née Jones), 142–3, 171,
  178, *193*, 193–4
Dutton, 106

Eat Right, Eat Well—the Italian Way
  (Giobbi), 131
ECA (Economic Cooperation Adminis-
  tration), 33
EGGPLANT STUFFED WITH LAMB, RED
  PEPPER, AND RICE, 279–80
Eisele, Betsy, 143–4
English Food (Grigson), 205
Epstein, Jason, 145, 146

Essentials of Classic Italian Cooking, The (Hazan), 96
European way of eating, 107–8

Fannie Farmer Cookbook, The, 16, 50, 121–7, 202, 219–20
Fanny Farmer Candy Co., 121, 122–3
Farmer, Fannie, 121, 123, 124
farmers' markets, 184
Fast Food Nation (Schlosser), 134–5
fat (body), fear of, 13–16
fat (dietary):
    changes in American palate and, 171–2
    fear of, 95, 131, 171
Feasts for All Seasons (de Groot), 75–9
fiction, food in, 147–50
Field, Michael, 79–80, *81*
fish:
    BROILED BLUEFISH OR MACKEREL OVER A BED OF FENNEL AND NEW POTATOES, 262–3
    Canadian rule for, 57–8
    GRILLED, GOOSEBERRY SAUCE FOR, 252
    SHAD AND SHAD ROE IN SORREL SAUCE, 250–2
    SWORDFISH-OLIVE PASTA, JAMES BEARD'S, 263–4
Fisher, M.F.K., *81*, 114, 119, 150–6, *153*, 196, 251
FLUMMERY, GOOSEBERRY, 255
foie gras, 175
food processors, 111
Foods of Israel, The (Nathan), 193–4
FOOL, GOOSEBERRY, 254–5
foraging, 176–8
Forbes, 127
Forgione, Larry, 111–12
Foster, Catherine Osgood, 165–6
Four Seasons (New York), 239, 247
Frank, Otto, *46*
Freedley family, 14–15
FREEFORM APPLE TARTS, 259–60
French Chef, The, 71–2
French food, 3, 40–1, 59–72, 81–9, 196
    boudin blanc, 35, 224–7 (recipe), *226*
    Jefferson's exposure to, 108–9

Judith's attempts at, after return to America, 48–50
Judith's first exposures to, 10, 20–3, 25–6
Parisian markets and, 36–8
see also baguettes; *specific authors and books*
FRENCHIFIED MEATLOAF, 214–15
FROZEN MAPLE MOUSSE, 261
fusion cuisine, 156

game cookery, 119, 144–7, 170–2
gardening, 163–6, 188–9
Gift of Southern Cooking, The (Lewis and Peacock), 189
Giobbi, Ed, 131, *164*, 164–5
Good Things (Grigson), 185
goose, 41, 86–7, 175
gooseberry, 173–4, 176
    FLUMMERY, 255
    FOOL, 254–5
    SAUCE FOR GRILLED TROUT OR SALMON, 252
    TART, 257
Gottlieb, Bob, 103
Gourmet, 65, 103, 113–14
"gourmet," de Groot's definition of, 75
Grant, Cary, 105
GRATINATE OF CUTLET WITH EGGPLANT OR ZUCCHINI SLICES, LIDIA'S, 266–8
GREMOLATA, 241–2
GRIBICHE SAUCE FOR COLD LAMB OR OTHER MEATS, 277
Grigson, Jane, 151, 185, 205, 224, 254–5
Gunther, Jane, 18–19, 29
Gunther, John, 18–19, 29, 30
Gurdjieff, 253

Hamilton, Alexander, 106
HAM TIMBALES, AUNT MARIAN'S, 202–3
Harper, 144
Harriman, Marian Bailey, 11, 42, 43, 200
Harvey, Peggy, 74
HASH, A GOOD, 228–9
Hauser, Gaylord, 44, 54
Hawaii, 156–9
Hawaiian food, 156–9

Hazan, Marcella, 93–6, 184

Hazan, Victor, 94–6

health movement, 130–1, 171–2, 174–5, 195

Henry, Mary Roblee, 151

Herald Tribune, 33

HERMITS, MRS. COONEY'S, 221–2

Hersey, Barbara, 57

Hersey, John, 56–8, *57*

Hill, Lewis, 174

Hirsheimer, Christopher, 170

Hook, Leslie, 176–8, *177*

Houghton Mifflin, 63

How to Live in Paris on Practically Nothing (E. Jones), 45

Hubmann, Hanns, *34*

Indian food, 90, 97–9, 105, 139

ingredients:

    available to American home cooks, 48–9, 127, 184

    back-to-the-earth movement and, 163–6

    expense of, 185–6

    farmers' markets and, 184

    recipe formats and, 58, 64–5

Invitation to Indian Cooking, An (Jaffrey), 97–8

Israel, *193*, 193–4

Italian food, 58–9, 90, 93–6, 131, 137–40, 192, 196–7

Italian Food (David), 58–9

I've Been Reading, 71

Jaffrey, Madhur, 97–9, 105, 115, 139

Japanese food, 140–2, 194–5

Jefferson, Thomas, 108–9

Jerome, Carl, 96

Joel, Yale, 23

Jones, Evan, 10, 51–2, *53*, *57*, 61, 86, 119, 126–7, 129, 152–3, 154, 156, 175, 192–3, *198*, 229, 241, 242, 253, 261

    beaver tail recipe of, 171–2

    bread books by, 143–4, 152, 160, 162

    cheese book by, 103, 104–5

    cooking and, 35, 48, 69–70, 73, 80, 96, 142, 143, 145, 171, 181–2, 224, *226*

    Judith's first meeting with, 33–4

lamb curry recipe of, 232–3, 278

    in Paris, 33–44, *34, 42, 46,* 186

    in Vermont, 160–3, *162,* 166–7

    wedding of, *46,* 47

    writings on American food by, 106, 108, 113–14, 128

Jones, Martha, 242–5

Jones, Russ, 44, *46,* 91, 242–3

Joy of Cooking, 50, 64, 122, 144

Julia and Jacques Cooking at Home, 260, 268

Kelly, Denis, 129

Kim, Nova, 176–8, *177*

Kinnell, Bobbie Bristol, 188, 190–1

Kinnell, Galway, 188, 190–1

kitchen equipment, 49, 54–5, 111, *112,* 127

Knead It, Punch It, Bake It! (E. Jones and J. Jones), 143–4, 152, 160

knives, sharpening, 141–2

Knopf, 127–8, 224

    Judith hired by, 53–4, 55

    Judith's first cookbook assignment at, 58–9

    see also specific authors and books

Knopf, Alfred, 55, 56, *57,* 59, 61–2, 64, 68, 105, 144

Knopf, Blanche, 53–4, 55, 56, 58, 59, 64, 105

Knopf Cooks American, 128–9

Koestler, Arthur, 18, 20

Kohler, Matteus, 174–5

Koshland, Bill, 60

Kuo, Irene, 99–102, *100,* 105, 234

L. L. Bean Game and Fish Cookbook, The (Cameron and J. Jones), 144–7, 171

Laber, Jeri, 123

lamb:

    BITKI, 210–11

    CASSEROLE OF, WITH MUSHROOMS AND BULGUR OR BARLEY, 278–9

    COLD, SAUCE GRIBICHE FOR, 277

    CROQUETTES, 280

    CURRY, EVAN'S, 232–3, 278

    EGGPLANT STUFFED WITH RED PEPPER, RICE AND, 279–80

    MINCED, ON TOAST, 281

    The Nine Lives of a Leg of, 276–82

lamb *(continued)*:
  SHEPHERD'S PIE, 205–7, 278
  SOUP WITH LEEKS AND FLAGEOLETS,
    281–2
Lambert, Liliana, 197
Larousse Gastronomique, 170
Latin American food, 90–1
Lee, Mrs. N.K.M., 250
LEEK AND SORREL PANCAKES, 249–50
leftovers, 80, 137–8, 191–2, 203, 209
Lévy, Calmann, 45
Lewis, Edna, 115–19, *117, 120*, 188, 189,
    190, 191, 217
Lidia's Family Table (Bastianich), 137–40,
    192
Lidia's Italy (Bastianich), 196–7
Life, 23, *24*, 35
Li Lian Xing, 195
Little, Brown, 110, 121, 144
Live Longer, Live Better (Hauser), 44, 54
local produce, 165
Lord, Sterling, 35
Luang Prabang, Laos, *194*, 195
Lucas, Dione, 69

macaroni and cheese, 133–5
MACKEREL, BROILED, OVER A BED OF
    FENNEL AND NEW POTATOES,
    262–3
Madrid Fusion food conference (2006), 135
Malraux, André, 18, 20
MAPLE MOUSSE, FROZEN, 261
maple syrup, Vermont, 172–3
Marbella, 103
Marshall, Lydie, 256
Martha Deane radio show, 70
Mastering the Art of French Cooking (Child,
    Bertholle, and Beck), 60–71, 144
    Volume II of, 81–5, 86
Master in the Kitchen, The (Pierce), 73–4
master recipes and variations, 61
McAllister, Russ, 172
McCall, Azure, 156, 157
McCarthyism, 52
McDonell, Marie Clare, 38
MEATLOAF, FRENCHIFIED, 214–15
Mehta, Sonny, 129
Mendelson, Anne, 175

Michael Field's Cooking School (Field), 79
microwave, 125, 184
Middle Eastern food, 91–3, 105, 193–4, 195
milk, 172, 175
milkweed pods, 166
    STUFFED, FRIED IN BEER BATTER,
    247–9
Milky Ways (Mendelson), 175
Miller, Josy, *181*, 184–6, *185*
MINCED LAMB ON TOAST, 281
MINI-CASSOULET, 275–6
Montoya, Carlos, 161–2
Montpelier, Vt. 10–11
Montpelier Tavern (Vt.), 107
Mont-Saint-Michel, 23, *24*
Moore, Sarah, 17, 18–19, 23–5, *24*
More Classic Italian Cooking (Hazan), 95–6
Moss, Julie, 130
MOUSSE, FROZEN MAPLE, 261
mushrooms, wild, 177–8
My Life in France (Child), 65

Naples, 19, 196–7
Nathan, Joan, 129, *193*, 193–4
Neal, Bill, 129
Nela's Cookbook (Rubinstein), 102–5
New Yorker, 33
New York Times, 54, 69–70, 94, 224, *226*
Northfield, Minn., 51
Now, 35–6
Nussbaum, David, 137, 139

O'Conner, Barbara, 23
offal, 4, 25, 174
    BRAINS WITH A MUSTARD COATING,
    239–40
    SWEETBREADS SAUTÉED WITH
    MORELS AND CREAM, 237–9
Omnivore's Dilemma (Pollan), 175
organic gardening, 165–6

PANCAKES, SORREL AND LEEK, 249–50
PAPRIKASH WITH LITTLE DUMPLINGS,
    MARTHA'S, 242–5
Paris:
    Joneses' annual pilgrimages to, 186,
    187, 195–6

Judith's years in, 17–47, 131
see also French food
Parsons, Jeff, 33
Pasard, Alain, 196
pasta:
 making at home, 96, 135–6
 SPAGHETTI AND CHEESE, 203–5
 SWORDFISH-OLIVE, JAMES BEARD'S,
  263–4
pastes, toasting, 97, 139
Peacock, Scott, 188–91, *190*
Pépin, Jacques, 224, 226, 260, 268
 DUCK GIBLET SALAD, 270–1
 Jacques's version boudin blanc, 225
 SKILLET DUCK LEGS WITH PARSNIPS,
  273–4
Perry, Hilda Hedley, *5*, 14, 39, 154–6
Peterson, Evangeline, 115–17
Petite Maison, La (New York), 10, 17
Pierce, Donn, 73–4
PIZZA, INDIVIDUAL, 231–2
Pleasures of the Good Earth (Giobbi), 164–5
Point, Fernand, 32–3, 128
Pollan, Michael, 175
Pomfret, Conn., 14–15
pork, 175, 234–7, 266–8
Port Manech, Brittany, 21–2
Price, Edie, 3–4, 8–9, 13, 134, 181, 205, 217
Price, Frank, 45–6
processed foods, 134–5
professional chefs, 124, 135, 185–6, 188, 247
Provence, 155–6
 Joneses' trip to, 86–8
Prud'homme, Alex, 65
Prudhomme, Paul, 128
Putnam, Sumner, 63
Pyramide, La (Vienne), 32–3

Quest, 143

RABBIT IN A SWEET-SOUR CHOCOLATE-
 ACCENTED SAUCE, 252–4
Rabbit Redux (Updike), 149
Real Beer and Good Eats (Aidells and
 Kelly), 129
Renggli, Seppi, 239
Restaurant Associates, 90–1
Reynolds, Carol, 179

Reynolds, John, 173, 178, 179–80
Reynolds, Travis, 179
RHUBARB AND STRAWBERRY TART, 257–9
rice, cooking small portion of, 234
risotto, 138–9
rocks, hot, cooking on, 193–5
Roden, Claudia, 91–3, *92*, 99, 105, 115,
 195, 209, 211
Rogers, Charlie, 38, 40
Rogers American Motors, 38–9, 40
Rombauer, Irma, 122
Rosenthal, Mel, 127–8
Roth, Bettina, 38–40, 41, 186
Roth, Jacques, 38–40, 41, 186
Rubinstein, Arthur, 102–5
Rubinstein, Nela, 102–5
Russell, Diarmuid, 152

safflower oil, 131, 164
Sartre, Jean-Paul, 18, 20, 55
sauces:
 béchamel, 37, 205
Saucier's Apprentice, The (Sokolov), 224
Saveur, 170
Schlosser, Eric, 134–5
Schrafft's (New York), 16
 BUTTERSCOTCH COOKIES, 219–21
seasonality, 118, 165
serving amounts, 58, 64
Sexton, Kay, 130
SHAD AND SHAD ROE IN SORREL SAUCE,
 250–2
Sheffer, Nelli, 193
SHEPHERD'S PIE, 205–7, 278
Sheraton, Mimi, 137
Shimbo, Hiroko, 140–2, *141*, 194–5
Simca's Cuisine (Beck), 88–9
Simonds, Nina, *194*, 195
Singapore, 195
Sister Age (Fisher), 154
smell of cooking, 125, 135
Sokolov, Ray, *224*
Sontheimer, Carl, 111
sorrel, 173
 AND LEEK PANCAKES, 249–50
 SAUCE, SHAD AND SHAD ROE IN, 250–2
 SOUP, 246–7
Southern food, 115–19, 129

SPAGHETTI AND CHEESE, 203–5

Spence School, 107–8

Splendid Fare (Stockli), 247

Spoonful of Ginger, A (Simonds), 195

Steingarten, Jeffrey, 195–6

STIR-FRY, THE VERSATILE, 234–7

Stockli, Albert, 247, 248

STRAWBERRY AND RHUBARB TART, 257–9

SUMMER BERRY PUDDING, 218–19

Susan Prince (New York), 9

Sushi Experience (Shimbo), 140–2

SWEETBREADS SAUTÉED WITH MORELS
     AND CREAM, 237–9

SWORDFISH-OLIVE PASTA, JAMES
     BEARD'S, 263–4

Tante Marie, 37

Taste of Country Cooking, The (Lewis),
     115–19, 188

taste:
     acquisition of, 132–6, 137
     new, openness to, 76–7, 155–9
     radical changes in, 171–2

television, 70, 71–2, 112, 152, 189

Thomas, Anna, 130

TIMBALES, HAM, AUNT MARIAN'S, 202–3

Time, 84, 128

titles of recipes, 58–9

Today, 70, 189

travel, learning about food and, 192–7

Twombly, Mrs. Hamilton, 59–60

Tyler, Anne, 148

Unsettling of America, The (Berry), 178

Updike, John, 149, 151

Vandercook, Audrey, 132, 133, 135–6,
     160–1

Vandercook, Chris, 132–3, 134, 136, 156–9,
     157

veal:
     LIDIA'S GRATINATE OF CUTLET WITH
          EGGPLANT OR ZUCCHINI SLICES,
          266–8
     SHANKS, BRAISED, WITH GREMO-
          LATA, 241–2

vegetarian cooking, 130

Vegetarian Epicure, The (Thomas), 130

Victory Garden, The (Morash), 221

Vivez Jeune, Vivez Longtemps (Hauser),
     44, 54

Volkening, Henry, 152

von Ott, Ursula, 153, 154

Vulcania, 18–19

Waihee, John, 157

Wales, Joneses' trips to, 163, 173–4

Waters, Alice, 165

Way to Cook, The (Child), 71–2

Webster, Daniel, 108–9

We Called It Macaroni (Barr), 129

Wechsberg, Joseph, 33

Weekend, 33–5

Weinstock, Herbert, 60

WGBH, 71–2

Whitehead, Alfred North, 181

Williams, Chuck, 54–5

Williams, Nina, *117*

Williams-Sonoma, 54–5

Wilson, David, 158

Wong, Alan, 158

Woodward, Anne, *15*

World-of-the-East Vegetarian Cooking
     (Jaffrey), 98–9

Yankee, 52

yeast, 95–6, 110

ZUCCHINI BLOSSOMS, STUFFED, FRIED
     IN BEER BATTER, 247–9

Illustration Credits

Frontispiece: Gene Kammerman
Page 24: © Yale Joel
Page 77: © 2007 Photograph by Sylvia Plachy
Page 92: Reg Green
Page 100: West Chester Rockland Newspaper
Page 117: John T. Hill
Page 120: Brant Ward, *San Francisco Chronicle*
Page 141: Jim Smith
Page 153: George Hurrell
Page 162: *Burlington Free Press*
Page 169: Bronwyn Dunne
Page 177: Chris Vandercook
Page 179: Carol Reynolds
Page 226: Gene Maggio/*The New York Times*/Redux

A Note About the Author

Judith Jones is Senior Editor and Vice President at Alfred A. Knopf. She joined the company in 1957 as an editor working primarily on translations of French writers such as Albert Camus and Jean-Paul Sartre. She had worked before that for Doubleday, first in New York and then in Paris. In addition to her literary authors, she has been particularly interested in developing a list of first-rate cookbook writers; her authors have included Julia Child (Judith published Julia's first book and was her editor ever after), Lidia Bastianich, James Beard, Marion Cunningham, Rosie Daley, Marcella Hazan, Madhur Jaffrey, Edna Lewis, Scott Peacock, Joan Nathan, Jacques Pépin, Claudia Roden, Nina Simonds, and Hiroko Shimbo. She is the coauthor with Evan Jones (her late husband) of three books: *The Book of Bread; Knead It, Punch It, Bake It!* (for children); and *The Book of New New England Cookery.* She also collaborated with Angus Cameron on *The L. L. Bean Game and Fish Cookbook.* Recently, she has contributed to *Vogue, Saveur, Bon Appétit,* and *Gourmet* magazines. She has been awarded a lifetime achievement award by *Bon Appétit* (2003), the James Beard Foundation (2006), and the I.A.C.P. (2007).

A Note on the Type

Pierre-Simon Fournier *le jeune*, who designed the type used in this book, was both an originator and a collector of types. His types are old style in character but are sharply cut in a manner that presages the modern style of letter, best known from the Bodoni types. In 1764 and 1766 he published his *Manuel typographique*, a treatise on the history of French types and printing, on typefounding in all its details, and on what many consider his most important contribution to typography—the measurement of type by the point system. It would be a further hundred years before a similar system of weights and measures began to be introduced for ingredients in cookbooks.

Composed by North Market Street Graphics, Lancaster, Pennsylvania
Printed and bound by R. R. Donnelley, Harrisonburg, Virginia
Designed by Peter A. Andersen